BIG BONED

From Empty to Enough
The Heavy Truth About Breaking Free from
Eating Disorders and My Love Affair with Food

LAUREN HANKINS

DISCLAIMER

As you'll soon realize, I'm barely an expert in my own health matters and certainly do not claim to be one in yours. The content in this book on eating disorders is based solely on my personal experiences, observations, and research. I'm not a licensed medical professional or an expert in psychology, psychiatry, or nutrition. *Big-Boned* and the information introduced should never be considered a substitute for professional diagnosis or treatment. I encourage you to consult with qualified healthcare professionals before implementing strategies or treatments discussed in this book. Every individual's circumstances and experiences with eating disorders are unique, and what works for one person may not work for another.

The experiences and events shared are authentic to my journey, but identifying details, some names, and some locations have been adapted or changed to protect the privacy of individuals.

Big-Boned

Copyright © 2025 by Lauren Hankins

For more information, email hello@laurenhankins.com.

Edited by Joy Sephton: https://www.justemagine.biz

ISBN: 979-8-89694-299-3 - Ebook
ISBN: 979-8-89694-300-6 - Paperback
ISBN: 979-8-89694-301-3 - Hardcover

MY GIFT TO YOU!

Wanting to be better, do better, and live better is just that— wanting. Practicing and creating change involves action.

In the *Big-Boned* companion guide, *Unearthing Your Worth: A Step-by-Step Guide to Becoming a Better Version of Yourself*, I give you practical advice on how to start the evolution of YOU today. So you can have the best experience as you read through *Big-Boned*, there's a QR code below to download and explore the steps before, during, or after you dive into the book.

This guide will help you implement the tools and next steps in *Big-Boned* faster and more easily.

Visit www.laurenhankins.com to find more helpful content!

DEDICATION

To my babies: I was once told a child is a mother's heart living outside her body. The second I gave birth, I knew that to be true. Your smiles and laughter inspire me daily, and in learning to love myself the way you love me, I'll help you become the best you can be.

To my husband: You're my greatest cheerleader and the one who introduced me to every aspect of living in the gray. Thank you. God blessed the broken road, babes. I don't know how we got here, but I'm sure glad it was you.

To my mom: I hope to become half the woman you are. In the most unconventional way, you've led me down a path of self-discovery that was necessary for me to evolve into who I am today. Love you more.

TABLE OF CONTENTS

DISCOVERING ED development of an eating disorder | early influences

DATING ED living to eat | in the trenches of an eating disorder

DIVORCING ED eating to live | getting to the gray

ENLIGHTENMENT things I learned | take them with you

Note: There is a Quick Reference Page Guide on the first page of each chapter in this section.

IMPORTANT NOTES

About *Ed*

In this book, you'll find unending references to Ed. Ed is an Eating Disorder personified. Creating a character out of a disease has long been a therapy tactic and isn't my idea. I find this tool incredibly useful for those of us needing to grab hold of our disease. Feel free to use this in your journey, though you don't have to stick with the name Ed.

I learned the tactic through the book *Life Without Ed* by Jenni Schaefer and Thom Rutledge. It was one of the first books I read after being diagnosed with an eating disorder. I urge you to dive into resources like *Life Without Ed* if your journey leads you to it. If you've struggled with addiction for any amount of time, you'll know it takes so much from us. We can use all the help we can get.

It might be high time you grabbed your Ed by the horns and started fighting back!

About Using the Name *Ed*

I want to clarify that I'm not trying to vilify the name. If you happen to have an incredible person in your life with that name, rest assured, the text within *Big-Boned* is not about them. This is a memoir about my personal experience with eating disorders, and the use of Ed is purely metaphorical. To all the great Eds out there—you're safe.

About *the Gray*

Much like references to Ed, I make plenty of remarks in *Big-Boned* about finding your way to the gray and about living in the gray. Gray is the in-between. A place for those of us who need a different understanding of recovery and what that means. When we're living life in the shadows of our addiction, it's a way to find some solace between the absolute worst parts of mental illness and being set totally free from what ails us. After all, the answer is usually somewhere in the middle, right?

A Note on Other Addictions

The strategy I outline in *Big-Boned*—living in the gray—is specific to eating disorders and is not intended as guidance for other forms of addiction, such as alcoholism or substance use disorders. Recovery strategies for other addictions may require strict abstinence or different approaches entirely, and my personal story and framework are not designed to address those situations.

About Sobriety

Just as someone may define an alcoholic's abstinence or recovery as being or becoming sober, in *Big-Boned*, I also make references to sobriety as it relates to an eating disorder. I talk a lot about sugar sobriety in terms of an absence or abstinence from stimulant foods, whether they be refined sugar specifically or other stimulants like white flour and caffeine. Within these pages, you can liken the words *sober* or *sobriety* to abstinence.

Male Readers

If you're a man who doesn't think this book is for you, I urge you to keep reading. Eating disorders and body image struggles don't discriminate by gender, and they affect far more men than most people realize. Research shows that **1 in 3 individuals with an eating disorder is male.**

This book is about real people with real struggles—not just statistics or stereotypes. There's no denying the universal need for self-acceptance and healing.

About the Stories in This Book

As a self-help memoir, my stories extend further back than memory serves. I've put this book off long enough, thinking I needed an exact timeline or accurate recounting of people, places, or events. However, I realize I won't get things down one hundred percent accurately, even with all the emotion tied to my stories.

That stated, did you know the more emotional an event, the easier it is to remember? That's because, in your brain, the amygdala assists the hippocampus in storing those memories more effectively. The amygdala and hippocampus are activated at the same time, resulting in stronger memories. How cool is that?

Either way, the goal of this book is the same. Helping you find your way to the gray. I want to bring realization to you as early as possible in your journey, regardless of how long you've traveled, so you don't have to go through the muck and the mud—or as much of it—as I did.

If just one person is struggling and my story helps you find the tiniest piece of silver lining or a tool you can use, this book has done its job.

GET HELP NOW!

"Resources Guide for Mental Health and Eating Disorders"

If you or someone you know is struggling with an eating disorder or mental health challenges, support is available. You don't have to navigate this alone, and there are people and organizations ready to help.

The comprehensive resources guide at the back of the book has hotlines, treatment providers, support organizations, and tools to help you get started. You'll find it in the Table of Contents, or flip to page number 301.

Quick Access to Support

Here are a few key resources you can reach out to immediately:

- **National Alliance for Eating Disorders**: Call 1-800-931-2237 (in the US)
- **Crisis Text Line**: Text HOME to 741741 (free 24-hour support in the US)
- **Suicide & Crisis Lifeline**: Dial 988 (in the US)
- **International Help Lines**: See the Table of Contents for the "Resources Guide for Mental Health and Eating Disorders" or flip to page number 301.

You're not alone. There is help, there is hope, and there are people ready to support you right now.

TRIGGER WARNING

Make no bones about it—I had to start things off punny—there's a good chance you may not be on the same page with what I have to say. I've got to put it out there, though, because I've yet to see it published or talked about, and it fills me with a fiery rage.

Perhaps that came across as a touch extreme, *but it leaves me absolutely flabbergasted that this topic isn't more prominent in the recovery community.* Trust me; I'm twenty-six years into this thing. *This thing* being addiction. Food addiction and eating disorders, to be exact. I'm even longer than that into obesity—thirty years, I'd say. I turned forty last year, which means most of my life has been a revolving door of dieting and dying to be thin.

That's the problem, folks. If you don't act fast, the relationship with Ed lingers as the rest of your life hangs in the balance. Emotional terrorism goes on for years longer than you could ever dream of.

There's no magical cure for getting free and clear, one hundred percent rid of Ed. If there was, you think I'd choose this many years of torment? Heck no! I would have bottled up that potion a long time ago and sold it instead of doing what I'm doing now: writing a book.

Quite honestly, if I'd just opened Merriam-Webster all those years ago and simply read the definition of addiction or eating disorders, I would have seen it—as plain as day.

Just like addiction, eating disorders present with compulsive behaviors and devastating impact. They're not conditions that can simply be cured; instead, they require—no, they demand—a lifetime of vigilance, treatment, and support.

Let that sink in for a minute. *Eating disorders are chronic; in other words, lifelong conditions that are treatable. Not curable.*

If someone had been as frank with me as I'm planning to be with you, I feel it would have shaved years off of my looking, searching, searching, looking for a cure *that does not exist.*

Oh, but wait!

Someone *was* that frank with me. Turns out I was so deep into my disease that I didn't listen. My hope, though, is that through my stories—and buckle up, buttercup, because there are many—even if I didn't listen, *you will.* If you can find recovery more quickly and easily than I have, it would be my greatest gift.

My goal is to fast-track the evolution of a healthy and robust you, plain and simple. But how do we do that? I plan to help you figure that out. The tricky part is that each person's path may look a little different. By sharing my stories, I hope I can help you unearth your own worth and start finding your way to the gray.

If Ed or obesity has never plagued you in the way they have me, or you happen to be reading this for some other reason, I hope you get a glimpse into how serious these issues are.

There's likely someone in your circle who has an eating disorder and, with absolute certainty, someone who struggles with obesity. I'll teach you how to deal with those things, too. For example, how to have tough conversations with someone you love without saying insensitive things to an alarmingly skinny or gaunt individual like, "Eat a hamburger," or "You're just withering away to nothing." What about saying to someone who struggles with being overweight or obese, "Why can't you just work out?" or "Have you ever tried portion control?"

Obesity is a disease. Eating disorders are a disease. They're not about some person lacking fortitude or grit. Genetics, biology, environment, psychology, and lifestyle choices all have a role in this play. Even medication!

Given the prevalence and complexity of eating disorders, it's essential to approach discussions about Ed with sensitivity and understanding.

Did you hear me? Be compassionate.

When I say be compassionate, it doesn't mean you need to fully understand or grasp what someone with an eating disorder is experiencing. Instead, it's more about recognizing in the first place that they *are* facing something difficult. For those on the outside looking in, it is possible to gain insight into what someone struggling with Ed is dealing with and how Ed can hold such power—and even appeal.

For those of you in the thick of it, I wish I could say the end goal of *Big-Boned* is, of course, for you to divorce Ed and leave him forever. Be eating disorder- and food-addiction-free! That after you stop reading, food will never plague you again.

But let's be realistic.

If you're in the middle of Ed, other than just how long he's hung around me, the reason I don't believe you can ever fully break free is because, just like a divorce on paper, that someone still exists long after the fighting and mediation and finality of divorce ends. They're always there in some capacity, and they'll come in and out of your mind in memory and in your curiosity forever. Because you once were.

Ed's no different. He'll never entirely cease to exist. You've got to learn how to handle him when he starts coming in and out of your mind. So how do you learn to live a lifetime with Ed? You must learn from him so you know exactly what you need in order to be—sort of—free. That's what getting to the gray is.

Who doesn't want a better life, even if it means they'll be *somewhat* free? I know I'd sign up for that again and again and again because that's way better than what I've been through.

There's a lot of life to be living, and ain't nobody got time for Ed to fill them with self-hatred or the need to purge or any mess like that.

So with this, I'm writing the book I needed to read.

While I wish I could, I can't promise you you'll never binge or purge again after reading this or that you'll drop two hundred pounds or gain a hundred. But I can promise you I'll share every bit of how I got there, to the gray, myself. It's not pretty, but it's real and raw, and you can take or leave anything you need from these stories and create your personalized roadmap to getting there.

Most importantly, I'm not saying you don't need help outside of these pages. The reality is that you probably *do* need extra support. I'll help you find that, too.

Now let's dive in and get you to your gray!

DISCOVERING ED

development of an eating disorder | early influences

CHAPTER 1

THERE IS NO CURE

**In this first chapter, we'll examine the
problem and look at the solutions—or
lack thereof—for eating disorders.**

I'd been "big-boned" my whole life. I came out a whopping almost ten pounds and, according to those around me, stayed "heavyset" my entire adolescence and beyond. Curvy or sturdy, they'd call it. Are you eye-rolling as hard as I am right now? If I was big-boned, I was for sure made that way, and there was nothing I could do about it. That's what I thought, anyway. More on that later.

I wish I could nail down the exact date of this conversation—around 2003, when I was nineteen. However, early on in my eating disorder or relationship with Ed, but far enough into it that my mom had already caught onto my secretive behavior and changes in my eating habits, she suggested I sit down with Melissa, our neighbor, and talk with her about my food struggles to see if it would help. Melissa had gone through similar struggles, and my mom thought a conversation with her, given our shared experiences, might just lead me in the right direction.

I remember it like it was yesterday. Just like her Glade Hawaiian-scented home—please tell me you remember those plug-in thingy ma-bobs—the memory sits strongly with me.

Melissa sat me down and said, "Here's what I'm going to tell you. If it's anything like my own struggle, you'll never get over this. Food will fill you with seasons of torment for the rest of your days. I've only found one thing that works to help me fight it."

She continued, "From now on, you're going to wake up every morning and make a series of decisions before your feet hit the floor. You cry out, 'Lord, take this from me. I can't do it alone. I want to eat to live, not live to eat.' "

Woah. *I want to eat to live, not live to eat.* Now that was powerful.

"And if you break that promise about eating to live," Melissa added, "you just keep making it to yourself again and again and again. And let's be honest, you will break that promise.

"It's like compounding interest. The longer you stay out of addiction, the more your portfolio—your sobriety—grows exponentially. You'll eventually start to have more good days than bad. But you'll never have a day when you don't have to make decisions."

What Melissa said to me that day was a lot to hear. Perhaps too much? Maybe I hadn't yet accepted that I did, in fact, have an eating disorder. Or maybe I absolutely knew I was sick but was in denial. After all, denial plagues most addicts. Whatever I did get from it, I know I didn't immediately take any action based on what she said to me that day.

Let's face it, this was a new, fine line I was walking, and well, from there, the actual problem started to get fuzzy.

So, what does the problem look like?

Through any lens, I think you'll see that these are muddy waters. Which is it? What do I actually have? What is it called? Do I need an official diagnosis?

Where do I draw the line between obesity as a disease, a food addiction, or a fully-fledged eating disorder? Am I bingeing or just overeating? What defines overeating or consuming too much—eating one hamburger or three? Is binge eating part of obesity, or does that just further define binge eating disorder (BED)?

Or what about the other side of the spectrum—eating far too little or restricting so severely that it mirrors or develops into anorexia?

I'm only skimming the surface here, but do you see where I'm going?

While I'll focus explicitly on the problems surrounding food addiction, eating disorders, and the recovery journey, these muddy waters also exist for other addictions—whether it be alcohol, drugs, sex, shopping, gambling, or anything else. Most forms of addiction share common behavioral patterns. Cravings and urges often look similar, as do withdrawal symptoms and the negative impacts on relationships, health, or work.

But how can we tell where we stand with our behaviors? When does normal behavior turn into addiction? Obsession? The answer often lies in psychological dependence. Regardless of the substance or activity, we go back to the thing we think can help us to be in control or offer relief. And while biological effects and social perceptions may vary, the core experiences of addiction are frighteningly similar.

Could eating disorders be the worst?

I'm going to lean in a touch more—and I plan to get plenty of hate for this—because I think that out of all the mental health diseases or addictions, eating disorders are the worst. Why? Because of what Melissa said earlier. We have to eat to live! I don't need to go to the street corner to get my fix when the fix is food.

What's truly heartbreaking is that most people will never understand just how prevalent and dangerous eating disorders are. I could be dying in broad daylight without so much as a glance of concern from anyone around me. Did you know anorexia is responsible for the majority of all mental health-related deaths? And what about suicide? We'll never fully measure the total number of suicides stemming from eating disorders, but estimates suggest that one in five people who die from anorexia do so by suicide. One in five. My heart breaks as I type that. And there's bulimia—an insidious force infiltrating both our youth and adult populations. It knows no bounds. Here's the heavy truth: every fifty-two minutes, someone dies from an eating disorder, and that's just the deaths we're able to count.

Almost ten percent of the global population struggles with an eating disorder. If you need a visual, that's all of Europe, people. All. Of. Europe. Talk about soul-crushing stats. If that isn't a wake-up call, I'm not sure what is.

I'll say this, and then I'll get off my soapbox because Lord help me if this topic doesn't get me fired up.

It doesn't help that there was a generational, societal thing happening in America during the early 1990s to early 2000s. I'm looking at you, elder millennials, because we're the ones who have been brainwashed.

Don't get me started on the disservice to us as consumers and also as citizens, one of which was the food pyramid. I bet, like me, you didn't know the food pyramid was created in Sweden in the 1970s, and not until the early 1990s did the US Department of Agriculture (USDA) vomit out to us their adaptation of this ridiculousness.

Even with a small amount of research, you'll find the original pyramid was published during a rise in inflation in Sweden, which is likely why the bottom third of the pyramid is heavily focused on carbs—six to *eleven* servings per day. Say what? Carbs are cheap and carbs are easy to access. Not only that, but worldwide, even then, there was fat stigma, so there was no distinction between healthy and unhealthy fats. All fat was bad.

For the USDA to put its spin on an already plagued pyramid—my temperature is rising as I type this—and not consider its people and a nutritional profile that serves us and doesn't make us sicker blows my mind.

In the same decade as the pitiful pyramid, the fast-food industry was welcoming and widely advertising the *super-size me* new generation of huge portions. On the other hand, we were being pounded with fat hatred. Oh, the land of all things fat-free!

Diabetes was on the rise, and back then, before the research was done, it was indelibly linked to people eating too much fat. Food manufacturers were heavily promoting fat-free or low-fat versions of every food you can think of, flooding grocery shelves with chemically engineered products disguised as "healthy." These so-called solutions were often packed with sugar, additives, and artificial ingredients marketed as better choices but ultimately making things worse.

Do you remember Snackwells? If I had a nickel for every Snackwells I ate back then, and the number of spray butter and fat-free American Kraft Singles I ingested! Y'all, I'd mastered the seventy-calorie, perfectly fake, and perfectly processed grilled cheese. Gross.

My point? As if obesity, food addiction, and eating disorders aren't tough enough, it kind of feels like we've also been set up to fail by a system that prioritizes profit over public health.

And that's what makes eating disorders feel even more treacherous. Not only are we navigating distorted beliefs about food, but we're also stuck in a cycle where we can't just walk away. Unlike other addictions where abstinence can be part of recovery, we can't simply quit food. We're forced to face it; there's no avoiding our "substance" multiple times a day, every day.

That's why I stand by what I said earlier: eating disorders might just be the worst. Because they don't just thrive in the dark corners of our minds;

they're fueled by a world that profits off our confusion and self-doubt. And finding the solution? It's not as simple as just eating less or just eating more. It's learning how to make peace with something we can't live without.

So what *is* the solution?

Obesity

First, I'm going to detour to focus on two prominent obesity solutions, but I'll tie it back specifically to eating disorders. This isn't intended to limit the lens on solutions for obesity, but rather, to highlight how they further muddy the waters, delaying someone from getting to their gray.

Weight Watchers is, without a doubt, one of the most successful weight loss programs out there. And I should know. I'm slightly embarrassed to say it, but I'm certain I was such a large source of their revenue that, at one point, you could have called me an investor. At least eight years of dues and weigh-ins. And don't get me wrong, I had great experiences with Weight Watchers. I grew close with a couple of my leaders. I was even the Weight Watchers facilitator for a Fortune 500 company I was employed by.

But here's the ugly truth for those of us struggling with food addiction or an eating disorder while trying to follow a weight loss program.

In my experience, the cyclical nature of these programs is putty in Ed's hands. And I stress, that was *my* experience. As you can imagine, those weekly weigh-ins and recurrent fresh starts are perfectly curated for him. I'll never forget the physical and heavy emotional feeling of walking into a meeting feeling that if I didn't get on that scale in the next minute and reset to another fresh start—because I'd spent the previous seventy-two hours bingeing incessantly—Ed would, quite literally, kill me. You see, it wasn't just me doing Weight Watchers. Ed and I were on the program together. But this was his playbook: restrict, binge—sometimes purge—guilt, shame, start over.

So for as much good as I thought they were doing, weight loss programs were incredibly harmful to my health for years.

And while we're reflecting on solutions to obesity and how they intersect with Ed, I'd be remiss not to bring up weight loss medications and the complexities surrounding them.

I'm talking about the class of not-so-new drugs known as GLP-1s, or glucagon-like peptides. Recently, they've been making waves as weight-loss medications—a new application for them. Sound a bit like the fen-phen craze? If you recall that era, you might see some parallels. You've probably heard about some of these GLP-1s by their brand names, like Wegovy or Ozempic, or their generic name, semaglutide. There's also Mounjaro, which goes by the generic name tirzepatide.

So what exactly do these drugs do, and why are people going bananas over them?

Well, they do some pretty fascinating things. For starters, they mimic incretins—hormones released from the gastrointestinal tract in response to food—that help regulate appetite and insulin secretion. Wild, right? This hormone mimicry reduces hunger and enhances satiety, making it easier to eat less. They also act on the brain's appetite control center, amplifying their impact on weight regulation. Essentially, these mechanisms make them incredibly appealing for those looking to lose weight.

And just like with weight loss programs, the administration of weight loss drugs revolves around a schedule. Weekly injections. Sometimes, weekly weigh-ins.

I'm all for lessening food noise; I just think it's a fine line we're toeing. That's what I worry about with these solutions and their rising popularity.

It's the same line I toed with Weight Watchers. How many people are taking these drugs while knowingly or unknowingly dealing with Ed? What if all these things are delaying someone from getting help for what's really going on? I know that's not universally true for all who either a) are on cyclical-in-nature weight loss programs or b) are taking weight loss meds, but I do think we're teetering on an unhealthy ledge. What if there's a way we can make sure these solutions only fall into the hands of patients who truly need and will benefit from them?

While I've begun to lose faith altogether in our regulatory bodies that govern food and meds—and that's being gracious—I do think there's a better openness and acceptance emerging for those of us who struggle with the very thing society has set up to plague us. And there's something special about lessening the stigma around obesity. People need to recognize obesity as a disease and worry less about portion control nonsense or not having the willpower.

Either way, it fires me up to see the industry preying on its own people because, in the end, who's paying the price? We are.

Give us a break. Give our bodies a break!

To clarify, this isn't intended to be a judgment on anyone trying to lose weight, and I'm not in the camp of don't. I'm just in the camp of do someone's behaviors around food trend more toward obesity or lean more toward addiction? I've tried everything possible, from an oral meds perspective, like taking legal speed, all the way to changing my anatomy to stop the food noise, so I'm not the one to be throwing stones. I address changing my anatomy in Chapter 12.

Once we have an understanding of what we're up against, then we can a) do our research, b) better assess risks, and c) get the support we need even before we begin the solution.

Eating Disorders

Now let's get back to solutions specific to Ed.

There are about a million camps when it comes to addiction recovery, each one claiming to provide you with its own version of freedom. You've got rehab, but within rehab, you've got inpatient or outpatient to choose from—if you can choose because minors may have parents who, regardless of consent, decide this route for them. Do you need a true detox, or can you use weekly outpatient meetings and check-ins? What about 12-step programs, and which one would be most effective for you? Or counseling, but do you go to a psychologist or psychiatrist? Do you seek individual counseling, or do you need a group setting? What about just a regular counselor? But maybe it's a family therapist you need to see, or is it one that specializes in eating disorders and addiction? Maybe you need to find one who treats your specific condition. Do they provide cognitive behavioral therapy? And let's top it off with the option to take a more holistic approach if you aren't into Western medicine.

We haven't even dipped our toes into insurance and affordability and transparency in the game I like to call mental health madness. When it comes to eating disorders and other mental illnesses, what's covered and what's not is unacceptable, and it's a shame that victims of addiction and these disorders have to be put through the wringer to get help while they're trying to cope and are struggling just to stay alive.

So what are they teaching in these million camps? Most of the eating disorder curriculum leans heavily on intuitive eating or abstinence.

If you're not familiar with the term, intuitive eating is something like "Buy the bag of Oreos and let it sit on the counter, and if you aren't hungry, don't eat it."

What a damn joke, am I right? Here's the scoop. I went through years of counselors and therapists who drilled intuitive eating into me. I read books on books about hunger cues and feeling your fullness. All the while, I was wondering what in the world was wrong with me, given that I was trying and trying and trying, and bluntly, none of that garbage worked. Because, guess what?

Your brain doesn't work like that.

Your brain can't work like that when your hunger and fullness signals are completely and utterly distorted in the first place. If you're anything like me, you have a difficult time distinguishing emotional hunger from physical hunger. I know I'm going to hit a nerve with someone right now, but for some of us, our lives depend on structure and counting and weighing. Just don't come at me with the listen-to-yourself voodoo crap. I've listened long enough, and what Ed got to say be crazy. Unhinged. We don't want him talking and causing a ruckus.

A treatment that wildly opposes intuitive eating—and which I'll get more into later but makes a lot more sense, though it also isn't fully sustainable—is abstinence. You know, more like what you hear from 12-step programs where patients are encouraged to stop stimulant foods altogether—sugar, white flour, caffeine—or, in the case of Alcoholics Anonymous, alcohol.

To me, it's freaking nuts that the two headliners of recovery from eating disorders are such polar opposites. Either the cure is a) just listen to what your body is telling you, or the cure is b) cut that stuff out entirely because you'll die if sugar ever hits those lips again. Those are your two options. Does that not sound like addiction itself? Sounds like *all* or *nothing* to me. We, as addicts, already have the disadvantage of lots of extremes in our thinking and behavior, striving for perfection, and difficulty finding a middle ground or moderation.

I realize this doesn't apply to everyone, but can the cure for your disease really be the very thing that contributed to developing the disease in the first place? Goodness, no wonder we're struggling—being told to fix ourselves with the same thing that may have led us here to begin with!

Well, all that sounded like just part of the issue, and that's because it is. Our current solutions *are part of the problem*. Remember when I said I was looking for a cure that doesn't exist?

Somewhere in the Middle

Here's the major point of this. The actual solution.

Have you ever heard someone say that the answer is usually somewhere in the middle? My husband says this all the time, and I love it because it resonates on so many levels.

What if we did live in the gray? While sometimes unclear or fuzzy, gray isn't bad. Gray is just saying that there's another way to perceive something that may not be as extreme as the obvious or more popular answers and options. Trust me, I'd love to say for sure that intuitive eating works or that hanging my hat on abstinence is the only way, but I'm finding the gray to be much more realistic these days. What if recovery is fluid? Why can't we have both? Why can't I have a little bit of total sobriety with some flex in there? What about all or *something*? What if my life depends on both? What if I need absolute sugar sobriety for a year, and then I can handle some intuitive eating for a couple of months, but then I need sobriety? What if I can't have ice cream, but I'd like a cookie occasionally? What if I absolutely cannot bring bread into my house, but I love making sourdough, and my body says to stop after the second slice, so I've managed to find some kind of balance?

I also love the phrase, "It's easier to say no." I feel that deep in my big bones. The phrase doesn't confine you to no forever. But we can say no for now if that's what we need in that moment.

What if, in my head, there will always be voices of Ed that I must fight off? Voices telling me to drive through Bruster's and begging me to give in? Indeed, these same voices may always be there, but we can work hard at telling Ed to eff off when he wants to be the only thing we hear.

For me, that's been the case. I'm neither fully cured nor recovered, but I'm definitely not *in* my disease like I was at one point. I move not so gracefully but definitely fluidly through my recovery journey, finding myself, now, twenty-six years later, in a good, healthy spot. Praise God! And part of finding myself is finally hearing what Melissa tried to tell me years ago.

There is no cure.

Sure, there's life-changing sobriety. And I have no doubt there are some unicorns out there who have been given the gift of true food freedom. But in the unprofessional court of Lauren's opinion and her history of eating disorders, Ed will never go away.

I'm sorry if you were coming here to get the rule book for stepping out of disordered eating or eating disorders forever, but this just isn't that. Ed will be with you your whole life.

What you need is a rule book for integrating your life alongside Ed—the gray part of all this.

But first, let's flash back, all the way to the beginning, long before I got to the gray.

For lessons learned and insights from this chapter, visit
"ENLIGHTENMENT on DISCOVERING ED"

CHAPTER 2

GROWING UP BIG-BONED

In this chapter, we'll look at my early experiences with and around food. We'll also address family and how those relationships can affect us in the long term.

Looking back, I wish I could say, "All of this began on November 28th," or something specific like that. Or what about, "I contracted my eating disorder in Eufaula, Alabama, after coming in contact with an infectious eating disorder virus-bug-thing."

Truly. What a gift it would be if we could pinpoint the exact time and date addiction begins—much like getting bit by a tick and contracting Lyme disease. Perhaps that would solve much of the heartache if, in recovery, we could find the root cause. Even better if there was a strong course of antibiotics we could take to rid our bodies of addiction!

But forget all that wishful thinking because you know as well as I do that this doesn't exist. Specific to my own story, while there are a few pivotal moments that I believe launched me into an eating disorder full speed ahead, I believe Ed's influence was surrounding me a lot longer than I have memory of. After all, when I rewind the childhood memory bank, I begin to unearth hundreds and thousands of triggers.

Starting with:

Mama and Me

Mama always said, "Honey, you're not fat; you're just big-boned."

I'm talking as early as I can remember. My dad did the same. Constantly. It was directed at me and about me, to others, to everyone. "I don't know how she keeps holding on to all this weight. She's so active," my mom would say.

Sure, I'd been overweight for some time—I don't remember being conscious of it or seeing a shift until around age ten—but I wasn't *always* that way, no matter how often I was called big-boned.

I'd always been active. From the minute I was old enough, my mom and dad had me in every sport, music, or dance class available. We hopped around from activity to activity, and afterward, it was nothing to go to Subway or Wendy's and order the biggest thing they had on the menu. And don't forget to supersize my Coke—or, gasp, even my Diet Coke, since that's what the industry was telling us, right? What an oxymoron.

We were in a hurry. Life was busy. When we weren't on the road, we ate plentiful meals at home. Every sit-down dinner had multiple courses. Always bread, lots of times a salad, occasionally something to start with, the main course and—voila—let's end it on a high note with some dessert. I'm not saying all of that is bad. I'm a fan of multiple-course meals and fine dining. I'm just saying it was in excess. And for what? A worn-out mom? To please my dad? Y'all. I can barely pick up a rotisserie chicken from the store some nights to feed my family. I don't see how Mom did it. She would slave over homemade gravies and decadent pound cakes with homemade icing.

I'm not calling out specific foods as being bad, either. Most of the time, I like to think of food neutrally. Most of the time, because I'm human. What I *am* saying is that the actions were wrong. The actions and language around food were dead wrong.

In my childhood home, it was waste not, want not. You sat militantly at the table and couldn't be excused until a) you'd finished your plate, regardless of whether you enjoyed the food concerned or not—I can hear "An empty plate is a happy plate" ringing in my ears to this day—and b) everyone else had finished their plate. Those were the rules.

Anyone else grow up under the all too familiar lens of food is love and the Clean Plate Club? How is any child supposed to benefit from the guilt of being told, "You better finish every morsel! There are starving children in Africa." Or, and I love this one, "Your aunt is going to have her feelings hurt if you don't eat the food she's prepared for you."

It was never about trying different foods or stopping when you felt full. Hunger cues or eating until you felt satiated were out the window. We'd paid for it and cooked it—even worse if someone else had—so it better not go to waste.

It was about others. Always about others. Please others. Do what makes others happy. Make a good impression on others.

Don't get me wrong. My mom, opposite of my dad, was and still is an absolute earth angel. To know her is to love her. She's read every Farmer's Almanac cover to cover since the year—well, I don't know. I'm not kidding. If you were to ask her right now if it's going to be a tough winter, she'd say, "Well, I don't know, honey, I ain't checked the husks on the corn yet."

How old-timer but totally endearing is that?

She's straight gold, that woman, but she had her faults. Less than the average number of faults, I'm certain of it, but those she did have contributed to unhealthy habits and treatment of herself and others—insert me—along the way. You see, her behavior was learned. It was so ingrained and stitched into her being that she couldn't see the forest for the trees. At forty, I've begun to realize and appreciate that it was simply that. It wasn't sabotage. It was her history. It was her experience. It was my mom being brought up in a generation that didn't ask questions. Didn't self-advocate. Didn't speak. Men ruled. Religion ruled. You stay private and quiet, little girl.

Can we talk about perfection for a second? Perfectionism is clearly linked to addiction, and Brenda—that's my mom—must have been the poster girl when the concept was founded. Perfection is the enemy of good, meaning that your increasing efforts typically pose diminishing returns, and diminishing returns they were. Here I am now, middle-aged, trying to rediscover who I really am and what I really believe.

So what I mean is that I was raised in a box. Not literally, just figuratively. Everything was black and white. To illustrate:

You must

Present yourself this way,

You must

Talk to people this way,

You must

Please your husband and submit to him this way,

You must

Respect your elders this way,

You must

Believe and worship this way.

Even if you don't feel like it, it isn't comfortable, you don't want to, or it doesn't make a damn bit of sense.

And don't you. Dare. Ask. Questions.

Y'all. Even now, and this is wild, my sweet mama comments on what I'm wearing to bed. She'll tell me, in her own poised way, that what

I'm wearing isn't sexy enough and how I should dress up more for my husband. Or she'll ask whether or not I've stopped to think about what Matthew will eat for dinner. Not our kids and not myself—but Matthew. Catching onto a theme here? What I do isn't for me, and what others do isn't for themselves. It's all about someone else and making others happy. Self doesn't exist. Self is less. Sure, some selflessness is good, but at what cost does so much of it come?

Folks, those generational curses were made to be broken. It's the responsibility of each generation not to repeat the mistakes of those who came before them, and the difference is that now I speak up. When Mama makes these remarks, I fire back. I stand up for myself. I don't care that she's seventy-eight and set in her ways. It's important for her to hear, ya know. I want her to know that there's a freer way to live, one that brings joy and happiness because it's not just about others. She's served others her entire seventy-eight years on this earth, so it's time to stop putting herself last. She deserves it.

My mom recently moved next door to our family, and while the topic of food will always be a stressor in our relationship, especially as I try to raise kids with healthy eating habits, the move has been a redemptive part of our story. I can tell her she's bananas when she tries to give my kids ice cream at 7 am, and we can laugh together, usually a day or so after the initial lecture, because I have a choice. A choice to help direct different behaviors. What's even better? I have a chance. A chance to change the old-school rhetoric, just as she can keep believing it if she so desires. And Brenda, as much as I want her to, ain't changing.

I thank God I've been given a chance at motherhood. I spend every day vowing that my kids will never know what a happy plate is and will never be made to feel as if their feelings are less important than those of others, whether that be with food or anything else. I'll make sure to do everything I can to see their self-worth grow stable and strong. For my kids:

We are

More strong, less skinny,

We are

More love, less hate,

We are

More praise, less judgment.

I'm redirecting the narrative and am so thankful to have the opportunity to do so.

Dad and Me

My dad was a lot. Racist is probably the first word that comes to mind. Yikes, I know. I equate racism to ignorance, selfishness, and a general misunderstanding of what it is to be human. Known by his initials, AC was tainted with health issues after health issues, both physical and mental.

I've learned to love him since his death and understand that he, too, struggled with mental illness, but I'm certainly not excusing his behavior. After all, the hurt he put on us is one heavy piece of messed-up baggage I've lugged around for many years. Favoring my friends over me. Showing up to only one football game during my senior year to escort me up the drum major stand. Asking me to have weight loss competitions with him and always commenting on things I wore or that the boyfriend I was dating had *too many layers of skin*, meaning he was too fat, or that he was *just right* because he matched me in size or big-bonedness. We'd be in the pool, and he'd ask my friends if they wanted to be thrown in the air while telling me to wait on the side since I was too heavy for him to handle. He'd tell me how ashamed he was that I grew up to be a n***** lover. Insanely brutal, but we're getting raw and real, right?

I've forgiven AC. I've been cured of his hate.

Have I forgotten? No. Never.

It took a long time to get here, but I have. Regardless of my new lease on our relationship, I know, beyond a shadow of a doubt, that he contributed to my eating disorder, body image issues, and much of my life with Ed.

Oh, there were some very special moments.

In high school, he'd lock me out of the house if I was one minute post-curfew. The door wasn't just locked. It was locked with him behind it, waving at me, saying, "Too bad, so sad. Pick another place to stay tonight because you ain't staying here."

Meanwhile, my mama would be behind AC, wanting him to let me in and crying hysterically.

I'd like to take a minute to thank my cousin, Sam, for providing me with a place to stay when that happened—with a hot toddy waiting for me at the door. Yes, she directly contributed to underage drinking, but those cocktails were a welcome nightcap after dealing with AC and his shenanigans.

Now picture this.

It was move-in day for my freshman year at college. On the way, I was pulled over for illegal window tint—on the car my dad purchased for me, no less. AC and my uncle were following behind me since it had been an absolute necessity to load multiple cars down with all the essentials for my new dorm.

As he passed by, AC witnessed me being pulled over by law enforcement. He immediately made a U-turn and peeled in directly behind me and the cop. He then got out of the car and yelled at the cop as loud as he could, "HOW FAST WAS SHE GOING? TELL ME! I'LL HANDLE IT."

Can you picture the embarrassment? The cop warned him to stay back and asked him if he'd like to answer for my illegal window tint.

Are you ready? My dad ignored the cop, marched back to his car, and left me on the side of the road. No bye, no nothing, nada. He missed a perfectly good opportunity to support me. Maybe even to save me from a ticket. Not only did he not help me get out of that experience, he created a worse one.

Even the cop recognized his poor behavior. "Wow, some dad, huh?"

Me to the cop, "You have no idea."

Above and beyond all of that, the most hurtful sting. It took him twenty long years to say for the first time ever, "I love you."

It was six months prior to his death, and I don't know if he genuinely meant it. I mean, he was so sick. Was he regretful and wanting to make amends? Did he want to make sure I knew that he loved me before he kicked the bucket? Or was he just that sick that he didn't know what he was saying as much as he didn't know who I was—thank you, Alzheimer's. However, in my head now, he meant it, and that's all I need.

Other Family

The evil spirit in my dad hadn't fallen far from the tree. My dad's mom, my grandmother, that bingo-playing fool, has to be one of the largest negative food influences I had growing up. I spent a lot of time with her until middle school, when she eventually passed, so perhaps it's more of a timing thing than a blanket bad influence, but alas. This lady would smoke twelve packs a day of whatever-she-could-get-her-hands-on cigarettes and make me run laps around her apartment building after breakfast because the toast THAT SHE'D JUST MADE FOR ME was slathered in butter. "It dare not go to those already thick hips, lady."

It didn't end there. She highly favored her other grandchildren over me. At Christmas, she made it extremely apparent by the doting and the number and kinds of gifts she gave them compared to me. I'm sure some of it was my own insecurity and the negative talk coming from my mom about how my grandmother, her mother-in-law, had treated her, too, given her size, but it was still evident.

My uncle, an alcoholic, also on my dad's side of the family, was extremely abusive not only to his wife but to many around him. He was a pompous asshole for no good reason. If he got the chance to slander or take a stab at you, he went for it. He always took the opportunity to tell me how something I was eating or drinking was going to make me gain more weight and how I should stop while I was ahead.

One night, my mom and dad left me with my aunt and uncle while they went to a class reunion. Naturally, my uncle had gone on a bender and came back absolutely hammered. I'd never seen my aunt like that; she was afraid for her life. I think she was worried about what he'd do to me, too.

We hid from him in the upstairs bathroom as he staggered up the stairs, intoxicated. I remember, so vividly, my aunt pulling the long phone cord—this was the early 90s—into the bathroom from the bedroom. She quickly locked the door and called my dad to hurry home.

I have questions, people. Of course, this was before cell phones, so to this day, I'm wondering how she rang him so fast and who she called. Maybe a restaurant manager? Shortly after that call, my uncle broke into the bathroom, pulling my aunt outside and down the stairs. All I could hear was her yelling, screaming, and telling him to stop.

I've no idea what happened between the two of them that night. All I know is that at the age of eleven, I was hiding under the bathroom vanity, thinking I was a goner, that my aunt and I were both goners. Thank God my dad and mom showed up. By that time, though, not wanting to fight with AC, my uncle had fled. There were occasional holiday get-togethers, but my uncle didn't show his face much after that. That was just fine in my book.

Years passed, and my mom asked that I go see my uncle while he was on his deathbed to say my last goodbyes. At that time, I was deep in my disorder and quite frail. I was so skinny that my upper ribs were poking through my clothes. I was dying to be thin—literally. I remember it so clearly: walking into the hospital room and my uncle reaching his arms out to hug me. A hug? This man had never once hugged me, not ever. Though sickened by the thought of hugging him, I gave in. After all, I was a certifiable people-pleaser—and he's dying, and there's that thing about respecting my elders, so maybe I should.

He then grabbed my arms and looked me in the eyes, "I've never seen you look so good. You're finally the way God meant you to be."

Those words immediately permeated every cell in my body and have been with me for years. On the one hand, I recognized his words were full of abusive behavior and lies, while on the other, I'd just received confirmation that killing myself was producing a positive outcome. Thank you, piece of you-know-what, for going out on such a high note.

Even More

It came from all sides, and I'm certain many of you can relate. There are probably fifteen other stories I could tell you, all linked to childhood and about being made to feel inferior by certain relatives and teachers and society as a whole.

Stories of Love

There were also plenty of stories of love, though. I don't want you to think my childhood was destitute or ruined by these experiences. I'd even say it was better than average—or maybe that's years of therapy talking. I grew up with a great foundation of love and friends and family. Some of the best.

The problem is that those negative experiences stick with you. They become stitched into the fabric of you.

It's Not One Thing

I'm sharing the bad apples in an attempt a) to reveal how those around you can have incredibly negative lasting effects, but also b) to say we shouldn't spend our entire lives trying to pinpoint the exact date and time, that a single thing became the universal cause of our addiction, or obesity, or mental illness—or you name it. In the court of Lauren's opinion, that's not feasible.

Research will continue to advance the understanding and investigation of primary causes, and for that, I'm thankful. Of course, there are more effective prevention strategies that need to be understood, and with that, treatment strategies tailored to individuals. But a bit like the roots of a plant, everyone's why about their addiction is made up of tissues and cells that have journeyed deep through various experiences along the way, forming the anchoring network that is their addiction.

This has finally gotten me to one realization: after my twenty-six-year struggle, my disorder isn't discoverable in a specific place or defined by one thing. That one place or root cause is an amalgamation of hundreds, if not thousands, of things.

That's why I say screw the why. You still need therapy. And it's okay to unpack the past. Do it. It's good practice for the puzzle pieces of you. But you could spend your entire life in therapy and still not have a clue as to what got you here.

Know This

It happened to you. It wasn't because of you. You didn't do anything wrong. You, the human, didn't cause this. You are not your disease. You are not your disorder.

Meeting the Devil

These next two chapters are tricky because as you read them, you're going to say to me, "You just told me the why is an amalgamation of things we can't precisely pinpoint, and *now* you're telling me these next pivotal moments led you to Ed?"

And you aren't wrong. The difference in these next two chapters is that the stories describe distinct introductions to Ed through friends and people who felt like family who were *already* dating him. So, while they don't wholly define my why, they make up a big part of it.

There are so many lessons to be learned from those who have eating disorders and are close to us. When Ed tangibly introduces himself before affecting you, it's a strange place to be. It's perhaps one of the most delicate situational experiences anyone already conditioned for an eating disorder can find themselves in.

So let's get to the pivotal moment in which I first met the devil himself.

For lessons learned and insights from this chapter,
visit "ENLIGHTENMENT on DISCOVERING ED"

CHAPTER 3

LOVE LETTER TO ASHLEY

**In this chapter, we're introduced to Ed
for the first time as he grabs hold of my
friend, and we look at how two lives
were drastically changed because of it.**

Have you ever thought, *What if I could go back?* Back to grade school or college or some instance that was pivotal for you. Did I just age myself by saying grade school? What if you were given the chance to do it all over again and totally transform your behavior or actions leading up to and around that crucial moment? This is one of those times.

Let me be clear. I don't think being given a chance to redo it would change my being diagnosed with an eating disorder, but perhaps it might have saved Ashley and me some heartache along the way.

We'll take it all the way back to elementary, middle, and high school, where friendship can run so deep it carries baggage that's equal parts true joy and heartache.

That was us. Ashley and I were thick as thieves. Pretty sure we rode the school bus home together three out of five days a week. Her mom and dad were my mom and dad. We joined every club together, cheered together, played softball together, and joined the band together. If she did it, I did it. And if I did it—you guessed it—she did it. We ate copious amounts of Tony's frozen pizza and farm-fresh hamburgers straight from the cows on her farm. And we drank Coke. The real "real thing." She was everything to me at that age. The sister I never had. We loved hard and played hard, and boy, did we live like we were on top of the world—whatever that means for young girls of that age.

Anyone remember Lisa Frank? Can I get a "Hell, yeah!" from all the 90s babies? If I had to introduce Ashley to you without you knowing her—which I'm assuming you don't—I'd say she was everything Lisa Frank was and made you feel. Happy, glittery Ashley.

We. Were. Dreamers. We dreamt about everything, from being real-life Ariels to the boys we wanted to date. We'd even film ourselves and each other talking about our future man and what he'd look like and how handsome he'd be. We'd stay up late talking about who our crushes were—spoiler alert; we had lots of the same crushes—and where we'd end up in life. We repeatedly watched *Wild Hearts Can't Be Broken*, and *Tommy Boy* on rotation—RIP Chris Farley. We knew every scene backward and forward. Quite the mix.

When we weren't in the pool playing mermaids, we'd slip 'n slide in the garage. Who needs Dawn and a plastic tarp to have a good time when you have good old-fashioned motor grease on a concrete floor? Those were the absolute best of times. You know, the kinds of memories that make your heart smile.

We did everything on Ashley's farm. We'd fish in her pond and chase cattle, though I don't advise doing the latter as it got a little dicey at times. Her dad was the most precious man ever, who I love to this very day. He called me *dry bones*—which was way better than big bones—because Ashley and I would search for cow carcasses. I know what you're thinking, "You're kidding me, right?" No! We'd hunt for said cow carcasses so we could paint the bones all kinds of wild colors. Very Lisa Frank of us.

What a childhood. It was pre-internet, so we didn't have tablets or phones. What we had was the outdoors and our imaginations. And oh, how our imaginations would run wild.

Remember how my dad never showed up for me? In almost fifty high school football games, he showed up for maybe two or three. And out of ten football games in my senior year and a handful of other band events where I was drum major, my dad showed up for one. One, people. Do you know who walked me up the stairs of the drum major platform at almost every high school football game and every band event? Ashley's dad. Total stand-in for my never-present father.

With that foundation laid, here's my caveat before we dive in. Ashley isn't the antagonist in this story or, more specifically, in this chapter. Ed is. Before you get your wires crossed, know that I deeply love and care about Ashley. I think of our history as one of those that will live on forever in my memory, and I pray my children are blessed with the same kind of childhood friends that Ashley was to me. A bond so tight that even after you've grown apart, you still feel threads of them woven into who you've become.

Ashley is where this all begins. She brought me to my very first introduction of an actual, factual eating disorder, so much so that this is where I can confidently say I met and started to fall head over heels for Ed.

You see, Ed got to Ashley before he got to me. I'm not sure how, but naturally, eating disorders don't discriminate. This would not only be my first intro to an eating disorder but also to several aspects—both anorexia and bulimia.

Dare I remind you what an outright disaster middle school can be in the first place—regardless of who your friends are? Boilerplate, even without this other stuff. I remember from 6th to 8th Grade feeling like I'd been thrown into a foreign land with no passport and no guidebook.

Middle school brings on an entire host of hormones and hell like you've never experienced before. I mean, as a girl, you're getting your period and trying to figure out your identity, all while maturing into a body that isn't your own. As a boy, you're—well, I don't know, but I'd imagine it's about the same or worse. And if you identify as anything outside of that, whew, I can only imagine: exhausting.

I remember Ashley staying in the bathroom for hours on end. I also remember her lunch box during that time. On a good day, she'd fill it with a bit of fruit, some raw vegetables, and saltines. But fruit only on good days because when she was feeling skinny, she'd allow herself to have the extra calories. So there was little to no protein, nothing of sustenance, and an overall scarcity of food in general. Forget Tony's pizza, and don't even joke about a hamburger anymore. Those were now a thing of the past. All of a sudden, there was an emphasis on weight control and what she was eating.

Drastically, Ashley's physique began changing. I noticed her weight drop quite literally overnight. I was curious about what she was up to, but she was always dieting or trying new things to lose weight, so I didn't suspect it was an actual eating disorder. Then, one day, I caught her throwing up in the middle school bathroom. We were now in 8th Grade, and I knew it. I knew there was something more to the story because, trust me, even I, in all my innocence, knew that people didn't lose weight so quickly unless they were sick. Yes, the lunchbox had been scarce for some time now, but this was more than just a lack of food. This was starvation on steroids. And now, realizing that she was purging, I knew it for sure.

This was Ed.

Ashley started drawing all kinds of attention from our totally platonic group of guy friends. Insert jealousy. I was soooo jealous. In middle school, as a people-pleaser, that's all I wanted—to be liked and loved. Popularity came before anything.

Happy for her, sure, but I wanted the same for me. I'd never had that attention from guys other than one, but even he was noticing Ashley in a different, more compelling way. Everyone was noticing Ashley now. It even seemed like teachers began to notice Ashley more. Did they appreciate her better now that she'd dropped some pounds? Why was she now more liked than before? It was the most perverse and twisted account of relationship dynamics I'd seen in my short twelve to thirteen years of life.

Regardless, I didn't care how she was getting there. I wanted in. It was as if she'd finally started living. Ashley was thriving.

Little did I know, she wasn't thriving at all. Ashley was dying.

Because of the little-did-I-know part, I committed myself to throwing up. I'm not sure I even had a name for it at the time, but I was going to do whatever Ashley was doing. If it was working for her, it surely had to work for me. If I looked like her, maybe I'd get the same attention. We had originally been the same size, so I knew it was possible to get there.

At that age, I equated being popular to winning an Oscar, and I'd act out whatever character I needed to be to turn heads like Ashley was doing. I remember planning it like I was gearing up for something special. I told myself, *Today is the day. You're going to hold your head high because your Oscar awaits.* Unlike Ashley, at least initially, it was more about disposing of the food I ate, not about what I ate. So I'd plan my escape directly after the lunchroom period and go into the bathroom on Yellow Hall. I'd then act out the unmentionable: I'd make myself throw up. Or, I should say, I'd try, because once I got in there, I kept poking and poking to no avail. Trying to teach myself how was miserable. I felt weak but had no success. How did she do it? Whatever, however, I just couldn't muster enough in me to keep going. A switch flipped in my mind: whatever this was, I decided, it was for the birds.

You have to remember, I never thought this was wrong or wondered how I could help her or anything like that. It still puzzles me to this day.

Was it my age? Was it my lack of knowledge about the harm she was doing or around eating disorders in general? Mental health was not yet an openly accepted problem to seek help for, and the internet, which could have been a resource to us, was barely a thing in average-income households. I could list a million other excuses for my actions, but the bottom line is I looked inwardly and not out. Selfishly, not selflessly.

For sure, I brought it up with her, but I wasn't asking with helpful intent. I was asking so I could learn more and execute better than the times I'd tried on Yellow Hall. "What are you doing? Why haven't you told me? Help me lose weight, too. Let's lose together."

And Ashley, of course, wanted to cover it up, respond as if she didn't know what I was talking about—she was good at that—and act as if she wasn't doing anything outside of the more natural watching of her food intake and exercising. And that's part of the addict mindset. First, deny, then redirect.

While my relationship with Ed hadn't yet blossomed, Ashley's continued, and this is where shit gets real. And scary.

Fast forward to high school. We were on a band trip, and band trips were everything. Who doesn't love being crammed into a charter bus with their closest friends and their portable CD player for hours on end? Band trips were also perfect for first kisses or, I dare say, something more, except that I was a career virgin, so that wasn't exactly in my purview. Either way, it was a time to let loose and see the world.

But terrible things happened on this one band trip in particular. We were in St. Petersburg, Florida, we'd already performed, and it was time to have fun. We had an amusement park day planned. Ashley had gone into the bathroom of our hotel room prior to our heading out and showed no signs of exiting the bathroom anytime soon. Imagine four girls sharing a hotel room and one bathroom. She'd gone in, turned on the shower, and—silence. For too long.

Things started to get uncomfortable. What else do teenage girls do but obnoxiously begin banging on the door, "Get the heck out, what are you doing in there?"

No response.

Minutes later, after telling a chaperone, EMTs were busting open the bathroom door, and there Ashley lay on the floor, looking lifeless. She'd passed out and, because of her *episode*, we'll call it, ended up missing the trip back for a short stint in the local hospital. Call it dehydration. Call it low blood sugar. I call it Ed fair and square. Don't even try to palm this off on something else. Was she actively throwing up when it happened? Did her body just give up in the moment and her blood pressure tank? Was her potassium level off? There could be a whole host of reasons for why and how Ashley went down like she did. But that was Ed showing off like he does. He'd done this.

I'd seen my dad pass out before—and even my mom—but seeing your childhood best friend being wheeled out on a gurney, lifeless, with an oxygen mask, succumbing to a disease that she couldn't see her way out of, was traumatizing in the absolute worst way. She was in the trenches, and no one knew how to help her out.

Punchline reenters the chat: I was still jealous. This would bring Ashley more attention. She'd be even closer to friends and boys and teachers now because everyone would be watching her. Everyone was already asking about her.

What was wrong with me? I cared, but, bottom line, I cared more about looks and attention than Ashley's health and well-being. That was a tough pill to swallow and still is.

Ashley recovered from the incident, and all was well. I mean—she was alive. While I was traumatized by her experience and how serious a problem it was, I also remembered her in a bikini at the pool just days before the incident, getting noticed by everyone. I thought everything that had transpired would be worth it for just a smidge of that same focus on me. How utterly messed up.

So that's the first big, pivotal moment: I met bulimia and anorexia, end of story.

As we got older and life happened, Ashley and I made new friends. New, close friends. I feel like there was one specific moment in high school where I pushed her away for the last time, but I'm unsure why or what happened that made it so detrimental to our relationship.

Our interaction now consists of a Facebook message once every five years. I don't know if or how Ashley ever got the help she needed, but I still care deeply about her and hope she's thriving. Her children and husband are adorable, and I still think of her parents often and wish them well.

Knowing what I know now, I wish I'd been a better friend. A more nurturing sister. I know there are limitations: I couldn't possibly have made her better, but I could've been there in a different capacity. Jealousy is a thing of evil; I succumbed to the comparison trap long before social media came on the scene.

As much as I'd like to think I could have acted a different way, I'm not sure I could have. You know, when you're young, and life hasn't yet offered you much perspective. How do we see beyond that, offering compassion instead of jealousy? How do children, teenagers, and adults support their friends? But also, how can we take action to help someone who's going through something similar?

These are just a few of the many topics I share with you in the chapter "ENLIGHTENMENT on DISCOVERING ED."

And wherever you are in life, Ashley, know that I love you. I love our colorful upbringing with you by my side. Our friendship was a thing you'd usually only dream about or watch in a movie. If I could go back,

I'd Bubble Wrap our little bodies and tell us we're perfect and beautiful and that we've been given such a gift in each other and never to let that go. I'd be a better friend. I'd choose love over jealousy. I'd choose encouragement over envy.

Bottom line, I'd choose you.

For lessons learned and insights from this chapter,
visit "ENLIGHTENMENT on DISCOVERING ED"

CHAPTER 4

RIP BELLE

This is my second pivotal moment in discovering Ed. We'll see how this time was different and how it affected my relationship with food moving forward.

Do not, I repeat, do not offer up your disorder to someone else. By this, I mean stop sharing the details. It isn't a competition, and you don't get bragging rights for being a certain size. Stop sharing numbers or how much weight you lost when you were sick. Stop talking about how you did it and how you hid it. That's *your* story. Those are *your* tools. Not mine and not theirs. Addict secrets should remain under lock and key forever. I say this because inquiring minds will ask questions and want to know. Don't tell them. People are impressionable. People are vulnerable. People love shortcuts.

I'm no different.

For as long as I can remember, I was searching for a quick-fix microwave solution to weight loss. While I'd spent years on Weight Watchers attempting to make sustainable change, I still tried just about every other weight loss program or diet imaginable. Keto, cabbage soup, grapefruit—you name it. There was South Beach and Atkins and Jenny Craig and SlimFast. Shakes should be easy enough, right? That's what I told myself, anyway. Even my doctor got in on the act, prescribing Sugar

Busters at one point. Then there was Nutrisystem. If there was a diet out there, I'd tried it.

There was even a church-inspired weight loss plan, I kid you not. We all had these teal blue binders that held our food logs and scripture that somehow tied back to weight loss. We'd go to church every week—in addition to the usual Sundays *and* Wednesdays—and weigh in and talk as if we were in a support group, which we were in a way.

I'd give anything to go back and be a fly on the wall just to hear Betty Lou and Geraldine talk about how the devil himself was interfering with their weight loss. "He tempted me too many times this week!"

Talk about a perfect target demographic. Well done, church-fad-diet-weight-loss-program creator.

I wanted to do it the healthy way, sure, and if others were seeing results, then so should I, right?

Here's the catch, though. Healthy and fad diets go together about as well as nourishment does with starvation. They don't!

Whether it's cabbage or grapefruit or shakes or rebuking carbs in the Lord's name, it usually goes something like this. First, we start with a restriction of sorts. Then, we lead ourselves into nutrient deficiency. Lastly, we binge because, at that point, it's only natural for our bodies to react in that way. Our bodies can't tell if we're just attempting to restrict a certain food or foods or if we're in a full-on famine, so they go, "Hey brain, I need you to go find food and eat it real fast."

Yes! So we end up getting off the rollercoaster that is fad dieting because we're seeking relief after such a ride, but we can't resist the next new and shiny ride to come along. See where we're going? It's an absolute vicious cycle.

Truth is, at this point in my journey, nothing was fast enough for me, and I was beyond fad diets. I wasn't just considering Ed; I was full-on flirting. So far, though, my attempts had failed.

Until the next pivotal moment.

It was when meeting Belle on Thanksgiving Day in 2002 that I was introduced to Ed for the second time in my life.

I still—for the life of me—don't understand how, when she left rehab, Belle didn't take with her the knowledge about not sharing. Or maybe she did, and she just thought her secrets were safe with me—meaning I'd never act on them. Sure, I came across as if I was chock full of confidence. I'd been perfecting the whole fake it till you make it act for years. So maybe Belle just thought I wasn't near as impressionable as I was. I sure had her fooled if that's the case.

It's an interesting thing in eating disorders, specifically, but perhaps for addiction in general. There are building blocks of mental health disorders and disease and, potentially, a singular instance that causes you to finally execute. Ever thought of it like that before? Is that true for you or someone you know? There are personal events, like the examples I gave from my childhood, that lay pieces of your why or even its whole foundation: why you go on to have an eating disorder, why you so easily pick up the bottle any time you're stressed, why you always seek out a particular dopamine hit.

But then, what about the exact instance that causes you, for the first time ever, to take the action that starts the doomsday domino effect? Of course, addicts go through gateway drugs or dabble in things before they get hooked, but what's the reason behind the one time they amp up and fully execute?

For me, it was tools. I'd been trying to execute for a long time, but this was the one event that was the catalyst that took me from Point A to Point Z at the speed of 0 to 60.

What took me to the next level was the explicit knowledge and experience of someone else. Belle—quite literally—handed me bulimia on a silver platter that day. It was as if the eating disorder gods and the Thanksgiving pilgrims got together and said here it is! Take it!

That's why I say stop sharing.

I was in my freshman year of college. Oh, the freedom! To anyone who's been to college, is there any other time in life when you feel freer than your freshman year? If there is, someone, please tell me so I can chase it. Moving out and living on your own for the first time is a hallelujah moment like no other. Suddenly, you're in charge of this absurd mix of everything: your schedule, your chores, your decisions, and, unfortunately, your finances. Ah, yes, finances. Kill me now. I was *terrible* with money. Thank goodness for my cousin, who owned a bank. Not some big fancy Wall Street operation, just a tiny branch bank, but let me tell you, it was the perfect solution for reversing my overdraft charges. I highly recommend befriending someone in banking if you plan to be a financial disaster.

I digress; we'll come back to this later.

So there I was, driving myself in my very own car, fueled by that unshakable freshman-year delusion of independence, on my way to Thanksgiving dinner. It was the first time I'd ever gone without my parents in the same car to a holiday gathering. I had my Saturn's sunroof open and the CD player was blaring Michael and Alan—last names Jackson, of course—as loud as it would go. I know, I know, but I do pride myself in my diverse taste in music. There are gems in every genre, folks.

I couldn't wait to get my hands on some of Mama's sweet potato soufflé, the guaranteed delicious smoked turkey, and the smorgasbord of desserts that would be there. All the usual suspects. Sweet potato pie, pecan pie, my cousin's homemade banana pudding and peach cobbler— Our family on that side had its share of musicians, so I knew we'd be making some musical memories that day, too. My cousin was hosting, as she always does. Thanksgiving is her favorite. I got there around 1 pm sharp. Time enough to socialize before we sat down to eat.

This cousin, y'all. Ann. I'd looked up to her forever. If you've gotten this far, you know things at my house were strict, more about structure and less about fun. It was the opposite with Ann. Nothing, and I mean nothing, was off-limits. She was forty years old when I was ten, but our age difference never got in the way. I was never afraid to talk to her. Why would I be when anything went? With Mom and Dad, it was you can't do this, you can't do that. Ann didn't care. Or maybe I should spin it as she did care. She loved me for me—just the way I was. She wanted to spend time with me and teach me everything she knew. She was like a big sis, a mom, and an aunt, all rolled into one.

Weekends with her while I was growing up were the best. She'd pack our days with all the fun. She'd do my hair—shoutout to the alter ego she'd style for me, bouffant Betty—and we'd go junking. We rode around in her Cadillac with the scent of Estee Lauder Cinnabar while Dwight Yoakam blasted on the radio. Life was good when you were around Ann.

Ann had recently moved to Eufaula, Alabama, to marry some guy. The only distinct thing I remember about him is I didn't see him much of the time. She'd made fast friends with Belle, a California native who had moved into town from Michigan, and she couldn't wait for us to meet. Belle and her husband didn't have family in town for the holidays, so naturally, Ann invited them to hang with us on that Thanksgiving Day. What a sweetie, right? Ann was like that. Equal parts generous and fun.

I walked in, and what did I see before me but a blonde bombshell. She was forty-nine and beautiful. She had that Cali vibe to her. I'd always, always equated skinny to beautiful, but her beauty was only amplified by her personality, which radiated love and acceptance right from the start. I was very excited to get to know her. Ann's Belle.

We made some initial small talk, but I didn't get to properly meet her until we got ready to sit down at the table. I remember it like it was yesterday. I, with a near-insurmountable pile of food on my plate, was about to dig in, but I'd forgotten my tea in the kitchen.

As I walked into the kitchen, I was startled. I didn't expect to see Belle there; I guess I hadn't noticed her absence from the table to begin with.

She was standing over the sink, putting the tiniest bit of smoked turkey in her mouth. She was so dainty as she took that bite. And so careful, as if the turkey was fragile or something. Since we'd had little in the way of actual, formal conversation, we started with friendlies. I'd heard about her, and she'd heard about me. She asked about my college experience and how excited I was to be there. What it was like. Was I dating anyone?

I was at the most vulnerable place in my life, and the Belle I saw was about five foot four and a hundred pounds soaking wet. I didn't care that she was thirty years my senior. I wanted to be her. I wanted her body. Her blonde hair. Her tan skin. All of it. Here I go again with envy. Hello, again, feelings of inadequacy.

I'm not exactly sure how Belle knew to start peeling back the layers, but she did.

I definitely don't believe this was all Belle's fault. I mean, there's just too much history to pinpoint. But I do feel strongly in my big bones that this was the jump-off. The catalyst that got Ed really going for me.

For whatever reason, I immediately felt comfortable enough to question her back.

"What are you doing in here?

"Why are you eating in private?

"Don't be silly. Come to the table."

Talk about pushy! I hate hearing me now.

What she said was akin to, "Well, I don't like to eat in front of people."

My head immediately went back to Ashley, thinking how she'd demonstrated some of those exact same food behaviors and mannerisms.

Belle proceeded to tell me that she'd had an eating disorder and gone for rehab at a well-known inpatient treatment facility in Arizona. She added that while she was now in active recovery, she still struggled with not wanting others to see her eat or what was on her plate. It bothered her to the point that she just preferred to eat in solitude.

If there was a moment I could go back to and stop, it would be this one. For myself, selfishly, because this is where my manufacturing of a disease begins. My curiosity had gotten the best of me. And. It. Was. On.

"Why? How? I mean, for an eating disorder? But what kind?"

"I was in rehab for laxative abuse."

Wait. What? I thought throwing up was it. Well, it was the one I was most familiar with, and I kind of thought the abuse of laxatives was a joke. But I was also thinking, *If this is real, there's hope.* I could do it a different way! After all, purging hadn't so far been successful.

Then, it all came out of her, rushing like a waterfall.

Belle went on to tell me how much weight she'd lost, the brand of laxatives she abused, how she abused them, when she abused them, tactics to make sure she kept things secret around her husband and friends, even down to the calorie count she knew she had to maintain just to keep standing. Because, naturally, this was risky.

If she could drop that many sizes in that little time and look this good, I wanted in.

I was taking notes, y'all. Fast and furious notes in my head. Okay, so I'd head straight back to school, stop off on the way at Belle-told-me-where, and grab everything I needed. Every single thing I needed in order to do exactly what Belle had been doing.

Let me tell you, the soundtrack to Rocky started playing in my head; I'd won the lottery. I'd never felt so victorious. Laxatives, I thought. Had I just been given the keys to the kingdom of bulimia? The true microwave version of weight loss I'd been looking for? I was diagnosed with IBS in middle school, so diarrhea was no stranger to me, and this would be easy. Pandora's box was open.

And as for Belle, I don't understand how it was okay. How, in her mind, it made sense to unload on me in that fashion. I never will, I guess. Rehab 101 teaches you ultimate discretion around sharing numbers, abusive habits, and anything that might equip another vulnerable individual to take on addictive or disordered behaviors.

I know I was the curious one. I asked all the right questions, but she gave me all the wrong answers. Well—the answers she shouldn't have.

Anyway, back at the table, leaving Belle to her own devices, I was viciously mapping out the path on which I was going to take this terrible disease, manifesting my bulimia within seconds of sitting down. Something had shifted in my brain that fast. I could get to eat whatever I wanted that Thanksgiving because I was going to follow Belle's steps all the way. I'd lose a ton of weight, and maybe it wouldn't be as detrimental to my health as purging. I wasn't harming myself that bad—or so I thought. After all, it was available over the counter and on the shelf. It was waiting for me.

And that's what I did. I went to Belle's store. I bought Belle's brand and took her dose. I followed Belle's timing, and eventually, I even used the excuses she'd given me. I went home and made Belle's journey my own. That. Very. Night. Bulimia, with the vehicle being not my hands, but laxatives. Lovely. Poop your pants lovely.

Back at school post-thanksgiving, I began to spiral. Every waking minute, I calculated what I needed to do to get to Belle's exact size—slowly trimming back what I ate, how I ate, and maximizing what laxative dose I took. I curiously studied the side effects I was having and graduated myself to the next intensity level. And my body somehow managed to muster up enough energy to get me through freshman classes each day, even with all the abuse.

I'd be sick all night and wake up—if I'd managed to get a wink in—to charge forth into my freshman classes with the stamina of a horse when, in reality, my body was suffering. What's sad is how blind I was to the havoc I was wreaking on my long-term health as well. My potassium levels were tanking, but I'd show up for every class, acting as if nothing had happened the day and the night before. I was ready to go. I had goals in my mind that must be achieved. I was on my way to being the blonde bombshell I'd modeled my disorder after.

I look back and think how wild that was. Here I am, now forty, and I can't imagine showing up to class on time after losing even one hour of sleep, much less getting gussied up after giving myself a drug-induced stomach virus the day and night before. Gross and shocking.

Diane, my college roommate, had started to catch on.

We came from two separate worlds. She'd grown up with housekeepers, for crying out loud. I'm certain she never once visited Walmart or McDonald's, which is about as real as real can get. We didn't get along much initially but later became close. I taught her how to wash dishes, wash her clothes, and all the finer domestic things she'd arguably been missing out on.

On move-in day, freshman year, her parents asked when the cleaners were coming. To which my parents responded, "This is a freshman dorm. Better not be no cleaners coming."

I may have been laughing on the outside to smooth over any awkwardness, but, for sure, I was dying on the inside. Talk about a diabolical difference in upbringing. I was from the lower middle class with a mama who always said, "If you buy a house bigger than you can clean yourself, you've bought too big of a house." We may have believed in happy plates, but we—bet your bottom—didn't believe in housekeepers.

A stand-out all-time favorite Diane moment was when she popped popcorn in my illegally-hidden-under-the-bed microwave for a whopping twelve minutes. Twelve whole minutes, y'all. The fire alarm in our freshman dorm could be heard all over campus. As I was leaving my first class, I rushed to see what was going on and could tell it didn't seem like such a huge threat until I got off the stairs at our level. All the smoke was coming from our room. Our dorm was built in 1911, I think, and let's just say she ignited the room. My white microwave was now black. The electricals were legit ripped out of the wall, and our room was forever changed. Long live burned popcorn smell. I bet it still carries the stench!

She confronted me with my laxatives one day after class. She'd found my stash and presented it to me while she intervened. "I know what you're doing. Why are you doing it? You can't keep this up. I care about you, and this cannot be healthy. What can I do for you? Can we go get some food?"

I don't know why it had to be about food with her, but it always was. She wanted to fix me with food. Such an oxymoron; food is a quick way to get someone with an eating disorder to shut down or push you out. In reality, I did need Diane's support, just not in that way.

My roommate had caught me red-handed, but I kept going. I kept going until I started to see some weight come off—a small fraction of the success I craved. Looking back, I'm not sure if I was genuinely satisfied with the weight I lost or just so sick and tired of worrying I'd poop my pants all day. Either way, six months in, I stopped. Isn't that strange? Even now, I ask myself how I managed to walk away from such an addictive behavior so easily. Maybe Diane's intervention struck a chord with me after all. I was done with laxatives—for now.

Here's the thing. Do I fault Belle for introducing me to laxative bulimia? Occasionally, yes. I'd be lying if I said I didn't. But even if you take Belle out of the picture, there's still me. There's still Mom and her complicated relationship with food. There's still Dad and his lack of I love you's. There's still my mean grandma, forcing me to run laps around her apartment building to lose weight. There's still the abusive uncle. The muck and the mud from my childhood were always there, long before Belle. So no, it wasn't all about her.

Oddly enough, as the years passed, Belle and I formed a bond. She became part of the family, someone I could turn to during the worst moments of my illness. I know it sounds strange, given how I half attribute my relationship with Ed to that day she handed me bulimia. We never spoke about it outright, but I think she knew. Somehow, without saying it, we both understood—and maybe that's part of why we stayed close.

Whatever the reason, I cared deeply for her, and I know she cared for me too.

Belle left us tragically in 2020 after suffering a heart attack, which brings me to the title of this chapter. Her loss was devastating to Ann and all of us who loved her. While no one can say with certainty what caused her heart to give out that day, I can't shake the belief that Ed played a role.

It's no secret that eating disorders shorten life spans, putting immense strain on the body—on the heart, the organs, everything, even years into recovery. I often wonder if Belle might still be here if Ed hadn't plagued her for so many years.

Even so, she lives on in me and in the good lessons she unknowingly taught me. As I write these words, I feel like part of her is here too, woven into these chapters, helping in her own way to heal those who suffer the same torment from Ed—even long after she's gone.

For lessons learned and insights from this chapter,
visit "ENLIGHTENMENT on DISCOVERING ED"

DATING ED

living to eat | in the trenches of an eating disorder

CHAPTER 5

GOODBYE BOOBS, HELLO BULIMIA

This chapter examines the escalation to a new level of the relationship between Ed and me, both before and after I underwent plastic surgery for the first time.

I feel like this isn't talked about enough. And yes, I'm realizing just how much I say that. Have you ever had plastic surgery? What about plastics during your adolescence? Wanna know the definition of a mental mind f***? Welp, that's it, folks. Imagine being rolled into an OR at nineteen. It's your first surgery—sure, there was the tonsillectomy at age three, but I'm talking about one you distinctly remember. You wake up, and part of you is gone.

I'm sure plastic surgeon speak would call it transformed. I call it double demolition. Dual destruction. Especially in the case of breasts. Saying buh-bye to my tig ol' bitties proved to be one of the most pivotal and possibly destructive chapters of my life. I didn't know how much of my identity was tied up in a body part.

I was a full D cup in 5th Grade, for Pete's sake. When all my friends were barely in training bras, I was going to the local department store to shop in the women's section for Bali underwire full-coverage brassieres. As if that wasn't enough weight to carry around, I managed to continue growing to a formidable size G cup before I'd land in talks with a plastic surgeon about breast reduction. I had permanent dips in my shoulders—those never go away, I came to find out—terrible back pain and a whole host of other not big-boned- but big-boobed-related problems.

I'd been asking for a breast reduction since I was about fifteen years old. *Fifteen.* Begging! I wore two types of bra everywhere I went: a minimizer below and a size smaller than I was just for extra security on top.

I'll never forget this one night when I was invited to a house party during my freshman year of college. To my surprise, the men's basketball coach just happened to be at the party. I'd developed a crush on him from day one. I still remember how I'd be rendered speechless anytime I was around him. I guess we'd both had enough to drink at the party, and it seemed the attraction was mutual. Anyway, we started making out, and things began to heat up. By heat up, I mean in an old-fashioned kind of way. There would definitely be no home plate hanky panky for me, but I let him feel around for fun.

He began by unhooking my first bra. Then blurted out, "What the—?"

Ha! He'd gotten to the minimizer and was absolutely baffled that I was wearing two bras. What a buzz kill! That broke any romantic connection we had, but we did have a good laugh and went back to the party. Pretty sure those two bras scared him off forever, as we never spoke again after that night.

I strapped those babies down with duct tape every formal I had. I have picture proof. Trust me, no dress was built for those bad boys of mine. My knockers were huge. They sat down at any restaurant table before I could. Boobs on the table, then my butt hit the seat. And running? Pffff. Entirely not possible when you have boobs that size. They needed to go.

But my dad refused. A breast reduction had been off the table—so punny—and out of the question for as long as I'd been asking for one. And as you know, my mom didn't argue with my dad, so that was that.

Dad was getting sicker, so naturally, he got softer. Things opened up for me. I'm sure the part where insurance was able to cover every penny helped, too, but still! He was open to it. And just like that, with his blessing in hand, I found myself meeting with a plastic surgeon in Rome, Georgia, and getting things scheduled.

My jugs—those overachievers that *felt* like they weighed four hundred pounds combined, but realistically, only about four—were finally going to become a proportionate and welcome feature rather than something literally dragging me down.

Let's say this:

Plastic surgery is a lot like those HGTV renovation shows. You know, the ones where a family leaves for a week-long vacation, and by the time they come back, their house has been completely transformed? Gone are the creaky floors, the peeling wallpaper, and the kitchen stuck in 1974. Instead, they walk into something beautiful, modern, and unrecognizable in the best way. And do you remember their faces? Pure shock and disbelief, followed by tears of joy. I lived for those moments!

With plastics, it's like that, but the shock of the transformation is magnified by infinity. Because it's you. The dwelling isn't just some mid-century brick-and-mortar home you moved into after you got your first job or got married. You've lived in this body, well, your whole life.

And while your body may be changed—drastically in some cases—the mind stays the same. That's where all of this gets highly problematic for someone with an eating disorder.

Fast forward to the summer before sophomore year. The boobs were finally coming off, y'all. It was time.

Here we go into dual demo. I woke up to pain and incisions that looked to me as big as Everest. I'd never seen so many bandages and so much tape in my life, and I had drains coming out of me on both sides. That sounds fully dramatic, and the doc had no doubt set expectations with me as far as post-operative pain and drains go, but when that lovely feeling of the anesthesia wearing off sets in, you kind of forget all the expectations stuff. Then there were pain meds as I'd never experienced them before, so both the highs and lows of that. And the wildest part: a totally new body. My saucer areolas had transformed. My boobs were no longer giant.

They were teeny tiny.

My whole body was changed.

When I look back, it's nearly unbelievable. I think that's because I have babies now and can't imagine them going through the same thing. That level of transformation, electively, at that age.

But here I was. I'd done it. It was inpatient at that time, and, goodness, was that a recovery.

Once I was wheeled to my room and the anesthesia fully started to wear off, I could see it. My flat chest. It was as if my chest was as flat as my stomach, and I was absolutely shaken to my core. They were gone, never to return. At that moment, I thought I'd made the biggest mistake of my life. I'd botched myself entirely.

My nurse asked me, "Would you like to see your chest tomorrow during bath time? Only if you're ready."

My answer was a firm no. I was worried about what that flatness might look like on me. I walked in with G's and came out with B's? That wasn't the plan.

"Doc, I was supposed to be a full C!" I exclaimed in fear and sadness.

He gave me some excuse about art and science and how he ended up taking out way more than planned to get the contour and balance my body needed, but I didn't care at the time. I was devastated. Here I was with unrecognizable small breasts. Just great. He told me to give it time and that I'd learn to love my new breasts. He also mentioned—which is interesting—that most patients do lose some weight after breast reduction because of how their torso looks with their smaller breasts. Or something like that.

Hmmmm, I thought. Little did I know this would come to major fruition for me less than twenty-four hours later.

The only positive thing about that day was Jane's visit. Diane and I were getting an apartment in the fall of sophomore year, and Jane would be our new roommate. We'd grown so close, Jane and I. Her mom, who I absolutely adore, came with her to the hospital. Guess what they brought? Titty balloons! Please, get you a friend that brings you boob balloons to the hospital after breast surgery. Those were so funny and quite entertaining for anyone who walked into the room.

It was day two post-op, and a new nurse came in to get me ready for the shower, a welcome event after such an occasion. She noted that the board said NO LOOK, which was nurse speak for "the patient isn't ready to see themselves." She told me we'd need to check the incision site and that she'd do that once we were in the bathroom, prior to my shower. It meant I'd have to get fully unwrapped and rebandaged before I got into said shower. So there we were, standing in front of the mirror. I was using the sink for balance. She kind of took turns walking side to side as the bandage loosened and came off.

I was making such an effort to avoid the mirror that was right in front of me, but she asked me to step back, and, in doing so, I loosened the last bit of bandage too quickly. Inadvertently, I looked up into the mirror. *No no no no! That—can't be me!* It looked horrific. Mutilation. I was all scar. What had happened to my body? I wasn't even a B cup. I was nothing. Maybe an A cup at best? Just pectoral muscle. *Heaven help; what have I done?* And my stomach! My rolls! I hadn't even known I had rolls. I began to feel lightheaded, and the next thing I recall is the nurse helping me get off the floor.

I didn't realize it at the time, but my boobs had become my security blanket. They were what made me cool and popular, or so I thought. After nineteen-plus years with them, they were etched onto my brain as part of my being. My shirts always fell nicely because of my big bust. That's why I'd never paid much attention to the rolls on my belly. Y'all, I'd never before seen the skin under my breasts. It was the craziest hyperpigmentation you've ever seen. I swear the large brownish-gray spots went all the way down to my belly button.

How young is nineteen to undergo major plastic surgery? The experience is so intense. I'm not saying it's not a good thing to have because, Lord knows, I needed the weight off my shoulders and back.

I just feel the surgeon could have offered more preparation for such a young patient. As in, "Let's get you in to see a counselor who's going to give you a look into what this surgery means for you and what to expect mentally and emotionally—because your life will never be the same. It'll be mostly good, but it takes a minute to catch up."

Instead, I was in a state of utter shock. It ripped me apart day in and day out as I put on my clothes. Who was I? Whose body was this?

Remember how quickly I adopted Belle's teachings? The same thing happened before I was even discharged. Given my history of dieting and weight loss programs, I was so intensely familiar with the popular points program that I got to scheming. I knew I couldn't possibly continue with this body. This body had a newly discovered torso. Rolls! As I write these very words, I'm sarcastically swooning, the back of my hand to my forehead, at my nightmare of those rolls. Rolls. Are. Normal. People. Rolls exist on every shape and size. But, oh no. I had to do something about it—and quick. I was over the laxative abuse, but anyway, I needed something much faster, and I didn't want to try Ashley's version again.

That's just it! I'd write my own custom quick weight loss program. I'd eat this much every day and not an ounce more. I'd have this many calories and not a calorie more. I'd consume only these specific foods and no others. I'd take the points system and turn it on its head, far away from registering any bit of what the body needs on a nutritional scale.

Do you know what my new, custom weight loss program should've been called? Starvation. That's the only appropriate name for it.

Fast forward a few months, and we were back at school. I was well into my first semester at this point, having given starvation a good run. My body dysmorphia had escalated big time. From the rolls to the hyperpigmentation and an overall misunderstanding of my newly constructed chest, I couldn't handle it anymore. Ed was taunting me.

Much to my dismay, I wasn't seeing the success I needed because of—remember?—the bingeing nightmare that recurs with restriction. I had to do something more. I needed immediate. I needed extreme.

But what did I know? I knew Ashley had lost weight quickly, so fast, so dramatically. She made it look easy, like it was just another thing to check off the to-do list. If she could purge, why couldn't I? Maybe this time, if I just tried harder, I'd stick with it. I couldn't give up so quickly again.

Some weeks later, I went to the cafeteria and straight to the bathroom afterward. After some trial and error, it finally worked. I stood there, shaken but triumphant, like I'd unlocked some secret code. I was so excited—disturbingly, sickeningly excited—about this new tool. My mind raced with possibilities; my heart pounded with the warped thrill of "success."

What I didn't realize in that moment was that I wasn't starting a quick fix or a phase. I was entering into a toxic, abusive relationship with Ed. The kind that consumes your thoughts, manipulates your body, and isolates you from everyone and everything. I'd just signed up for fourteen years—fourteen *whole* years—of obsession, self-destruction, and pain. And the most horrifying part? I didn't even know it. To me, it felt like a victory.

For lessons learned and insights from this chapter,
visit "ENLIGHTENMENT on DATING ED"

CHAPTER 6

SKINNY PRIVILEGE

In this chapter, we'll look at my college years with Ed, my navigation through both skinny privilege and people catching on to my disorder, and how this affected me.

I have a *lot* to say here. I'm not quite sure how to fit it all into one chapter or, heck, even one book. I mean, those next years were loaded with some of the best and some of the worst times in my life. From the most memorable to the most horrific. It. Was. Messy. College was messy. My disease was the messiest.

After the boobs came off, my obsession with losing weight and losing it at warp speed kicked in and didn't stop. I was doing everything I could to control my intake and then my output through purging.

I'd just entered my sophomore year in college, and I was about to experience something so strong—dare I say violent?—that I'd chase after it. It's like a drug that fuels you to keep going, keep doing the very thing that's killing you.

Whether you like it or not, whether it's wrong or right, there's this thing. This one hundred percent messed up thing that's all too real in our world. And it, my friend, is skinny privilege.

Oh yeah. It's a full force. A way of life I never knew existed until the fat started to fall off and my frail frame began to appear.

I want to be very clear. There was nothing wrong with me to begin with. Truthfully, I think I was probably a better version of myself before I lost it—not the weight, but myself. My personality, my love for people, my trust. I lost it all to and because of Ed. Dating him meant full surrender. But in return, I had this gift. Or maybe *curse* is a more appropriate term.

It was a wild ride from hiding under my skin all those years—at three hundred pounds—and becoming more and more visible the smaller I got. Don't get me wrong; I was always well-liked in school. I had a self-deprecating humor that I thought attracted folks. But now, for whatever reason, I became more visible but with less there. You get me? I felt seen for the first time ever, even though more than half of me was gone, and just like that, skinny privilege joined the chat.

The weight was falling off of my frame in a continuous drip—almost daily. So much so that my clothes size changed drastically by the month. I was barely getting in enough calories to sustain good grades, and the calories I did get in had to come out.

Somehow, among all the chaos with Ed in my sophomore year, I was able to land my first official college boyfriend.

We loved all the same things. I found him both attractive and interesting. He was already popular, even in the short time we'd been at college. He was a leader, Type A through and through, and I was just like him. This has always been a weird thing for me; he shared my dad's birthday—my high school sweetheart also shared my dad's birthday—and, because of that, I thought it was meant to be. I know that's bizarre since my dad was pretty terrible, and there's the part about my high school boyfriend not working out either, but there we were.

Lucas and I liked fancy parties and getting gussied up to entertain or be entertained. We sang songs in the car at the top of our lungs and talked about what we'd name our kids one day. We both enjoyed musical theater and challenging each other in deep conversation about heavy life topics. We had a closeness that didn't require true intimacy, and since I was bound and determined to hold onto my V-card for a while, that was important. The lack of intimacy foreshadowed the eventual demise of our relationship, but at the time, it worked. We watched countless movies together on my apartment living room couch. We took trips to his aunt's house and sang and danced on her coffee table into the wee hours of the morning after copious amounts of wine. Or maybe that was just me.

I loved how connected he was. Connected to me but also to everyone else. Lucas was—important. And being with him made me feel the same. I also loved that he was a bit numb to my disease and, I thought, didn't know much about Ed, my reality. Men usually don't, in my experience, but of course, Lucas was different than other men.

The best part? His full name. Lucas Camden Love. Tell me a better name exists, please. I'll wait. Of course, I was attracted to Lucas himself, but the name made it all the more so. It fit perfectly with his personality.

I majored in biology pre-med and wanted to become a dentist. I'd be lying if I said I didn't practice writing Dr. Lauren Love. All. The. Time. I even pictured my future patients saying it. I'd travel to the ends of the earth doing free clinics, and there would be write-ups about how Dr. Love was changing the world. In my head, it was already written on the business sign on the front lawn of my practice. In lights, it would say, *Lauren Love, DDS.* What an oxymoronic paradox that was: the desire to become a dentist while Ed was ruining my teeth.

Spoiler alert: I didn't end up being a dentist, and Lucas and I never married. But we'd go on to date—get this—off and on for nearly a decade. We likened our relationship to baseball. There were nine innings, folks. Yep. Count 'em. We dated nine different times.

If you've ever had a default or fallback boyfriend, be thankful, as long as it was a healthy one. I swear Lucas and I saved each other through it all.

Our relationship allowed Lucas his own freedoms and me some as well. Sure, we were on again, off again, but Lucas was always there, always in the background, a constant in my life. And I loved Lucas, and still do, for his consistency and loyalty to us. To me. Not that it mattered in the end, but oh, it sure as heck mattered then.

I'd sometimes go home to Rome on the weekends and hide everything. Or at least I thought I was hiding it. I was notorious for thinking I was good at that, remember? I'd keep bags in the closet to be able to purge without going to the bathroom and risking someone hearing me. Mom or Dad catching me in the act would have been devastating. The horror and shock of it all would be too much. I accumulated garbage bags throughout my stay-at-home, thinking no one smelled the stench. Can you imagine? The smell of vomit had become something so familiar to me, so normal, I didn't think anyone else smelled it.

I had the city mapped out perfectly to continuously execute my disorder while I was there. I knew every gas station in Rome that had a singular bathroom stall—bonus if it had a fart fan. I loved knowing I could purge without someone next to me. There's no chance anyone would hear me if I went into the single-stall bathroom. Ed and I would do our dance, I'd wash my face and feel energized once more. A release. I ask again: can you imagine? Thinking no one could hear me when everyone could.

On Sundays, I'd enter my home church feeling confident and skinny. I was shocked when I walked into Sunday School one morning, and Myra, who had been my Sunday School teacher for at least four years, looked at me like she'd seen a ghost. It seemed she barely recognized me.

"Lauren??"

"Hi!" I said, going in for a hug and carrying on my merry way to my seat. I thought she must have noticed the positive change I'd made. That's what everyone else there was saying, anyway.

Things like:

"What are you doing to lose weight, Lauren?"

"You look so great now that you're slimming down."

"You must feel so much better."

"Tell me your secret!"

"Are you exercising *and* dieting or just watching what you eat?"

"I need to do whatever you're doing!"

Those exact words—verbatim—were uttered to me in the pews of the church.

Myra's shock, though, wasn't quite in line with what others were saying. She pulled me to the side after "big church." "I barely recognized you with your hair and— Lauren; you're just— So skinny. Are you doing okay, health-wise?"

I'm guessing my frailty had given her clues, but I was so confused by her lack of positivity. I responded, "Myra! I finally cracked the code on losing the weight I had to lose."

And on the ride back to school, heading down the highway, I'd rid myself of those closet bags full of vomit I'd collected. As I threw them out the window, I felt a release run through me. I'd just gotten away with it again. It was so easy. And don't come at me for being a litterbug. I know it's awful. I was sick in body and sick in mind, not knowing the harm I was causing to others, including God's green earth.

Most everyone loved new Lauren. New Lauren was cool. She wore a tiny size and still appeared healthy, except to Myra—and some others, I'd soon find out. New Lauren was getting the attention of boys and girls. Faculty and staff. Churchgoers. New Lauren had skinny privilege.

Skinny privilege, I was discovering, was everywhere.

But then there was this collection, if you will, of instances when friends and colleagues and professors started showing up for old Lauren. They knew something was very, very wrong.

Back at college, I'd just left the shower and was walking into my bedroom when I heard the main apartment door shut. We lived in a four-bedroom, two-bath apartment, so the left two bedrooms shared one bathroom-vanity combo and the right two bedrooms the other. Diane was perpetually gone, so I knew it wasn't she who had just run out of the door, and our other roommate, Alyssa, was usually in class at this time of day. So it must have been Jane. Remember the boob balloons? *That* Jane. I guessed she was heading out to the lab or the gym or something. Weird she didn't tell me because we were like that—keeping each other informed about what our day looked like and where we were off to next.

Then I saw it. I always migrated over to my desk after each shower to plug in my 10x magnification mirror, obsessively clean out my pores, and do my makeup. She knew. She knew exactly where to put her letter so I'd notice it the second I stepped out of the shower and into my room. And this wasn't just any letter because we didn't write letters anymore. Maybe in high school, but not now.

I opened it.

Jane had never spoken a word to me that entire time about my disorder, either because she didn't know what to say or because she knew her words would likely fall on deaf ears, given the severity of it. Her letter was about to make up for lost time, though, because in twenty years, I haven't forgotten that letter and the words on those pages. They still haunt me in the best way.

Lauren,

I am having a hard time confronting you face to face, so as of right now, this letter is the best I can do.

I know what's going on with you.

I'm not stupid, and I went through the same thing and used all the same tricks. It is not just a way to lose weight; it's a disease. You are killing yourself slowly. I don't think anyone else has the guts to say anything, but honestly, I can't let my best friend in the universe do this to herself. I love you too much. I will do whatever it takes to get you to stop. I will go on the strictest diet with you, and I will work out and run all day long, but I cannot let you keep doing this. This is not just concern; this is my job as your friend. Please think about this! And if this makes you mad, well, frankly, I would rather you be mad at me and healthy than happy with me and still doing this to yourself. Nobody knows that I have written this letter so don't worry. I am here for you and will always be here for you. Please think about this. I am begging you. I know that you would do the same thing for me. I love you with all my heart.

Jane

By the way, this has definitely given me diarrhea. Sorry, I had to say it. We always talk about our poop. :smiley_ face:

Oh, Jane. In that letter, I felt the love and the hurt and even the laughter at the end. She was scared. She cared. It brings me to tears, reproducing it here. I feel like she's giving me a giant hug, even now. That's what she was trying to do then. If I'd only been more receptive to her offer, how life-changing that could have been for me and our relationship then and there.

What Jane did was successfully pin me into a corner where I knew I couldn't act out so comfortably anymore. So while she may not have gotten me to check myself into rehab right away, she did what she could to push me in a direction that made my disease harder to execute. I was now conscious. I was exposed. If Jane knew, that meant other people knew.

That consciousness wasn't enough, unfortunately. For the skinny privilege I was gaining, I would continue on my path and not allow some letter to get in my way. Of course, I'd be more careful, but I found new, inventive ways. Pain in the butt ways, but I'd do whatever it took to keep up this new way of life. This—skinny privilege.

That included hiring a trainer to get me into shape. This trainer was a friend. She was super fit, and I thought, since she didn't know about my disorder, she could help me stay on top of it if I wasn't able to purge as much anymore. We'd run five miles every night. Remember, I was barely fueling my body. Rarely eating, and purging what little I did, so the rigorous exercise routine had me sleeping late in the mornings. I started to miss class. I started to get weak. I was incredibly lethargic.

At one point, my doctor told me my potassium levels were enough for her to call an ambulance and get me admitted immediately. I wish she had that day. Maybe *that* would've been what I needed to break up with Ed.

I kept praying during every purge, "Let me hit rock bottom, Lord, so I can stop." But what is rock bottom? I didn't want to die. I just wanted to stop. I wanted Ed to stop. I wanted something so scary to happen that I'd never let Ed hurt me again.

Then my sorority big sis came back to our college for homecoming weekend. The weekend was going to be a magical one, as most homecoming weekends are. Full of partying and reuniting with your closest sorority siblings, packed with all the festivities imaginable.

I'd gotten in very late on Saturday. Much later than my big sis Jorgia—no normal *Georgia* for her. She was already in Diane's room, sleeping the night away.

To my surprise, sitting in the same spot as Jane's letter was another one. What in the world? I mean, letters—handwritten ones—were a thing of the past! She'd taken unlined paper out of my printer to write this. She'd sat at my desk and written it. And what was this? She'd cut the size tags off my clothes and taped them to the top of the letter! She was trying to make a point. And the point was made, believe me.

To: Lauren (read immediately when you get in)!!

From: Big Sis

For Lauren's eyes only!

I love you, and I hope you know that. If you need me after this, come into my room!

Lauren,

I wish I could be more proud of the above, but in all honesty, I can't because I'm so disappointed in you. You used to be a fighter, but now you've chosen to take the easy way out, and I don't understand why!!! The thing that confuses me the most is that you know you have a problem but still choose to do nothing about it. Why have you become like this? What drove you to the point where you are now? Honestly, to me and others, you've changed so drastically - losing the most amazing things that made you so beautiful!

For one, your personality is so different. The lighthearted, fun-loving girl I used to know and love has become a heavy-hearted, withdrawn young lady. Your beautiful smile has weakened because of all the harm you have done to yourself. Your beautiful face has become sunken and sickly, and your beautiful hair is gone, slowly but surely. All these have lessened because you have been so consumed with an idea of how you should be just to be "more accepted"!!!!

I'm not saying any of this to be hurtful in any way, but because I love you, and I'm worried about you! I know things haven't stopped.

It's obvious just by looking at you and observing your habits and constantly listening to everyone at school. I hope this letter somehow triggers something in you to change because you can't continue down this treacherous path. The worst is still to come if you do!

I LOVE you and care about you and always will, but I cannot sit by and watch you DESTROY your life like this because you are not only hurting yourself but all those around you who love and care for you. I love you and will always be here for support but not for praise of how good you look because it's been done in the wrong manner.

Lauren, you could DIE!

Do you realize this? I mean, I'm sure you think it isn't going to happen to you, but it could. Just know if you continue down this road, all of your hopes and dreams could vanish because of your vanity to be skinny and "accepted"!!! Please know that I love you and want to help with all my heart because you are an amazing person! If you want to talk to me, I'm here. If not, I will assume you don't want help and are satisfied with the way things are.

Love you, Jorgia

I think you'll understand why I had a hard time facing her the rest of the weekend. I avoided my own apartment like the plague.

Jorgia had done the only thing she knew to do. She wanted to help. She cared. She was scared, just like Jane. And this letter has also stuck with me.

I wish I could have turned Ed off as easily as Jorgia thought I could. I wish I'd known the why of it, too. You think I chose Ed? That's just the thing about him. He took control without asking my permission and had become bigger than Lauren. I'd have to figure out how to stop surrendering or, at least, make him a bit smaller before I ever had a chance to fight back.

Outside of Jane and Jorgia's letters, others were also noticing, just as I'd feared.

It was a quick interaction but one I'll never forget. Partying late into the night at one of the fraternity houses, Phillip came up to me out of the blue. He lovingly and supportively took hold of my arms and told me he knew what I was doing and that I needed to love myself just the way I was. He said with conviction, "Lauren, you're special. So special, in fact, that you have something others don't."

At that moment, I was afraid the very thing he was talking about was certainly too far gone. *I've already lost it.*

He continued on and on, "People care about you. I'm telling you, people love you just the way you are—or were. Don't lose it."

Even he knew. Even he knew I was losing it: myself, my love for people and life. He then told me how he cared for me and would try to help, but that I was the only one who could truly help me.

To this day, I'll never understand how Phillip mustered up enough balls to say that to me. He cared enough to say something to someone he wasn't even that close to. We were close after that, though. I *had* to keep him close because he knew. He knew my deepest, darkest non-secret of all time.

There was something about the way Phillip showed up for me in that moment. Something so bold and so comforting. He was right. I was the only one who was going to get myself out of this thing.

Ed and I were pretty deep into our relationship by this time, and I was heading home to Rome for another weekend. If somewhat strangers like Phillip had started to catch on to things, Mom was certainly starting to catch on. My small frame was becoming more and more noticeable.

I remember it like it was yesterday. We'd planned a shopping day at our favorite mall, Hamilton Place, on the way to Chattanooga, Tennessee. We were in and out of stores, amassing large quantities of clothes together as we usually did on one or two big shopping trips a year.

We walked into the NY&Co store. There weren't two dressing rooms open, so we decided to share one. It was plenty spacious, and we'd both found some cute things to try on.

Mom went first, and when she had her stash ready to check out, it was my turn. She handed me the first item and commented on the size. "Lauren, this size?" she questioned.

To which I snapped back, positively confident, "Yes, can you believe it?"

Mom continued, "I don't think this is healthy, Lauren."

As I ignored her comment, I put each leg in and pulled up the pants, fastened the silver hook—and—they fell. Dropped onto the floor with all the heaviness in the world.

My mom fell to pieces at the same time. She let out the most emotion I'd ever seen. Right in the middle of NY&Co, my mom lost it. And y'all, my mom's cry isn't pretty. I don't know if there's really such a thing, but her cry sounds like the wail of a large sea animal. Her cry makes others cry—or laugh if they're awkward like that. It's that bad. You could visibly see the hurt through her tears. The reality of my relationship with Ed was evident like never before. She knew this wasn't just weight loss. Her daughter was sick. Dying even.

She'd had enough. After watching clothes drop onto the floor and tops spill off my big bones, she realized it was time to help. It was still the early days of Google, so consider this. My mom knew only one person who had been to a therapist. It was her friend at work, Susan, but it turns out he was no therapist. He was a psychiatrist, and Mom's friend had been going because her son had recently committed suicide. So Mom booked me an appointment with the same doc because, naturally, it sounds like a good fit. Nice try, but no.

Off I went to Cartersville, a town southeast of Rome, to see this man, Susan's miracle worker, about Ed. If he'd saved Susan, then surely, he could do the same for me. I'd never before spoken a word to a mental healthcare professional about having an eating disorder, so this was new territory.

I began sharing my story and this man was finishing my sentences.

"When I'm purging, I feel—"

"—immediate gratification?" he'd finish.

Was this voodoo? Holy mind-reader, this guy got me. He knew exactly what I was going through. He knew exactly what I needed.

Quite the reverse. He *thought* he knew what I needed. And that was a drug. The drug he'd prescribe was going to *cure my bingeing*, he said. "If we cure the bingeing, you won't have a need to purge."

Can I tell you something? This miracle drug royally screwed me up seven ways to Sunday. I had zero appetite. I was nauseous all day. I had the worst case of paresthesia—pins and needles in my hands and feet—and my neurocognitive functions were declining. What was happening to me? I was so sick in my mind that I kept on taking it anyway. This drug, this doctor's miracle drug, catapulted me straight into anorexia.

Jackpot, I thought. There was less purging because I could barely eat. The bingeing was gone, just like he'd said. So I was getting better, right? Far from it. I'm still perplexed to this day how that man hasn't killed someone yet. Or maybe I should be complaining about the drug itself. Maybe this drug has already killed someone.

That drug successfully got me down to the lowest weight—and grades—that I experienced throughout my entire college career. What Jorgia had said in her letter was coming to fruition. My hopes and dreams were beginning to disappear with my escalating illness.

Speaking of grades, I'd always, always been a straight-A student. Now I was showing signs of language impairment and confusion—so much so that my professor picked up on it.

Dr. Bagwell. He's one of those professors who's so wicked smart you're not sure he can get down to your level, you know what I mean? We'd always had a very professional relationship. All business. I came to class, he taught, I did the work, got good grades, and went home.

One day in anatomy class, when I'd been on this therapy for about six months, Dr. Bagwell told me—in front of the entire class, I died—to meet me in his office once we were dismissed. I knew I was struggling, but I didn't think it was *that* evident, which is laughable considering how badly I'd begun to fail. He'd called on me in class that day, and while I thought I'd given the correct answer, it was totally wrong. He knew I knew the answer but was somehow handicapped. He moved on so as not to attract too much attention, but I knew that was likely what he was going to talk to me about. My As had turned into Cs, and that, along with the troubled-for-words part in class, was concerning.

We sat down in his office. He looked at me and said, "Are you okay?"

I, not wanting to draw attention to myself, said, "Of course. Sorry I got confused back there."

He went on. "Lauren, I know you're sick. Something is killing you, and I won't let it happen. You need an outlet. Something to get your mind off of you. I've noticed every day just how ill you're getting. You're declining in both mind and body."

He offered to meet me at the pool for some exercise before class each day. His daughters were excellent swimmers, I recall. He said he didn't know if it would truly help me, but he was willing to do whatever it took to make a difference.

Talk about compassion. I'm still floored by it. I've thanked him maybe twice via Facebook messenger, but I love that I can document his compassion here for the world to see, along with that of Jane and others. How great Dr. Bagwell was to show up for one of his students like that. I'll never forget it for as long as I live.

Turns out, Dr. Bagwell wasn't the only angel in his class. There was another one, but this time, it was a peer. Her name was Kasey. She'd transferred from Mercer in her sophomore year, so we didn't have a longstanding relationship, but we did share the same major, so we were beginning to see one another quite frequently between labs and such.

We were in anatomy one day, and I overheard Kasey telling her story. She'd once dated Ed herself! What? My same Ed? She went on and on about how sick she once was, the treatment she'd received, and what it was like being in recovery. She seemed so full of life and well on her way to being better. She wasn't trapped anymore. I mean, the whole point of this book is that you stay trapped in some capacity, but I could tell she'd tasted freedom.

I wanted what she had. I don't remember if she said it to me first or if I reached out for help, but either way, she'd go on to share with me that I needed to get into therapy asap. And possibly rehab. "Just talk to someone—anyone," she'd say.

As much as she could, she shared recovery tools and explained certain therapies she'd found successful. She helped me research local therapists in our college town, and I made my first real appointment with someone who specialized in eating disorders.

While this therapist was far from what I needed at the time, and all she did was throw books at me about intuitive eating—which I was clearly not even close to being able to handle—at least she wasn't some whack-a-mole doc who wanted to hop me up on his eff-up-your-frontal-lobe-pharmaceutical.

Kasey began to watch out for me, knowing how close to death I was because she'd also traveled down that road. She was the first person I could share all the real and raw moments with because she knew. She'd call me on the carpet the second she saw me show up to class with broken capillaries around my eyes. If I took a swift exit after eating in the cafeteria, she'd catch up to me before Ed and I could properly do our thing.

I felt like I could be me with her. The old Lauren *and* the new Lauren. Kasey started to weave through me the desire for recovery. One, I could see her success, and two, I was sick and tired of being sick and tired because of Ed.

All this positive influence didn't keep me from betraying others, though, even Jane. I was now being driven by new Lauren. If you remember, I'd always been on the hunt for cool. Becoming popular and being accepted was still everything.

Three super-cool sorority sisters of mine asked me to join them as their fourth roommate for senior year, and I up and left my bosom friends without so much as a goodbye. Diane had already moved back home by then, but my friendship with Jane and Alyssa drastically waned as new Lauren professed her love for her new friends and couldn't be bothered with any parts of old Lauren. If you remember, Jane had made it very challenging for me to continue dating Ed, so in a sense, if I got rid of Jane, I could hide again. After all, my new roommates didn't know what I was up to. They didn't know how much harm I was doing to my body. They didn't know as much as Jane knew.

This was my jailbreak and reentry into a hot and heavy relationship with Ed. I'd traded kindred hearts for coolness, and I was ready to conquer my last year at school in my new skinny body with my new skinny privilege. They wanted me? I couldn't believe it—those girls would never have asked me to be their roommate if I was still fat.

Do I regret the closeness I'd go on to create with them? Not one bit. Senior year was a blast, even amid the shit storm that's Ed, and I developed some lifelong relationships with those sorority sisters. Those girls—now women—got me through life that year and far beyond. I had them pegged wrong. They didn't ask me to be their roommate because of my size or weight. And over time, they came to know me for who I truly was—the good, the bad, and even Ed. We went on to raise kids together, vacation together, and share life's celebrations.

But for the longest time, I couldn't shake the nagging guilt about how I'd treated my old friends who had been there through all the ups and downs. The ones who knew me best. The one who cared enough to write me a letter telling me to break up with Ed. The one who stood up for old Lauren.

Years later, Jane and I found our way back to each other. Life has a funny way of bringing the right people back when you need them most, and somehow, our friendship grew even closer than before. Jane never needed an apology; she just wanted me, the real me, and she welcomed me back like no time had passed. Diane, on the other hand, had her own battles to fight. We stayed in touch over the years and connected on an entirely different level. Her struggles with addiction mirrored my own, though the substances were different. There was an unspoken understanding between us, a shared pain that bonded us.

While I'll always carry the guilt of how I treated them, I'm grateful that time and life allowed for healing. Jane reminded me what true friendship looks like, and Diane showed me the strength in shared vulnerability. They taught me that even when you stray, the people who truly love you will still be there, ready to meet you where you are.

And the V-card I held onto? I lost it that senior year, but it wasn't to Lucas. His name was David. I still vividly remember how it started.

Jackie, one of my three new-cool-sorority-sister roommates, walked into my room one night and said, "Remember my friend from Tallahassee who came into town yesterday? He really liked you. He wants to take you on a date."

"Who, me?"

Much like when I convinced myself the cool girls only wanted me as their roommate because I was skinny, the doubts rolled in again. "There's no way. He must've gotten the wrong girl."

I didn't date people like that because people like that never went for people like me. David was older, taller, and drop-dead gorgeous.

We dated for a few months before it happened—I finally lost it. My V-card. He was blonde, beautiful, and everything you'd want for your first. Except he wasn't.

He left me a month later. I don't know if I was too naive for him or if it was something else, but it was soul-crushing. I'd held onto that part of myself for so long, and poof, it was gone in an instant.

I couldn't stop obsessing over why he left. Surely it was the loose skin on my abdomen or my thighs. Even with my drastic change in size, I still had cellulite—yes, my thighs, with all that cellulite. I was convinced he'd seen it. Or maybe the sex wasn't good; how would I know? He wasn't a virgin like me.

I cried for days, maybe even weeks. How could he take this from me and leave? I was no longer precious in *His* sight—if you catch my drift. I wore a mental and emotional scarlet letter everywhere I walked on campus. God was absolutely positively frowning down on me. I was ruined. Who would want me now? I wasn't pure anymore. My commitment to God was—broken? That's what I'd been taught, at least. Brenda and the church made it clear: "You must remain pure for the Lord." By not having sex until marriage, you demonstrated your true commitment to God.

Statistically speaking, you *will* have sex before marriage, soooo— But there was nothing helpful like, "Let's talk about safe sex just in case. I'm going to educate you so you don't have a teenage pregnancy and you don't get an STD."

Because of the negative sex talk my entire life, I called Mom and asked for Ann's number.

Ann always had the right words. "Honey, don't feel bad. It's a good thing. You needed to try on the shoe to see if it fit anyway. I mean, what if the shoe didn't fit; then you'd be in a real pickle, wouldn't you?"

She made me laugh and feel validated again: worthy of love, of giving it and receiving it, as long as it was with the right person. In that way, David, for all the wrong, ended up being right.

While Ann's words helped soothe my heartache, they couldn't touch the deeper insecurities still rooted in my body. While I came to terms with losing my virginity, I still carried the weight of self-loathing wherever I went. For the rest of my college career, Ed was always there, whispering lies, pulling strings, and keeping me from fully embracing the person others so badly wanted me to see in myself.

My desperation to escape my own reflection reached its peak before graduation. I would have done anything to quiet the body dysmorphia that had me convinced I still weighed three hundred pounds, no matter what the scale or others told me. That's what led me to plastic surgery. I underwent multiple procedures during senior year to remove the loose skin I thought was holding me back.

Even the doctor, to my disbelief, validated my obsession. "If we take off the loose skin," he told my mom, "Lauren won't see her old, three-hundred-pound self anymore. She'll finally see her new self and all the work she's put in. It may even help her gain weight." He framed it as a solution, a cure. Fixing the skin, he promised, would fix me.

My mom believed him. To pay for my surgeries in an effort to rid me of Ed, she took out loans we sure as hell didn't have the money for. This, we thought—because I wanted to believe as badly as she did—will do it. Once the skin was off, I'd see a flat tummy or smaller thighs, and I'd be healed.

I will say that things did slow down with Ed. Sure, there's the reality of how terrible it is to binge and purge while being post-operatively stitched up. No one wants to mess with that. And while that did bring a welcome break, it wasn't entirely the actual plastics that slowed things down. It was everything. Lucas. Jane. Jorgia. Phillip. Dr. Bagwell. Some therapy in between. Kasey. My mom. All of them and all of it. But also the new roommates. My relationship with Ed had been more difficult, as I didn't want to risk being discovered in the same way I'd been with my prior roommates. And we know how much popular and cool meant to me.

Maybe, more than any external influence, I was tired. Mentally and physically. I was an absolute disaster trying to maintain my lifestyle with Ed all the way up to graduation day of my senior year at college. I remember staying up late the night before. The night before I'd walk across that stage, shake the hand of the president, and ready myself to enter the real adult world.

I was too embarrassed to purge. There was zero chance I could be discreet due to the sheer number of people crashing at our apartment. Everyone was in town, and it seemed as if everyone had found themselves at our place. On our couches, in our beds, and on our living room floor. We did, for sure, break some kind of fire code that night.

So I resorted to old habits. Belle's habits. I don't know why I thought laxatives were the answer over purging—as if that would be any quieter—but that was the poison I picked on that night for that occasion—the night before college graduation.

The reality of my eating disorder and the depression from knowing it was still with me almost four years later sank in the next morning as I awoke feeling the lasting effects of Ed.

I'm still sick, I thought.

I knew I didn't want to be in a relationship with Ed anymore, but I also wasn't exactly sure how to get away from him, divorce him once and for all. I did know one thing. Walking across the graduation stage wondering if you're about to shit your pants in front of the entire college isn't fun. Perhaps it would've left a lasting impression, though.

After the ceremony, the crowd surged as all of us graduates spilled out of our seats and into the arms of waiting families, and I saw her. Belle. Right there, Ann at her side, cheering for me with the kind of over-the-top excitement that makes you feel good from head to toe.

Once I got through the crowd and to family, Belle pulled me into the tightest hug.

And that's when I felt it.

Her body frail and brittle against mine. Her sharp edges pressed into my sharp edges. Her thin arms barely wrapping around me. We were mirrors of each other—two bodies consumed by the same relentless force. Belle's frailty wasn't new; it had been there for a long time, and right then, it hit me like a ton of bricks.

Ed was still with her.

And Ed was still with me.

Because he never leaves.

Belle's body, so like mine, was living proof of that. As I held her, I realized something that felt both terrifying and inevitable: Ed was as much a part of me as the air I breathed. And as much as I hated him, as much as I wanted him gone, in my not-so-big bones, I knew he wasn't finished with me yet.

For lessons learned and insights from this chapter,
visit "ENLIGHTENMENT on DATING ED"

CHAPTER 7

LOOKING FOR LOVE IN ALL THE WRONG PLACES

In this chapter, we'll explore my new drive for success while having two very distinct relationships, one loving and one abusive, and what happened between the two.

Can someone please write a manual that explains how life—real life—hits you upside the head after you graduate college or after high school if you don't go to college? What a great gift—or warning—that would be for someone about to embark on this next chapter.

Because here we are, out in the real world, and out in the real world is a weird place, am I right?

You have to find a job, manage money maybe for the first time ever—bills, gross—find a place to live, and navigate new relationships in and out of the workplace. What about safety once you're out of your cocoon? What about changing towns entirely? I mean, the bedrock of your life is about to change, and forever.

Of course, the finding a job and earning money and paying bills part was bananas, but much of it came almost naturally to me, and I figured out early on how to navigate the workplace. I was a go-getter and knew I wanted to be successful even though I didn't understand how. I was also leaving behind any signs of the pre-dental/pre-med biology major I'd worked so hard to achieve the previous four years, thanks to stupid meds and stupid Ed. However, I was ready to make some money of my own.

While it wasn't a bit exotic, directly out of college, I settled into my first role—as a mortgage advisor. I had the West Coast, and thanks to a hot real estate market at the time, my first commission check was *very* pretty. So much so that I thought I'd hit the jackpot and spent it all in one place. *The* mall was across the street in Buckhead. I'm talking about luxury designer brands, stuff you couldn't get at Hamilton Place. Every two weeks, when that commission check would hit my bank account, I was in Bebe and Bloomingdales buying shirts and designer jeans for two-thirds of my rent check.

I was so money-stupid. But let's be honest, Mom and Dad hadn't particularly set me up for success when it came to money, so there's that. I racked up as much credit card debt as I could and would live many years trying to reverse the damage I did in those next few short years.

And if you think Ed was replaced by my shopping addiction, think again. Sure, I felt a renewed drive from my professional life—a sense of purpose—but Ed was still with me every step of the way.

Even as I threw myself into my new career, I found I was restricting more and more, clinging to that false sense of control in a world that felt anything but stable. Inevitably, life would happen, and I'd break my own food rules, or stress would overwhelm me, and I'd fall back into purging. If I slipped too far after days of allowing myself to eat just enough to function, he was always there, like a safety net. A twisted insurance policy I kept in my back pocket that would make things "right" again.

My dad's health was in severe decline, and eventually, Mom needed me at home more than I needed my job at the mortgage company. She still worked full time and couldn't afford assisted living or the like for my dad, so he needed caretakers. I moved home, working a few days a week at a friend's internal medicine office, which allowed me to bring in *some* income to pay off the high-interest credit card debt I'd accumulated. Two days a week, I'd be home with AC, usually transporting him to every doctor's appointment imaginable. On the days I worked, his Masonic brothers would come over to the house and watch him till Mom or I could get home. They'd make him pineapple mayo sandwiches; he loved those and loved spending time with his brothers.

On days we were together, AC would always ask for Krystal on the way home, and for whatever reason, he had to eat inside the restaurant. We could never go through the drive-thru, and I grudgingly obliged. He was dying, after all, and making his requests happen was something small I could do. I was always so embarrassed, though. Mortified. He had Parkinson's and late-stage Alzheimer's at that point, and he'd make a whole mess of himself before we left. I doubt half the food ever made it to his mouth, but he'd leave with a cheeky grin on his face that told me it had been a success. Looking back, I wish I'd enjoyed that time with him more.

The debt was stacking up, so I had to make a move. I couldn't keep up with my bills, given the hourly wage I was getting and the limited weekdays I was working.

When I say I started a new job in the midst of my father's death, I'm not kidding. I had to take time off the second I started. While it was the worst timing ever, the focus on a new job helped me get through a rocky time. I left my small potatoes part-time gig and moved to phonebook sales and marketing. That's right, the phone book. For those of you too young to know, you once had to look up phone numbers, limited to the area you lived in, in a book. I know what you're thinking. *Wasn't print dead, even then?* And you're not wrong. It was on its way out for sure, but it paid more than the doctor's office, and I could put gas in my tank and pay a bill or two, so that was worth the expiring industry.

This job came with a new set of challenges. Dealing with male-saturated staff and leadership, male-saturated clients, and a risky sales strategy altogether posed concerns straight out of the gate.

The Dalton phone book was up first, and my main focus was selling upgrades to existing clients. I walked into this established account excited at the potential for what I could do with a particular company's ad campaign. The owner already had good real estate in the book, but I wanted to prove to my team that I could grow this account even more.

Thank God there was a witness because one day, as the owner and I sat down at his desk, he said to me, "I bet you a dollar I can make your titties shake without touching you."

I'm not sure if I went straight into shock or what, but I froze. I'd never heard that come out of someone before. He then reached out and grabbed my chest as tightly and as forcefully as he could. I pushed him away with all the strength I could summon.

He threw a dollar at me, "Here you go. You're right, I can't."

I frantically loaded up my things as quickly as I could, visibly shaken and in tears, and ran out of the office. As I left, I made sure to look up at his admin lady, who had been sitting directly across from us in the same room. Still crying, I said, "Did you see that?"

"You're lucky that's all he did."

Her comment sounded as if he'd done way worse and that, in some sadistic way, she was okay with it. I burst out through the main door as fast as I could and drove back to Rome. I think I spent all forty-eight miles in hysterics. I felt sick to my stomach; I'd been violated in the worst way. I called a coworker, letting her know what had happened. To her credit and my benefit, she called our boss and told her before I could even get back into the office for our compulsory end-of-day check-in.

When I walked in, without so much as a "Hi," my boss, one of the only females in leadership at the time, told me, "Get in my car right now."

We drove straight to Dalton PD and filed a police report. She gave me the most amazing empowerment speech on the way, and for the first time in my life, I felt my true worth as an individual, as a woman. I deserved more, and I would demand it, starting with consequences for this man. What he'd done to me was bad enough, but I needed to make sure no other woman would experience it. After weeks' worth of investigation and picking him out of a lineup—talk about trauma-inducing—that man was ultimately charged and convicted of sexual battery, all because someone stood up for me.

Despite the amazing leadership and unwavering support, I knew the job wasn't fulfilling my goals and carried its own limitations, especially given my past experiences there. Though my biology degree hadn't unfolded as I'd originally envisioned, I knew I still wanted to work in healthcare and in some meaningful way. So I decided to reach out to Diane's dad. Remember roommate Diane? Her dad was a senior executive at a Fortune 500 global healthcare company. That's who I'd talk to!

I'll never forget it. I called her up one evening. "Diane, when is your dad home?" He was always traveling, so I knew I couldn't just show up at their doorstep and expect him to be in town.

"He's coming home on Thursday."

"Great. I'll see you Thursday. Tell him to expect me. I want to talk to him about getting into healthcare."

I rolled up, so excited to see Diane and the entire family but also ecstatic to talk to her dad. He'd help me get a job at the company. I didn't care what job I got. I was ready to start at the bottom with the absolute worst-paid job available. I just wanted in. Being there would mean I could compensate in sales for what I was missing out on as a wannabe healthcare provider. Instead, I'd be a healthcare professional.

After posing a few questions, Diane's dad went on to give me sound advice. "Lauren, I can't land you a job. You have to do that yourself, but I can help land you an interview, given a recent acquisition and what seems like your zeal for sales."

That was all I needed. Within forty-eight hours, I attended my first interview. Then, within two weeks, my second, and then I was signing a contract with dollar signs bigger than I'd ever seen. Those numbers were, of course, total compensation. I was given a baby salary but a large potential for extra earnings if I performed.

It took me a while to settle into my corporate life, but I soon found myself very comfortable as a healthcare sales professional in a suit, with heels as high as I could buy. When I tell you the TV show *The Office* could have been based on my team members' working lives, I mean it. We were a cast of characters who became more like family, going through everything together while starting our true professional careers.

I started working there in 2008, and about a year in, I was already up for my first promotion. I'd go from direct sales to managing our channel business. I had around forty-five business partners in my portfolio. Our team in Atlanta had been acquired alongside a business out of Seattle. They'd come here. We'd go there. For sales meetings, training, all of it.

The Seattle team had flown in one week for a meeting, and I suggested a Braves game the night prior to break the ice before our crazy agenda followed. I don't know how, but there was one Seattle team member I'd never met before.

As my cohorts were leading our way down the stadium stairs, I locked eyes with this man. I recognized that he was much older than me, but I was already curious about his story. I noticed there was no ring on his finger, and I got excited. Okay, fair game, I told myself. I *had* to get him to sit next to me.

Before I could utter the words, though, he exclaimed, "I'll sit right here, thank you." And just like that, he slid into the seat right next to mine, almost as if I'd manifested it.

It was as if he knew what I was thinking, what I was feeling. Could it be? Did love at first sight exist? Whatever it was, it rushed over my body as strongly as a rip current, and I was head over heels. He had a hold on me, and I'd only known of his existence for about fifteen amazing minutes.

Call it pheromones, call it stars aligning in the sky, but I was in love. Maybe for the first time ever.

We spent the next few days and nights together on a whirlwind romance, only for me to see a wedding band on his finger on our last morning of the sales meeting. Married? No effing way. Naturally, I brought it up as soon as I saw it. He was at a round breakfast table with about seven others. I crouched down beside him and spoke so no one could hear me but so he'd get the point.

"You played me?"

He immediately reassured me that I had nothing to worry about and asked me to meet him outside in the hallway. With his best friend beside him, they told me not to sweat it. He was separated from his wife and nearing divorce.

I don't know for what in the Sam Hill reason I thought his separation gave me the green light to keep talking to this guy, but I did. He then told me he had a kid at home. I spent the next hour or so on the drive home questioning myself. For one, people with ex-spouses—and certainly married exes—had always been off the table for me. I didn't want someone else's baggage. I wanted new. New to me. New to marriage. And if they had a kid, that was even further off the table.

So what was happening here, then? Must I just desert everything on my own man-bucket list for this guy because he was giving married-man-but-separated-not-yet-divorced butterflies? The kind that feel so right because they're soooo utterly wrong. I guess so. I was willing to give up all my non-negotiables for a guy living three thousand miles away whom I'd just met.

This relationship, I'm embarrassed to say, went on for a couple of years. Flights back and forth. Excuses to be in the Seattle office. It was something out of the movies; you know the type, a wild romance with the Other Woman. While it kept going and going, his wife found out pretty quick—after my very first trip out there. She spied with her little eye a couple of wine glasses sitting in the dishwasher when she got home to his "bachelor pad" orange walls and black leather furniture. Not your typical happy family, happily married decor.

So we were caught red-handed early on. But he was getting divorced, so it wasn't wrong, right? Anyway, the affair continued for a ridiculous amount of time. He said he'd choose me over his family. I was just too dumb and ignorant to know that married men rarely leave their families.

The fake attorney letters encouraged my credulous tendencies. And yes, you read that right: he had fake attorney letters sent to me, proving he was knee-deep in a divorce from his supposedly bat-shit crazy wife. Plausible? Sure. After all, he was a con artist through and through. But that was just the beginning.

He mistreated me in ways that still make me shudder. Once, he hurled a wine bottle at me in a fit of rage. Another time, when something I said set him off, he yanked my car into park as I was speeding down the interstate at eighty-five miles an hour. My wheels locked, the car spun out, and I found myself on the shoulder, heart pounding, terrified.

He controlled everything. What I wore, what I did, even my money. Every spare dollar I had, despite my debts and rent, went straight to him. He demanded I buy him expensive things I could barely afford, bleeding me dry both financially and emotionally.

I was brainwashed and vulnerable and too scared to leave. Why would I leave in the first place, though? He gave me a high I'd never felt before. He was intoxicating to be around. I was addicted to him just like I was to food. My perception of reality was tainted. During those years, I would never have admitted it was abuse because, at the time, I didn't know I was a victim. Hello, low self-esteem and fear.

The loving was good when it was good. I thought he cared about me, and I believed his acting out was my fault. I couldn't leave him because he controlled me. From Seattle to Atlanta, he controlled me. That, my friends, is how people stay in abusive relationships. Mind games. When they ignore you, you feel the urge for more, and then you're hooked to the very thing, the very toxic relationship that's abusing you.

And I was just one of his victims. Persuasion had become his profession, stringing innocent women into his web of lies. Isn't it sad how our emotional damage positions us to enable repulsive people and stay in unacceptable situations for too long?

I wish his wife had written me such a pointed letter much earlier than she did. "Nothing he tells you is true," she said. "He's a rotten piece of garbage, and the only reason I'm staying with him—if I can stand it—is because my kids need a father."

The final straw in that letter was a family picture with her *newborn* in Santa's arms. Yep. She'd gotten pregnant during this time. She said I'd messed up her milk production, and surely this photo would give me the proof that their marriage was very much alive, albeit not well.

If I was ever going to save myself, this was my chance. And that was that. It ended as quickly as it started.

Here's the deal: there's a link to addiction and staying in abusive relationships. We're used to abusing ourselves, so why would it be that much different having someone else be the abuser?

Feeling unwanted and unworthy after spending years with the wrong person, I found myself drifting from one relationship to another while working on my executive MBA at the University of Georgia.

I was always searching for more.

If a man's acceptance and approval weren't enough, maybe a degree would be. I thought if I couldn't make an impact as a dentist, traipsing around Africa to pull teeth or put up free clinics to help serve and save the world, then perhaps I could start an eating disorder clinic or become CEO of a hospital. I wanted to feel seen and valued in a way that, from an early age, I'd never been.

Though I don't regret my MBA, I now see that it was partly an attempt to find acceptance and status and pedigree. I was starving in every way because my body wasn't nourished, and neither was my sense of worth.

And that's the thing; when I felt the emptiest, Ed was always there. Only by that point, he was beginning to look a little different. Restriction had once felt like my superpower, but in this new season of love lost, bingeing began to take over. A desperate attempt to fill the void inside me.

I'd still restrict, sure, mostly during the day, convincing myself I could stay in control, that I could strongarm Ed. But, by night, I'd find myself bingeing—all that control reversed. Stuffing down everything I didn't know how to face.

I was still purging, but less often. Of course, I kept telling myself that if I restricted harder the next day, I'd erase the damage. If I could outsmart my body, my mind, I could keep the chaos from swallowing me whole— there I go with the puns again.

Looking back now, I realize that I didn't need to travel across the world or build a career with a fancy title to make an impact. I didn't have to become a dentist or a CEO to serve others—those opportunities were all around me, closer than I ever realized. But back then, I was too consumed by my own need for validation to see the truth.

Ask yourself:

What do you want to do with your life?

Why do you want to do that with your life?

If it doesn't happen in the way you've forever visualized, what's the alternative?

Don't shrivel up and die; find other ways to satisfy that need.

And now, back to looking for love!

Lucas, my Lucas. He was still very much a part of my life, and a solid chapter of it, I might add. Our relationship was woven through all the ups and downs of my life.

We spent New Year's Eve, 2012, in New Orleans, and what a trip that was. I think it's one of the reasons I don't drink that much anymore. Ever heard of Hurricanes? Best to stop after one of those—or don't even start, for that matter. Anyway, citing the usual suspects that he had too much international travel and I was busy with my studies, we broke things off—the 9th inning—a couple of months after the trip to Louisiana.

Fast-forward to May, and I got the call. I was in Athens finishing my residency that week, and Lucas asked if I could meet him at a coffee shop. I just knew it. He couldn't shake the last breakup and was going to ask me out again. He was tired of playing games and couldn't stand it anymore, especially if we were meant to be together forever.

He'd always been the one who loved me right, the one who knew and loved old Lauren and new Lauren. We were grownups now, and we were destined to be married. It was high time we finally, once and for all, got it together.

And yet—

I was dead wrong.

I remember parking at Land of a Thousand Hills and getting out of my car with a little pep in my step. I knew what was coming. I was excited and nervous, but I was ready to commit this time around. This would be forever.

There was a coolness to the air that was still spring but wanted to be summer. Looking back at it now, I think the whole day had a sort of symbolism to it. The shedding of a season into something new and beautiful. But not new to Lucas, just new to me.

We hugged. It was different. Something was off, but the smile on his face when he saw me wasn't different, so I ordered my sugar-free vanilla soy latte and didn't think much more of the vibe. We zeroed in on an available highboy and sat down. We exchanged sighs and a quick "Hey." "Hello."

Then, there it was, the most earth-shattering but confident statement ever. The pressure had built up so great the walls of Lucas could no longer hold it in.

"Lauren, I'm gay."

Deep breath. I'll never forget that exact moment. We both burst at the seams.

I was bawling, not because of sadness but because of joy. Okay, there was sadness for such finality to a chapter that had been almost ten years of our existence on earth and knowing that was it, but his happiness mattered more. Lucas was finally living for his true self, and my sadness was also because he'd had to wait so long to do so. Maybe I felt a little guilty, too? I was a mixed bag of emotions that day. My best friend, my now gay ex-boyfriend, was evolving into who he knew himself to be with no more hiding.

And someone else would, eventually, come to know Lucas as I had— though in a way that was both deeply personal and profoundly intimate, reaching beyond what I could offer him. It brought me peace to think he'd find that with someone who could fully reciprocate and support him in the way he needed to move forward in life.

We ended the coffee date in joyous tears and understanding and with an appreciation for what we were. What we'd been all those years. I'd argue that he's one of the things that got me through living, and there's something magical about our relationship to this day. It was never, ever hard.

And I know what you're thinking. "Come on, Lauren, you didn't know?" And the answer is, honestly, no. Apart from never having had sex, there was nothing that indicated to me that he was gay.

The best part of my story with Lucas is that we're still part of each other's lives, not romantically, but in a way that feels just as close and meaningful. It's as if we were always meant to stay connected this way. Honestly, given that our relationship was never consummated, it was probably easier for us to stay close, and things might be strange now if it had been different. I like to think we were brought together to support each other through a difficult time and, as a result, were gifted lifelong friendship that left room for us to find our own true loves.

Now Lucas and his partner live at the beach. We have a close-knit friend group that gets together every few months; we travel, we chat often, and we still call each other for advice. My kids know their "Uncle" Lucas and the special, unbreakable bond we share. So, while I may have been looking for love in all the wrong places, Love found me and is here to stay, even in a my-ex-boyfriend-who-is-gay kinda way.

For lessons learned and insights from this chapter,
visit "ENLIGHTENMENT on DATING ED"

CHAPTER 8

SETTLING DOWN AND SAYING I DO

This chapter goes through all the messy about how my husband and I began our relationship but, of equal importance, how I began to move toward the gray.

When my dreams didn't seem to be lining up, both in the relationship department and that of doctordom, I shifted my focus.

I decided to channel all my energy into my career and completing my Executive MBA. Out in the real world, I'd trade popularity for success, and that would be my new form of acceptance. I'd be accepted because of my success.

I was now approaching thirty, though—just a couple of years to go—and life began to feel different. I vowed that if I *did* entertain a new relationship, what I was looking for would be fundamentally different. I wanted friendship over lust, a deeper connection like the one I shared with Lucas, not something superficial. I craved intellect and wisdom, not just passion. I didn't need butterflies to feel fulfilled. The physical side of a relationship would be welcome, of course, but only if it came with someone who could genuinely be my life partner, supporting my career aspirations and dreams along the way.

Matthew, who comes from Viking blood, we like to say jokingly after doing 23andMe DNA testing, happens still to do all the yucky love stuff—

name that movie if you're an elder millennial—while, at the same time, giving me the deeper connection and intellect bit too. You see, we have a history. We were friends in college. He saw what I was going through and never treated me any differently. He knew old Lauren—before Ed took over entirely—and new Lauren, who eventually found the gray. We had the kind of connection that you develop entirely out of the blue but with years of friendship behind you.

About four months after Lucas and I had broken it off for the last time, insert the most unexpected, loving relationship ever. It didn't come without heartache, though. What a doozy. You see, one of my college roommates and best friends had dated Matthew beginning in high school. She'd since found new love in college, though, so free game, right? I mean, they hadn't been together in almost eight years.

It was as innocent as innocent could be. Matthew DM'd me one day about coming over for a barbeque. He happened to be home after the World Series of Poker and was getting some college friends together, so he insisted that I come. I hadn't seen that group of friends in years! I went excited, with zero apprehension but also zero clue as to what would transpire.

At that point, I was in what felt like a steadier place with food, or at least steadier than before. I wasn't purging as much, and I'd convinced myself that was progress. But in reality, I was still eating in a way that felt chaotic and out of control at times, numbing stress with food one day and restricting the next to "make up for it." It wasn't balance, but I told myself it was close enough.

We cooked out. I posted a picture of what we had on the grill and noted my location on Facebook.

Katie texted me while I was still there. *"Are you at Matthew's?"*

"Yes! He's in town! He hosted a bbq to get some college folks together, and I wanted to see everyone."

She didn't say anything after that. Was she upset with me? She'd always been hung up on him. *Oh no, should I have invited her?* That wasn't right, though. This was Matthew's party, and I was just there to see friends.

After hours at his place, I announced my departure, and he said in the most attractive, respectful, and manly way, "Let me walk you to your car."

Then it happened.

He asked me out!

Where was this coming from? *What? No no no no.* This could not, must not be happening.

"No!" I blurted out, and I had to tell him why. "Matthew, you're off limits, and you always will be—what about Katie?"

"Yeah? What *about* Katie?" he jerked back. "She broke my heart years ago. I think you can go to Jason's deli with me for lunch."

He was right, and it would go nowhere. I mean, I'd never once had romantic thoughts about Matthew. We'd stop seeing each other after this singular date, and I'd never even have to mention it to Katie.

I set some expectations. "Okay, but just Jason's Deli. Don't expect me to come over afterward or anything."

A few days later, we went to Jason's. Hello, salad bar and soft serve ice cream of my dreams. He insisted that we get it to go. I didn't like where this was heading. "I don't think we—"

"To go," he repeated before I could finish. Next thing I knew, we were sitting in his living room, talking about life, love, and other things.

I was laughing at his jokes. This guy was so funny. And, holy smart, I thought, I liked everything he had to say. He was tall and strong and behaved like a true gentleman. He was genuine. He was—real.

SETTLING DOWN AND SAYING I DO

It was two weeks later, and the actuality of where this was going—and fast—was settling in. It was exactly the reverse of how things should be going. But I did like him. A lot. A lot a lot.

I needed to contact Katie and tell her before it went any further. I mean, she was in love with the guy she'd been with all this time—they may have even been engaged at that point—so she'd be able to get behind it. It had been eight years; it wasn't like they'd broken up six months or even a year earlier.

I emailed her and asked her to accept my apologies upfront, but that she must know Matthew had never once been on the table for me. And that these feelings were just as shocking to me as they would be to her. I wanted to continue our friendship, I said, with the hopes that she'd still support and love us wherever this new relationship was going.

Two weeks went by, and as I was pulling into a DoubleTree in Pittsburgh, excited to get the usual warm cookie at the lobby front desk, my cell rang. It was him. No, not *him*. It was Katie's boyfriend—or maybe fiancé, like I said.

The gist was how dare I break trust with Katie when I knew better than to go out with Matthew. According to him, it was because of my recklessness that Katie hadn't been able to eat or sleep or—

I shut down. This was ridiculous, I thought. Why was he calling me about Matthew? Wasn't this a red flag for him? Alas, here we were at a crossroads; I knew I didn't want to lose Matthew. He was worth it, I'd decided. I couldn't listen to it anymore, and I hung up.

Another three weeks went by, and I was surprised when I opened my laptop at work to see an email from Katie! I was sure she'd come to her senses by then. We'd dance off into the sunset as best friends and forget this ever happened, me still with Matthew, of course. Turned out I was a bit—or a lot—naive in that thinking.

In Katie's mind, I'd betrayed her, and she'd never be able to be around me again since being around me meant being around Matthew. She got nasty, telling me she was going to expose all my deepest, darkest secrets to Matthew's family. I mean, maybe it cut deep, but that's too far.

However, in a way, she did our relationship a favor.

Matthew and I got real close, real quick. What else are you supposed to do after someone says they're going to read your diary out loud? I came out of the closet with all the information about my past. Information no new boyfriend should have to endure.

Matthew's response to my belaboring old stories? "That was your past. None of that matters. Who cares?"

And just like that, my friendship with Katie was over. I'd lost a beautiful relationship in the midst of building a new one.

Was it worth it? A resounding yes! Katie's total irrationality helped lead me to my soulmate and DCT—my dream come true—and this was perhaps the best worst decision of my life.

During those first months of dating, my body started changing quickly. I was gaining what some might call "happy weight," but deep down, I knew it was more complicated than that. I wasn't just celebrating love and newfound security—a security that led me to loosen my grip on restriction—I was eating to quiet the anxiety that still simmered beneath the surface.

And that anxiety? That was Ed. He lingered, but something else was starting to take root too—something steadier, something healthier— because it was Matthew who ultimately helped me find my way to the gray. For years, I'd been trying to write *Big-Boned*, but it was Matthew who, in his own way, pushed me to start telling my story. His influence shifted my perspective in profound ways.

At first, this shift was subtle; it started in my understanding of faith.

Things had always been black and white from a religious and spiritual perspective. I was told from a very early age that all I had to do to get into heaven—and not live a life of eternal damnation in hell—was to say the salvation prayer, thanking Jesus for the sacrifice he'd made, confessing my sin, and asking him to come live in my heart. This would make me a bona fide Christian. And at age six, that's exactly what I did.

Of course, the eternal damnation part wasn't fully explained until later, but that became a large driver of how I lived my life as a Christian. Scared. Fearful. Fully and completely overwhelmed with the idea of hell and what that would look like if I didn't perform.

It's important to acknowledge that these dynamics aren't unique to Christianity. Many religions have their own versions of rules, fear, and control. People across different faiths wrestle with the weight of religious expectations all the time. For me, it looked like this:

You can

Do this, not that,

You can

Say this, not that,

You can

Feel this, not that.

And that's how the relationship continued. Rule-based, scary religion. Sure, there was a smattering of a real relationship and spirituality in there. I longed for the closeness I knew *could* exist. I'd talk to God all the time; I'd ask him for signs of various things, to lay stuff on my heart, or even, sometimes, to speak to me out loud.

Ultimately, though, religion and rules dominated. Because, through rules, you get answers. You get black and white. You get—control.

Which is a great place to live, considering there's nothing you have to figure out. You've got it all down perfectly.

And that same rigidity was what kept me in a box. And kept God in a box! My beliefs were confined to a very specific set of rules, and nothing outside of that was able to fit in.

Not only did I have control, but because I was a Christian, I'd be shown favor. Favor meant I had power and protection and approval and blessings. Abundant blessings. Power to pray a plane to stay up in the air, and it would. Power to tell a storm not to hit my house, and it wouldn't.

So why couldn't God, wouldn't God stop Ed?

That mindset lasted until Matthew explained things to me in a way I'd never heard before.

I remember flying home from another work trip, headed back to our first house, which we'd bought before we were married—oh, the scandal! It was one of the worst flights I'd ever experienced. The shortest flight, from Charlotte to Atlanta, but it was through a hellacious storm. We were the last flight cleared for takeoff before a ground stop was called for the next twelve hours. By the time I finally made it home, I was still shaking.

I told Matthew how hard I'd been praying. "I knew that flight would go down if I didn't pray. I never stopped. It was so bad." My palms were sweaty, and tears were rolling down my face as I relived the evening. He came over to me and said, "Honey, God isn't going to keep a plane up in the air for you. He lets nature exist on its own. Of course he created the heavens and the earth, but he doesn't get in the way. And your faith, while meant to be strong, doesn't mean bad things won't happen. Most things that do happen are out of our control, even if we're believers. That's just nature."

"Uhhhh, what?"

I didn't have the power to rid the skies of turbulence and storm? That was just silly. I'd gotten myself out of many bad pickles with prayer; I was certain of it.

But wait. Maybe he was onto something.

The next day, while sharing the horror of the Charlotte flight with my boss, Dustin, I told him about the conversation I'd had with Matthew. Given how frequently we traveled, Dustin and I often talked about logistics and travel mishaps, but we never discussed matters of faith. So I was surprised when he shared his own story to illustrate a similar point—how God allows nature to operate on its own, choosing its own path.

To set the context, Dustin explained that cleanup efforts were underway in his neighborhood after a recent natural disaster. Both he and a neighbor, Mark, had suffered inconceivable loss after a hurricane. Mark had lost his entire home. Another neighbor, Will, who Dustin had grown close to, met up with both of them to help. As they surveyed the damage, Will remarked, "I'm so thankful God answered our prayers yesterday and spared our home."

As I recall, I'm not sure if Will knew the extent of Mark's loss, but regardless, it struck me as an incredibly tone-deaf comment to make after such a traumatic event in the community. Dustin shared how Mark responded.

"Wait. Are you saying we didn't pray hard enough?"

He and Dustin, still reeling with frustration and bewilderment, kept on with their efforts.

My boss added how impactful it had been, and, in that moment, I felt it, too. I was beginning to consider that maybe God allows the natural world, and even my body in the case of illness and so on, to work according to their own systems, not as punishment or reward, but because they're part of his creation. Hurricanes and storms happen because they're part of nature's order, not because someone did something wrong or didn't pray hard enough.

Dustin's story gave me a lot to think about. It wasn't that nature's power was unleashed because of sin, either, or that we could control it through prayer alone. It was just nature doing what nature does. And sometimes, we're caught in its path. Matthew's point became clearer: maybe prayer wasn't about asking God to control the storm but asking him to steady us through it.

This sparked something new in me, a shift in my beliefs. Perhaps God worked alongside nature but didn't necessarily intervene, even through prayer, at least where nature was concerned. Okay, so my prayers needed to change. But how? What was I supposed to pray for now?

"Pray with a thankful heart," said Matthew. "Pray for yourself, your family, and others, not things beyond your control. Nature is beyond your control. Pray for strength and courage and steadfastness. Let bygones be bygones. Pray for the qualities to do what you need to, not necessarily for the outcome. Don't pray to be a hundred and ninety pounds; pray to have the discipline to wake up every day and work out."

He made it sound so easy, but it's tough to change your core beliefs. For so long, I'd believed I could calm turbulence with prayer. But this moment marked the beginning of an unraveling, a kind of deconstruction of my faith. I know people cringe at that term, but it fits perfectly here, so I'm going to use it.

I still believed in God. I still felt his presence, but suddenly, I didn't know how to pray. And I had so many questions.

Things were about to get even more complicated.

Enter Hillary. She was the head of HR in California at a startup where I'd landed a new job. I didn't know then that she was originally from Maryland; to me, she was the epitome of a California girl. She talked preppy, drove a convertible, had blonde hair, and knew all the greatest hangs along the Pacific Coast Highway. We became fast friends, and oftentimes, I ended up forgoing my hotel stay so I could bunk at her house with her cool, in-a-band husband.

One day, she totally called me out on my Christianity. Out of the blue, she said, "I know you're a bible belt girl. I can just tell. We can be friends, but I don't need you witnessing to me, blah blah blah."

I might've done that years ago in high school or college, but not then. Maybe she saw me bless my lunch once; either way, she'd picked up on something. Raised as a Jehovah's Witness, she told me that at the age of sixteen, she ran as far as she could from religious abuse, leaving Maryland and her family behind.

Years into our friendship, I knew Hillary had addiction issues; I'd seen her with alcohol, and it was u-g-l-y. She struggled with food, too, dabbling in eating disorders. I just didn't know how bad it was. A couple of months before she died, she came to visit me, and her alcoholism was on full display. She got our house into a pitiful state—empty bottles, vomit throughout the upstairs bathroom, a mess everywhere. I was furious. When I confronted her about the severity of her condition, she looked wounded, but I couldn't let it go without speaking up. Maybe I was too harsh. She left for the airport upset, and that was the last time I spoke to her.

Shortly after that visit, Hillary died tragically of cardiac arrest—by which I mean alcoholism. It was addiction that killed my friend.

The news hit me like a wall. I was working for a company in Colorado when I learned of her death on social media. I flew home immediately, heartbroken. I called Hillary's mom when I landed in Atlanta to give my condolences. All she could muster was something largely pathetic about the church and how Hillary's time on earth had been a waste.

That's what you have to say about your daughter's death? I couldn't imagine then, and certainly not now, how the focus wasn't on the loss of Hillary but on a life wasted because she'd turned her back on the church.

So let's add some salt to that wound, shall we?

I reached home, and after Matthew enveloped me in love, my mom, who was there to spend the weekend with us, did the same, but as she held me, she said, "We must pray for Hillary."

"Why is that, Mom?"

"Well, we know she wasn't a Christian—or so we think. We need to pray she had a reckoning. You know—that she was led to the Lord recently."

I chimed in again, trying to lead her to the sinister—and also ridiculous-sounding—conclusion I knew she was about to share. "Why, Mama?"

"Well, honey, you know. If she stayed a non-believer, she's in hell."

I mean, what in the *Left Behind* series kinda answer was that? Could you say anything more messed up to someone while they're grieving? No.

From that exact second, the foundation of my faith started to crumble.

All the answers I thought I had were gone.

I knew that what my mom was saying was wrong on so many levels. I mean, Hillary had already suffered her hell here on earth. And with what relationship I did have with God, it didn't make sense that God would let her, his child, continue living that hell in the afterlife. What I envisioned and felt deeply was Hillary walking through those pearly gates, literally falling at the feet of Jesus. His loving arms picking her up off the ground and holding her. Rocking her. That she was surely feeling safety and love like she'd never felt here on earth. Something we couldn't possibly comprehend.

Something that Brenda couldn't believe—

Maybe God is bigger than our brains can comprehend. Bigger than I'd always given him credit for. I had to imagine something different, something out of the box! Right then and there, hell was turned upside down for me, and God would never be back in that box.

Y'all. My midlife crisis became not about cars or money or material things but more an existential crisis of religion and my own spirituality. Realizing I don't have all the answers is a hard place to be. I had it figured out for so long. What if things I'd experienced growing up were more toxic faith and religious trauma than a true relationship?

After all, our youth group would travel to a hell house every year, conveniently leading up to Halloween. If you don't know what a hell house is, just think of a haunted house, but specifically for Christians. Or to freak you out so much that you'd become a Christian. Displays of gore, tragedy, and eternal damnation played out right in front of your eyes. I remember the bus rides home being silent and still. You'd leave there terrified with tears in your eyes, a victim of quite possibly the worst fear-mongering you can imagine, believing those wooly booger Satan characters were going to haunt your dreams forever if you didn't fall on your knees instantly and invite the Lord into your heart.

And what's worse was if you already *did* believe but second- and third- and forth-guessed yourself. So you ended up inviting the Lord into your heart every hour on the hour until, well, a lifetime passes you by.

I lived scared, full of fear.

And we haven't even touched on the rapture. There was constant anticipation and uncertainty around when to expect the rapture and second coming of Christ, *so you better be ready or else.* Or else what?

I'll never forget this moment. Tiffany, an old friend, ran into me at Barnes and Noble years after we graduated. As we embraced like old friends do, she told me I was the person who pushed her away from God. "You frightened me. Do you remember what you said?" She went on, "You asked me if I knew where I was going when I died, and frankly, I was too young to consider it, so I told you I wasn't sure. You went on to threaten me! 'But what if the Lord comes right now? That means you'll go to hell, so you need to get right.'"

I said that? Me? No way.

Okay, okay.

I also went on witness missions with the church. We were given tracts, set free on the streets of Myrtle Beach, and told to go up to as many people as we could by the end of the night, give each a tract, and make sure they were Christians. If they didn't know where they were going, we'd pray the salvation prayer with them and get them to ask God into their hearts.

I was thirteen when I went on my first witness mission. Let out on the streets of Myrtle Beach. Thirteen! And it's not like we were venturing out at 10 am when it was plenty bright outside, and folks'd had time to sober up.

No. We were let out on the streets when it was prime party time. Late into the night. What an excellent time to speak with coherent individuals of sound body and mind who are willing to come to terms with good and evil and accept Jesus Christ as their Lord and Savior.

I shudder. I would never send my thirteen-year-old child out to do that. Ever. I have difficulty reconciling these events, as you can imagine.

There's a story lodged deep in my hippocampus somewhere, and it's too good not to share. It's about the time a friend's mom dragged me out of the church nursery because she'd decided I was living a life of sin and needed a wake-up call. She pulled me into the sanctuary, and what I saw floored me—literally, as it turned out.

Everyone, and I mean everyone, was lying on the floor, covered with blankets. If you're unfamiliar with it, when someone falls to the ground, overcome by the Holy Spirit, this is called *being slain in the spirit*. But our church was massive, so it wasn't just a few folks. It was rows upon rows of people, flat on their backs. What in the hallelujah was happening? I mean, I still believed in the Gifts of the Spirit, but really? Everyone? It looked like God blew out a candle or something, and everyone just dropped.

I know that sounds like I'm poking fun, but I was genuinely shocked. Then, before I could fully process the scene, there he came: Brother I-Won't-Mention-His-Name, Bible raised high, striding toward me with absolute intent. My heart stopped. What was about to happen?

Then—bam!—he smacked me upside the head with the Bible, and before I knew it, I was also on the floor. Was I supposed to close my eyes? Open them? Call 911? Make sure the person next to me was alive? The whole thing was so surreal.

You can't make this up, people. This kind of thing—this head-hitting, Bible-wielding display—should be what's called blasphemy. It insults the church, disrespects God, and, most of all, harms his people. Nothing looks worse on faith than a Mr. Evangelical-Pastor-with-a-Head-Hitting-Bible-Fetish.

Let me put it this way:

Beliefs, faith, and spirituality? They're sacred. But the rules people make up within the church to control or manipulate? Those are the least important. These *rules* turn faith into a rigid system, creating businesses and denominations out of what should be a deeply personal, spiritual journey. I feel it's not God himself who hurts people; it's the church—the people in the church—who hurt people.

As I continued on my new quest for a more mature faith and spiritual relationship with the Lord, Matthew and I were growing together as a couple. I began opening up to this notion that both God and nature coexist and that God, while having the power to do so, doesn't fool with nature too much. Matthew's faith had shown me an opportunity for growth, or gray, in my own beliefs. A less black-and-white way to look at things.

But even as I moved closer to finding the gray, my struggles with Ed remained. Matthew's love was steady and certain while my relationship with food was anything but.

After a remodel from you-know-where took almost an entire year at our house in Alpharetta, we were finally in a place to host. Excited and knowing we were going to have both families at our place for Christmas dinner anyway to show off the house, Matthew suggested it would be cool if we invited a justice of the peace and got married on Christmas Eve. At our home, in our yard!

I was aghast. *He's crazy.* If I was ever going to have a wedding, it would be The Wedding, a blowout for certain. I'm talking designer gown, swans, and ice sculptures. *Father of the Bride* was one of my all-time favorite flicks, and I'd be willing to shovel a lot of money toward my own wedding to be able to ride off in an Austin-Healey just like George Banks himself—and I'd do it without so much as an ounce of regret. Oh, and did I mention? It was only two weeks before Christmas.

"Ha!" I said. You know how you do when you're feeling awkward. You don't know the correct response and need an extra minute to contemplate what's been said.

Then, after letting the idea sit with me for a bit, I thought, *Wait. That's fun and unexpected, and OMG.* "Let's hire a film crew and go shopping! Let's do it!"

The very next day, I had to fly to New York for work, but I wouldn't let that stand in my way. I got off the plane, having pushed my meetings back, and went straight to the nearest mall, where I started looking for casual wedding dresses. I'd forego the designer gown, given that I wasn't sure the occasion fit such a dress anymore. Something simple and white would do. Or maybe ivory since that bit about my V-card— *Ha!* I'd already successfully booked the film crew and sent out inquiries to a few photographers. Things were happening so fast.

I was about to walk out of the mall, slightly saddened by not saying yes to any dress, when I saw BCBG. I hadn't been to that store in ages. *I'll give it a whirl,* I thought.

In the clearance section hung the most beautiful, elegant ivory—praise be—dress. It was. Just. My. Size. How was this all coming together in the nick of time? Apparently, two weeks is all you need to plan a Christmas Eve front-yard wedding with you, your DCT, and twelve of your closest relatives. We'd register my cousin as an officiant. He's a real-life rock star and would play the part perfectly.

We filmed a tiny toast before everyone arrived so we'd have something to send out on Christmas morning to our two hundred would-have-been guests.

The best part? It was a surprise! In an attempt to conceal our shenanigans, we asked our family to arrive dressed to impress. We told them there would be lots of cameras and a film crew there because my friend, the videographer, needed footage for a commercial, and this setting, our newly remodeled house with a big holiday family gathering, would be the perfect backdrop. *Ha!*

Once everyone had arrived—my mom wore a 1980s sparkle-bedazzled tracksuit, can I just say that—the crew asked us to gather in the kitchen in such a way that all eyes would be on Matthew and me. Don't worry, we were still in casual clothes; well, fancy enough for a commercial but still casual. They said they wanted to get Matthew on film giving a toast to begin the festivities.

Matthew started in, "We want to thank you—" His speech continued for a minute, and then, slightly nervously, he said, "Lauren, will you marry me—tonight?" To which Matthew's mom let out a happy holler like you've never heard. My aunt squealed with excitement while my uncle asked, "Well, who's going to marry them?" As if we hadn't thought of that. My cousin, of course. Shawn would marry us.

We changed into wedding attire and stepped outside into the night of our dreams. Trees lit up with soft white Christmas lights, not the harsh LED kind that has a hint of blue. I can't stand those. We'd made an aisle that was also lit up. The lights illuminating our sweet home were just perfect. My bouquet, made for me just days before without anyone knowing, was still fresh. Our neighbors watched from next door by their overhead garage lights like something out of a Christmas movie. The Allman Brothers played first, followed by Rascal Flatts, "Why Wait?" Some of our family members danced while others embraced, taking it all in.

It was magical. The most magical night of my life. So sweet, so intimate. After dinner, we left our family and continued celebrating at the Mandarin downtown.

Our wedding was idyllic but not at all what I had in mind. And I wouldn't change a thing.

In the end, I can't say for sure whether it was God or nature that brought Matthew into my life. What I can say is this: I don't think God is orchestrating every moment like a grand puppeteer. He gives us the freedom to write our own stories, leaving room for a bit of mystery and maybe even a bit of magic. Leaving room for some gray.

For lessons learned and insights from this chapter,
visit "ENLIGHTENMENT on DATING ED"

CHAPTER 9

AHA! ABSTINENCE
(my holy shit moment)

Throughout this chapter, we'll talk about the lightbulb moment that catapulted me into looking at rehab as a solution to rid myself of Ed.

Oh, the days of leisurely reading, book in hand, hearken back to me. Sure, I'm into my Audible subscription and all, and I can really get into some psychological thriller audiobooks here and there—when the kids aren't in the car. But I'm talking about how I miss the smell of print, the desire to flip pages endlessly, dog-earing my spot, and the thrill of a finished book sitting on the shelf as I stare at it with pride, knowing I've read every lick of it. Even better if I pass it on to someone else to experience the same thrill.

Those days are long gone for me, not to return until—well, I don't know. A kidless vacation, perhaps? I mean, I know there are people out there who have kids and still enjoy reading, but tell me, how do you do it? I guess instead of writing this book, I could be reading, but that's not an option right now. This story is about to burst out of me, so *Big-Boned* is priority one. I suppose that after I retire, I will be able to read books again. I have a neighbor who makes sure each room has a reading nook. I just love that. There's something so cozy and comfortable about it.

Anyway, it was 2016, and Matthew and I were about two years into our marriage. And with no kids in the picture, that still meant lots of reading for me. I also wasn't so tied to my phone, you know what I mean? Doomsday scrolling at night or cackling my way through Instagram reels. Back then, I'd read a few chapters or more of something every night and drift off to sleep. Depending on my plans, I might get in another chapter or two during the day as well.

It was just before the holidays, and I can't remember what attracted me to this particular book in the bookstore. Probably something to do with the color and the striking title. I've always been a sucker for the self-help section and solid front covers. While *Life without Ed* was instrumental in my health, this one, *Better than Before: What I Learned About Making and Breaking Habits*, is the book that certifiably led me to rehab.

It's written by my idol author, Gretchen Rubin. If that name doesn't ring a bell for you, she's a bestselling author known for her work on habits, happiness, and humans. *Better than Before* dives into the nature of habits, discussing both how they're formed and how individuals can effectively change their habits, radically improving their lives. In this specific book, Gretchen provides readers with insights and strategies for creating better habits and breaking bad ones.

How exactly did her book change my life? What struck a chord?

I'd curled up one night, ready to read and drift off per usual. The first little bit I read was already chock full of great, effective content. Then I got to a chapter titled "Free From French Fries: Abstaining." I didn't know at the time, but this chapter is where Gretchen talks about her inability to stop at one donut. Her friend was the same with french fries. Naturally, I felt the tug from the minute I read the title. Had I missed this somehow? Were we about to talk about food?

One of the things I love about Gretchen is she gets right to the point.

Early on in that chapter, she talks about a quote from one of her favorite writers, Samuel Johnson, an essayist from the eighteenth century. Just as Gretchen's words inspired my journey, Dr. Johnson had positively changed hers. I'll share the same passage from Gretchen's book with you:

> "When a friend urged him 'to take a *little* wine,' Dr. Johnson explained, 'I can't drink a *little*, child; therefore, I never touch it. Abstinence is as easy to me as temperance would be difficult.'"

Gretchen almost shouts through her pages:

> *"That's me,* I realized, with a sudden thrill of identification. *That's exactly how I am.*
>
> "Like Dr. Johnson, I'm an abstainer: I find it far easier to give up something *altogether* than to indulge *moderately.* And this distinction has profound implications for habits."

And there I was, shouting at her pages, "That's me, too!" I kept reading, excited for what else I'd find:

> "When we Abstainers deprive ourselves totally, we conserve energy and willpower because there are no decisions to make and no self-control to muster."
>
> "Abstainers do better when they follow all-or-nothing habits. Moderators, by contrast, are people who do better when they indulge moderately."
>
> "Abstaining is a counterintuitive and nonuniversal strategy. It absolutely doesn't work for everyone. But for people like me, it's enormously useful."
>
> "As an Abstainer, if I try to be moderate, I exhaust myself debating: how much can I have? Does this time count? If I had it yesterday, can I have it today?"
>
> "... abstaining cures that noise ..."
>
> "By giving something up, I gain."

The words on these pages were making too much sense! *OMG, OMG, OMG!* This could be it! This could be *the* cure. The fatal blow for Ed.

Why hadn't I—in my umpteen years of attempted recovery—found a therapist or doctor or eating disorder clinic that mentioned this? Such a small concept with such massive impact. I couldn't put the book down. I was reading every word and, almost in disbelief, coming back for more, it was that good. Gretchen was reassuring me with each line, capturing facets of myself that I inherently knew but had never seen articulated professionally or in a medical setting. Something so profoundly individual and personal and life-changing.

I'll add more passages that resonated with me on a transformative level, but I highly recommend that you read the book for yourself.

> "For Moderators, the first bite tastes the best, then their pleasure gradually drops, and they might even stop eating before they're finished. For Abstainers, however, the desire for each bite is just as strong as the first bite—or stronger—so they may want seconds, too. In other words, for Abstainers, having something makes them want it *more*; for Moderators, having something makes them want it *less*."

> "Abstaining sounds demanding and inflexible, so people assume that they're moderators even if they have never successfully followed that strategy, but counter-intuitively for many people, abstaining is *easier*."

> "Research—and my own experience—suggests that the less we indulge in something, the less we want it. When we believe that a craving may remain unsatisfied, it may diminish; cravings are more provoked by possibility than by denial."

Something had clicked. I'd found my answer! Finally, freedom from food and freedom from Ed.

I wasn't sure if Gretchen had faced Ed like I had, but her words spoke directly to my soul. This was unlike anything I'd encountered before. Finally, I'd found a perspective beyond the usual intuitive eating advice— or hogwash, as I like to call it.

I wasn't a moderator. I was an abstainer. I *am* an abstainer. No matter how hard I tried to moderate, it always ended the same way. My mom could easily set aside half a Snickers for later; why couldn't I do that? I'd felt crazy all these years, but now I understood. The moment sugar touched my lips, I needed more. Much more.

Gretchen's friend had found freedom too; she'd once thought she was a moderator, but learning otherwise had freed her from french fries.

Energized, I leaped out of bed and ran to tell Matthew about the chapter. I read it to him word for word—I wasn't going to water down the impact with a summary. Certain lines I repeated for emphasis, committing them to memory. I wanted never to forget. This was my first real Aha! moment with food.

As I read, a mental list began forming. *It's sugar,* I thought. *Carbs, especially the sugary, fatty ones. And definitely peanut butter.* Peanut butter was my kryptonite. I hadn't bought it in years, yet every time I visited family, I managed to find the sugary Jiff and almost finish the jar.

Hmmmm. How would I do this? *I'll just take it all out.* I'd make my list and implement my new, abstinent life. Piece of cake.

For the next few weeks, I dove headfirst into my *Better than Before* quest. But as weeks turned into months, my resolve started to crack. I couldn't shake my old habits. And I knew why: Ed wasn't just a habit. He was a raging, rip-roaring eating disorder—a relentless disease. This wasn't a relationship I could just ghost and move on from.

I should've expected this—Ed luring me in, convincing me, like always, that I'd be able to manage just one bite. Every time, I'd find myself right back at square one. It was a constant, unrelenting push and pull, as if Ed knew every trick, every weakness, and every excuse. He wasn't going to let go so easily.

Each slip-up felt like a failure but was also a lesson. I began to understand that breaking free wouldn't be as simple as flipping a switch. It was about learning, stumbling, and learning again. This wasn't going to be a clean, easy break—but for the first time, I felt like I had a path forward, albeit imperfect.

However, things got ugly and dark. I was so far down the road into my relationship with Ed that this wouldn't be the cakewalk I'd imagined after reading that book. The breakthrough I so desperately needed felt out of reach. I was killing myself, after all, and the challenge was now figuring out how I could stay alive long enough to reach abstinence.

By this point, Ed and I had been dating for nearly fifteen years. I had no idea how this story would end, how I'd find my way to freedom, how I was going to become abstinent. I prayed for wake-up calls, often crying out over toilet seats, "Lord, take this from me." I realized, then, just how deep the sickness ran.

I thought rock bottom would be my savior—that if I just fell far enough, I'd finally find the strength to rise. It's a dangerous illusion, though. Inspiration isn't what gets you sober, and rock bottom doesn't work like that. Why? Because things *can always be worse*. So what exactly would rock bottom look like for me? Passing out? A stroke? A heart attack? Or worse, would it mean death? And we know there's no wake-up call after that. Rock bottom would never come in the way I needed it to.

I was constantly waiting for the other shoe to drop, yet I had no idea what that moment would look like.

The truth is, sometimes being abstinent is bigger than you. It's bigger than a habit, bigger than a resolution. It's bigger than just declaring, "I'm done with peanut butter." It's more than attending a few meetings—though those can be powerful. I needed something separate from the *perfect* life I'd constructed.

When we bought our home in 2014, I made a promise to myself: I'd never bring my disorder into this place, our sanctuary. But that vow didn't last for long. Eventually, I caved. *Just this once*, I told myself. *Matthew's not home; it's convenient.* That once was all it took. Soon, I was missing hours of work, bringing food home, bingeing while Matthew was away, and ending the cycle by purging it all. The commitment to keep Ed out of our home had vanished, and with it, my sense of control.

After reading *Better than Before*, my desire to stop grew so intense that it almost seemed to make things worse. Does that make sense? The more I craved abstinence from certain foods and food groups—the ones I'd convinced myself I couldn't live without—the deeper I felt myself spiraling.

With each binge and purge that followed my reading of Gretchen's book, it became clear that I needed something more. The book was an open door, but I still needed a way forward—a vehicle to drive me to abstinence. Otherwise, I'd soon drive myself off a cliff. I'd reached my limit.

I don't know where I found the courage. For fifteen years, I'd resisted the idea of rehab, convinced it was an *easy way out*. Sure, you could go to some oasis in the desert where a chef, meal plans, and round-the-clock therapy made recovery seem almost idyllic. But six months after Gretchen's words had shaken me and abstinence had become my mission, something shifted. Driving down Northpoint Parkway, desperation urged me to look up eating disorder rehab centers. I was at a red light, by the way!

I knew of a few places—three, to be exact. Over the years, those three had each given me one of two messages, sometimes both:

1. I'd need to refinance my house since rehab costs a small fortune. Only kind of kidding.

2. According to evaluations I'd had, I would need at least six months as an inpatient.

Predictably, those same rehab facilities topped my search results, no doubt paying top dollar for a Google ad campaign. I skipped them. I didn't have that kind of money, and I couldn't just leave my husband for half a year—I was the breadwinner that year, and we had bills to cover.

But then, there it was: an option with a shorter stay that felt almost manageable. *If rehab can ever be called attractive,* I thought, *maybe this is it.* Later, I clicked the link without knowing anything about the place, its location, its reputation, nothing.

Restoration Wellness Center, or RWC. *Alright.* I scrolled to find the phone number. *Got it.*

It didn't take much to click, but as the phone started ringing, every part of me felt like bursting open and hiding at the same time. I took a deep breath. *Thank you, Gretchen Rubin, for getting me here.* If this worked, maybe I'd leave RWC not only better than before but better than ever.

For lessons learned and insights from this chapter,
visit "ENLIGHTENMENT on DATING ED"

DIVORCING ED

eating to live | getting to the gray

CHAPTER 10

FINDING SHADE IN THE TEXAS HEAT

In this chapter, we'll dive into rehab and all the gifts it gave me. We'll also talk through what happened at rehab and how I still carry those tools with me on my journey today.

"Recovery Wellness Center, this is Lisa. How can I help you?"

The sweetness in her voice caught me off guard. I wasn't sure what I'd expected, but it wasn't Lisa—her compassion, her patience. I could barely speak, my tears heavy, words light, yet somehow, she understood.

"Take your time," she said gently.

She'd probably been on the receiving end of that phone call many times, with many patients who were far worse than me; I was sure of it. Yet, Lisa made me feel like I was the only patient she'd ever wanted to help. She was genuinely happy I'd reached Recovery Wellness Center and excited to offer me a chance at something better. She talked to me as if I were a friend. She didn't care about my demographics or how I'd found their number. Lisa was pouring into me already. I realize rehab is a business, too, but dang it if she wasn't the most perfect person for that job.

"It's okay," she kept urging. "We've got all day. I want to help you."

After I'd gotten out as much as I could muster, Lisa continued, "I think you need what Recovery Wellness has to offer, and I'd like to get you here immediately, but we're at capacity for the next few months. Let me check the quickest possible availability."

She put me on hold, and I felt both relieved and devastated. I mean, I did need some time to tell Matthew, my boss, and maybe one or two select others. And I'd expected a wait. Those places always have one. But the hopefulness in her voice and the desperation I could feel in mine left me wanting to jump on a plane immediately. I'd go in a heartbeat if I could.

When Lisa came back, it was with news that stung: the next opening was months away. I felt crushed. She encouraged me, though, assuring me that she'd do her best to make it happen sooner. "Hang in there," she said, and somehow, her belief in me was enough to hold onto for now.

Not an hour had passed before my phone buzzed. Unknown number. I answered, hopeful.

"Lauren? It's Lisa. What are the chances you can book your flight and get here in two weeks?"

Here meant Texas, and, let's be honest, I'd travel to the ends of the earth at this point if it meant ridding myself of Ed. Bursting into tears at every seam, I blurted out, "I'll buy my ticket today!"

Just before we hung up, Lisa added something I'll never forget.

"Lauren, I'm going to tell you something. These next two weeks, you'll want to treat every meal like it's your last. No matter what I say, you'll probably do it anyway, but I'm asking you—try to get here alive and in one piece."

She explained that they advised all residents to start abstaining as soon as possible, no matter the addiction. I was to take out all stimulants—including caffeine, white flour, and refined sugar—starting today. Otherwise, I'd spend much of my time there in withdrawal, which would limit the benefit of both my therapy and my investment.

"We want you to have the best experience possible," she finished. And I felt ready to start.

Abstinence, I thought. She said the word abstinence! That must be part of RWC's treatment plan. I knew I was going to rehab because I couldn't bootstrap abstinence on my own. But hearing the word aloud drove home just how deeply I needed this. I was an addict, and I needed rehab. After years of doubting whether it would work for me, I finally believed that rehab could get me there. I felt the change beginning. *This is it!*

Even though I hadn't told Matthew yet, I could finally breathe. For the first time in ages, I felt certain of what was coming: health and healing. I didn't know exactly how it would happen, but I knew RWC was the vehicle that would get me there.

You know the saying, never say never? I'm singing it as I write these words—thanks, Justin Bieber. That was me. I'd always been extremely vocal about my doubts regarding rehabilitation facilities for eating disorders. "Of course I'd get better there," I'd say, "but what about coming back to reality? What about living with all the influences of daily life? What about grocery stores? Restaurants? How do I learn to do *that*? What about the fact that I can't just quit food?"

In my wildest dreams, quitting food would have been my answer. Like an alcoholic or a drug addict, I could go cold turkey and never look back. No more meals to haunt me, no more anxiety around parties, holidays, or family gatherings. Rehab could offer me tools in a controlled environment, but I'd been convinced I'd relapse the minute I came face-to-face with ice cream, pizza, a croissant, or peanut butter.

But for years, I'd tried everything. I was at the end of my rope, and rehab was my last resort. I knew something had to give. And at this point, Matthew knew something had to give. He knew my views on rehab, especially inpatient or intensive rehab, but he'd watched me fight and fail to beat Ed on my own. I came clean to him about my ongoing struggle—

the lies, the cover-ups, the broken promises, even in our own home. Being the supportive person he is, he said, "Babe, if this is what you need, go do it. Come back to me *Better than Before*. I completely support you in whatever you need to do to get *you* better."

Of course he'd react like that. It's in his DNA.

We decided to keep the news from our families until I returned. We didn't know what to expect, and we wanted to manage how and when we'd share the outcome.

There was just one other person I had to inform. And there was no getting around this one. Telling my boss was nerve-wracking on another level, but I've been blessed with some of the best, and Dustin was no exception. However, he'd never known of my struggle in the first place, so it was like confession time, coming clean about Ed, and "Oh, by the way, I need to take some time off to go get rid of him," all in one breath.

He responded quickly, "Don't even bother putting in PTO for this. Go to Texas, get what you need, and come back to us."

The rest of his sentiments went something like, if I happened to need more time—another week or a month or six months—we'd cross that bridge when we got there, and not to worry. My health was the most important thing in the world, and he'd hold down the fort for me.

Dustin's allowing that space for me to grow and heal without judgment or critique did so much for me as an employee. His support showed the kind of empathy and respect we should always have for each other.

I was set. I could go to RWC without anything weighing me down. Except—

Lisa had me pegged. I'm not sure I'd ever binged or purged the way I did in those weeks leading up to my time at RWC. It was the last supper at every meal, just like she said it would be. I tried taking out caffeine and limiting the other things she'd advised, but that didn't stop my behaviors.

I even planned a binge at the Dallas airport, thinking it would be my final one. I'd binge and not purge, and that would leave me satisfied—taking in every last morsel with me I could before I had to abstain—forever. But by the time my connecting flight was in the air, I felt miserable. My body wasn't used to holding in that much food, especially all that sugar, the very thing Lisa had warned me to avoid. It left me bloated and aching, an uncomfortable reminder of why I was on this journey in the first place.

My emotions during that flight were a whirlwind: pain from the physical discomfort, anxiety over the unknown, and a glimmer of joy at the thought that, in ten days, I could be returning home healthier than I'd ever been. Yet, as I inched closer to that new beginning, I found myself mourning the loss of Ed. He'd been with me for so long, a twisted comfort I didn't know if I was ready to let go of. Without him, who would I be? Clearly, he'd been my best asset when it came to coping. The feeling of that emptiness, facing the world without him, terrified me.

Once we landed at the small, almost deserted airport, a wave of nervousness washed over me. As clearly as I remember its size, I remember stalling—except I guess it wasn't all stalling. I'd wanted so badly to tell one specific friend. One specific roommate, Jackie. Over the years, Jackie had become more of a sister and even, sometimes, a motherly figure to me. You know the kind. The one who has better sense than you do when you're about to make some not-so-good decisions. She'd been that for me a lot. And for whatever reason—even if I was stalling a bit—it was heavy on my heart to call her and let her know what was happening. And she probably wouldn't answer after all; it was midmorning.

Miraculously, there she was. "Hey!" Jackie's voice, so warm and so familiar. It always is.

And there I was. "Hey, soooo—"

Abashedly, I gave her the cliff notes version that a lot had transpired, and I'd finally made up my mind that I couldn't fight Ed alone anymore.

I was checking myself into rehab. Like today. Like, as soon as we hung up the phone. They were waiting for me outside, but I was nervous, a blubbering mess. While Jackie wasn't in the actual airport with me, I could feel her presence almost as if she were sitting next to me. Her words were full of reassurance, even from hundreds of miles away.

I still remember most of what she said, "You're about to do one of the bravest things anyone could ever do: you're choosing yourself. This is your moment to rewrite everything Ed stole from you. You don't have to carry him anymore. Remember, you're not alone; you're surrounded by people who love you, believe in you, and are cheering you on. You are stronger than any voice that tells you otherwise. And on the other side of this? There's a you who's at peace, living the life you deserve. Trust yourself. You are going to do this and get through it. I'm so proud of you."

We hung up, and with Jackie's words echoing in my mind, I stepped out into the thick Texas heat. I swear I could feel her words wrapping around me, almost like armor. I would carry her faith in me, along with every ounce of her love and encouragement. It was as if her strength had become my own, making each step a little easier. Holding onto her words, I knew I could face whatever awaited me.

I'll never forget seeing Lisa standing beside the passenger van. I knew it was her—not just because she'd told me she'd be the one picking me up, but because it was entirely obvious. I was the last person to walk out of the tiny airport from the most recent flight.

I even remember what I was wearing that day. Jeans, a purple blouse— and I hate purple, so this still surprises me—and a black suit coat clearly screaming "Corporate America employee who doesn't know how to dress outside the office," and my Madewell leopard loafers. My face was surely flushed, and my stomach felt bloated as I walked toward that van, taking in the thick, humid air.

As I got closer, Lisa's welcoming smile drew me in. Once I was close enough, she opened her arms, waiting to envelop me in love as if she knew my entire story already. Of course, she knew parts of my struggle from our calls and the application process, but something about that moment made me feel like everything I'd carried was finally safe to release. I knew I couldn't abuse or hurt myself anymore. All the cards had fallen right where they needed to be so I could get the help I was meant to receive. And just like I lost it with Jackie, I lost it again. I'm talking full-on ugly cry, complete with snot and gasping breaths, right there in the Texas heat. Lisa brushed my hair out of my face as the wind from the nearby planes whipped around us. I don't think I'd ever experienced a release like that before. Just by being there—by taking this step—I'd already come so far.

Once in the van, I was introduced to Claire. She'd be one of my three roommates, but I didn't know that at the time. I was looking at her, and I'm sure she was looking at me. She looked totally normal to me. Claire was—average. Not fat, not skinny. She was just right. Her body was exactly what I'd wanted for myself. So what in the world was she doing there? Wait, maybe she was RWC staff? That must be it. But she had bags with her.

The corporate, networking side of me wanted to come out and ask a million questions, but then there's an awkwardness that comes with riding on a passenger van with complete strangers to a rehab facility you know nothing about beyond a Google search and a few phone calls. I mean, what was I supposed to start with? "Hey, so what brings you to RWC? You work here? No? Drugs, alcohol, Ed? Oh, alcohol. That's cool."

After we'd exchanged names, I decided to stay quiet.

What felt like two hours later, probably because of the silence, but only lasted thirty minutes, we'd arrived at RWC. It's weird, but to this day, when I think about getting out of the van, I still feel it. The heaviness. A heaviness that place held onto. I'm not sure what expectations I had;

maybe I thought rehab would have more of a sterile medical building-type feel. There was just something about the yellow buildings that sat under the trees. They were very house-like. Homey. Dry and yellow and, well, older. Much more retreat than center, with dirt paths leading patients from one building to the next.

Those who came before me have left all their burdens here. Work had been done there. Hard, intense work. Something told me that I, too, would be leaving it all behind at RWC.

We got out next to the dining building, where lunch was already prepared for us, each tray labeled with a name. My confidence flared for a second. *This will be easy, with meals ready and no temptations.* No peanut butter. Just chicken salad, some crackers—no white flour, of course—and some raw vegetables.

I thought nothing of it, but I didn't know I was being timed: down the hatch in seven minutes, to be exact. We were being monitored, someone watching every bite. More on that later.

Lisa had warned me that I'd have zero communication with the outside world once I got on campus. One thing she failed to mention is that there would be no clocks; watches weren't allowed. And RWC was no Vegas casino, folks. Talk about learning you're a control freak. During the first meeting that night, I popped up my hand so fast.

"Do we have a schedule for the week? What will our days look like? And—time? Does anyone know what time it is?"

Not only had I not worn my watch to Texas, but now I was without my phone, which they'd taken after our last call home when we arrived. I realized that no one around there knew the time!

Patsy, owner of RWC, called me out, almost laughing while doing so. "Ohhhh. You're one of those."

She didn't have to say the word; I knew who I was, and she wasn't wrong.

"You're going to have a really tough time here if you're already worried about an agenda."

Looking back, I'm thankful for the lack of clocks. I mean, who would want to see at the beginning of each day that they have eight or more hours of therapy left? At the time, I didn't know what I didn't know.

And as if the clock conundrum wasn't enough to upset my apple cart that first night, Patsy brought up group therapy. "All sessions will be group sessions."

"Uhhhh, this must be some kind of mistake," I gave my two cents. "Group is optional, right?"

I hadn't come here to share my demons with the rest of the addicted world, I thought. I wanted the best RWC had to offer, and surely, that included individual therapy. If I was leaving here without Ed, I was convinced group sessions wouldn't be the ticket. I was living in my own paradox, though, because that was a very unaware justification, considering my prior fifteen years of therapy had all been individual and hadn't gotten me any further down the road.

"We work and heal together, Lauren. If you think you've got problems that someone else doesn't, you're fooling yourself. We can all learn from one another."

Patsy went into a whole host of reasons why group reigned supreme over individual, citing emotional support along with sharing of experiences and how group sessions reduce stigma around all types of addiction. So while I was still fuming inside, I let it go. I'd bring it up tomorrow after not getting what I'd paid for.

Patsy was equal parts stern grandmother and angel—tough love with a touch of tenderness. I'll try to explain her presence, but words won't do her justice.

Have you ever been around someone who you felt knew more about you than you knew about yourself? Someone you've just met, but somehow they know all your secrets. It's like a true crime show where the detective calls you in for questioning while already knowing that you committed the crime. You're vulnerable, almost putty in their hands. That was Patsy. She just knew things. This was a woman who had stared down evil, devoting her life to a kind of personal exorcism. At RWC, she witnessed Ed leaving people's lives, the weight of years of torment lifting. Maybe she knew Ed's tricks too well because she'd faced those demons herself. Patsy was a force—one Ed had to reckon with every single day.

I won't go into detail about every session or experience at RWC, but I will say my time there was the best and worst of my life, all rolled into one. The therapy was raw and relentless, forcing me to confront parts of myself that I'd spent years avoiding. It was like stripping my entire identity down to the foundation—painful but necessary. I learned hard truths about the severity of my disorder and how much of a hold Ed had on my life, but I also found hope. I was given tools and insights that, piece by piece, began to rebuild me. It was the kind of healing that breaks you before it builds you back up.

We started every day off with exercise. Just some basic cardio to get the blood flowing. Exercise? At a treatment center? And for Ed? But it made total sense. We'd walk—not run—alongside Patsy. She was right there with us every step, every morning. Telling us stories, getting to know us, and us getting to know Patsy. It was time to create friendships and build unbreakable bonds. We'd then head directly to breakfast, load up on decaf coffee—sprinkle with cinnamon for an extra treat—and afterward get into our first therapy session.

Sometimes, I wish I could recall more, and other times, I'm thankful I only remember what I do.

Early on in the intensive, there was one therapy session that stuck out. We were met with large pieces of paper and chalk. We had to draw ourselves—a chalk outline of our bodies as if we were lying dead on the ground at a crime scene. Except we were drawing, not tracing, and just the image we had of ourselves in our minds. Then we lay down on our paper, and our neighbors drew our *actual* chalk lines, tracing our true physical shape. Body dysmorphia, folks. That's what this activity was illustrating. Just how messed up your own version of you is. Turns out, we weren't even close to what we'd outlined. Most of us had drawn a much larger version of ourselves because of the lies and assumptions we had in our minds—the lie that we were a hundred or more pounds larger than our actual selves—while our neighbor drew the truth. Reality.

Can I tell you what's mind-blowing? This activity was so much more than that chalk line. Our therapist for this particular exercise peeled back a million layers in that session. Did you draw a small head or a little head? It wasn't just about our stomachs or legs and arms. The size of your head was very telling as it showed how you judged your own intellect or experienced feelings of inadequacy—and this proved very true for those of us who drew an unrealistically smaller head.

She went into questions like, "What do you see?" After highlighting all the areas of concern and allowing us time to take it all in, she continued, "Are you willing to see yourself differently?"

We left there with paper in hand and some new tools in our toolbox. Most, if not all of us, weren't what we'd thought we were, and that alone gave us hope.

Also early in the week, there was another type of body awareness activity. Or maybe this practice leaned more toward body exposure. Whatever it was, with all sincerity, I thought this session was going to send me to the psych ward. I'm not sure of its formal name, and I know my description won't do it justice, but I'll try anyway. We weren't forced to be uncomfortable, but we were encouraged to step out of our comfort zone by revealing to the group what our least favorite body parts were and why.

I realized early on, as our therapist went around the group, that this was going to be complex because I couldn't even make up my mind. Every body part sucked to me. *My legs.* Thighs, to be exact. *I'll go with those.* They were dimpled and loose and uncomfortable. I didn't like the way they looked. I didn't like the way they rubbed together. I didn't even own a pair of shorts. You know what else I didn't own? A sleeveless top. I knew that my arms sucked too. Major. They were flabby from years of abuse to my body. They had lots of stretch marks. *Even my arms have stretch marks,* I thought with disgust. I'd never been caught dead in shorts or a sleeveless top.

Until it was my turn. My turn to, with great reluctance, go and put on some shorts and a tank top. My turn to expose my least favorite body part or two and talk about why. Then we'd work with our therapist to relearn and retrain the brain to think more appropriately about said body parts. This exercise not only gave our therapist an idea of how much body disturbance we had, but it also gave us an idea of how messed up our minds were.

I was mortified. Standing there in horror, worried both about what my peers would think of me and what I thought of myself. As I stood there totally exposed, feeling naked while fully clothed, it was devastating.

Tears stream down my face as I type this. I still remember shaking as badly as if I'd just done a cold plunge in the Arctic. A dark cloud came over that room, and I wasn't sure I'd ever recover. Did it kill me? No, but how badly I reacted to exposing my arms and legs took me completely by surprise. In my inexpert opinion, I look back at this cold-turkey activity as somewhat questionable. I don't know what other approach you could take with an intensive program, though, as there's no good way to progressively slide into showing more skin.

I still have a lot of healing to do in this area. I bought a pair of shorts this year for the first time in—well, a long time. I'm working on a more gradual approach to body acceptance and neutrality, but it was at RWC that I first learned just how loud the lies were that I'd been telling myself. So maybe I *am* thankful that they helped rip the band-aid off.

Probably my favorite session of the entire intensive was one particular guided meditation. It focused on inner child work, a phrase I was all too familiar with, given years of therapy. However, this exercise was new to me. We were asked to lie down and start envisioning not just a room but our whole childhood home. She was nowhere near striking to other people, but to me, she was the embodiment of home. I could see her plain as day, sensible and lovely. Naturally-brown vertical cedar siding hung with a sage green trim. A formidable front porch with my favorite swing and a yard full of tulips or buttercups, depending on the season. And Juniper. I still love Juniper. And my absolute favorite climbing tree, the most beautiful dogwood you've ever seen.

Patsy asked us to walk up to the front door and let ourselves in. Once inside, she asked us to walk to our childhood bedroom. There, we'd find our inner child sleeping. "Let's wake her up," Patsy said. "Let's ask her for permission to walk around. She'll need to give us a tour so we can remember it like it once was."

I gently nudged her, my inner child, from her nap. She obliged my request for a tour. We walked down the hallway, turning right into the dining room, and there sat my dad in his normal spot. He was always in that spot, I thought, exactly the picture to which my mind had led me and my inner child. He was reading the newspaper. I could smell the all-too-familiar cocktail: the fragrance of Old Spice and his English Leather aftershave. My mom wasn't far off, in the kitchen, cleaning and doing the dishes. Always busy, that one. A clean house was never up for debate; it was mandatory. She had a pound cake in the oven and fresh cornbread on the stove.

Patsy spoke softly, asking us to take note of how our parents greeted us when we walked into the room. Did they say hello? My dad hadn't. My mom had dropped everything for a quick embrace, but it was just that: brief and back to her duties. Were they interacting with each other? They weren't, not a word. I don't remember them ever talking a lot to each other, come to think of it. Were they paying me any attention at all? If so, what were they saying? Were they loving? Was their attention centered on me as I walked past them?

I realized, at that exact moment, that our house was very quiet. There was very little interaction with me and definitely a lack of interaction between my parents. Still, I could have stayed all day. I kept catching myself looking at my inner child less than at the scene. I wanted to stay there and speak to her, the small, innocent version of myself before she broke. I wanted to squeeze her so tight and protect her forever from harm. Harm from herself and from Ed.

I was utterly overcome, emotions crashing over me in waves so powerful and raw that I couldn't contain them. I cried out loud, my voice breaking into the stillness of the room, knowing that I was probably disturbing the quiet reflection of others. But the release was unstoppable. It was as if all the hurt and love, regret and forgiveness needed to burst free.

Patsy came over, her presence grounding me, and she took my hand, assuring me it was okay. "You're having a breakthrough," she said gently, helping me understand that this was a moment of transformation.

With her support, as I continued the meditation, I knew it was time to tend to child Lauren. We went back to my room, and with all the tenderness I could find within me, I tucked her in. I told her I was sorry, that she didn't deserve the pain we'd been through. I promised her I'd keep her safe, whispered my love to her, and, as she closed her eyes, I let her know she wasn't alone anymore.

Patsy continued, "Now I want you to walk out to the front yard and turn around as you leave your childhood home. Is there anyone on that porch waving goodbye to you? Who's there? Who's been in your corner supporting you? Do you see them? What are their names? Are both of your parents there or just one, or maybe neither? Grandparents? Aunts? Uncles? Cousins? Friends? Who's rooting for you? Are they shouting goodbye or just waving? Do you see smiles or sadness on their faces?"

This continued as she described what it all meant. What each face, each expression meant. And I felt the biggest relief and release I had in a long time.

Through that meditation, Patsy was demonstrating a lot, but my biggest takeaways were identifying underlying causes and releasing shame and guilt. Patsy's approach helped me reframe my perspective, showing me that I had allies, too—even if they were far away or not always present—and that Ed was never my fault. By reconnecting with my inner child, this practice gave me a framework to care for her and to approach my health with self-compassion and acceptance.

One of the last practices I recall just as vividly as I remember the meditation was a pairing of sorts. I'm not sure what RWC would formally have titled it, but my research has led me to family constellation practice partnered with psychodrama or anger release therapy.

Have you ever heard of family constellation practice? Talk about mind-bending. Picture this. Your therapist knows you well enough that they've been able to take some notes about your past. They've heard the horror stories about how your grandmother treated you, maybe your dad and an uncle. Others.

Unbeknownst to you, they've built up enough content over the course of the intensive to do this activity, so you enter your therapy session and are seated with your back to a group of staff members, each one a character in your life story. They proceed to beat up on you in just the way you remember. They talk to you as your family members and other influences did. They call you names. They mention how weird it is that you can't lose weight since you're so active. They talk down to you about how you're the biggest in your dance class. They ask friends around you if they'd like to be catapulted into the air while saying it's impossible for you since you weigh too much. They call you big-boned.

Then, after the practice is over, and now that you've built up a well of emotion, Patsy proceeds to lead you into the anger release portion, where you physically exert your frustration through a series of body movements. Let's be real; you punch and kick the heck out of stuff— pillows, props, and so on. Sounds bananas.

At first, it was awkward. It's not like I'm used to beating up on things, but where else can you do that and not look ridiculous? Gradually, I got into it. Like, really into it. And there was another release, just like the one I'd experienced with guided meditation.

Sure, it was a hurtful session in some ways, but it was a way for RWC staff to help me see the trauma firsthand. Family constellation was a way to witness or relive it as RWC revealed the trauma of my past, while the anger release or psychodrama portion was a way to address it. It was how to deal with it once and for all, both pinpointing and letting go of resentment toward those who had harmed me.

Every session was a good session. The reason I say those days in Texas were the best and the worst days of my life is because, while they were good sessions, sometimes even great, they were hard. Mega hard.

It wasn't just about therapy sessions, either. I could write an entire book on simple tactics they provided education on. Life skills: tools we should all carry with us. Things like conflict negotiation, setting and maintaining boundaries, emotional regulation, and so much more. The best part? I still use these tools on a daily basis. And it's not limited to your personal life; you can also use these tools in any professional environment. I'll admit that setting boundaries is one I still struggle with, but I'm working on it.

Along with the other tools, RWC taught me how I simply need to practice more often. With my mom, with my kids, at work. Boundaries prevent burnout, resentment, and unhealthy relationships. I'm not good at saying no.

I never have been. So boundaries are an absolute necessity in order to assert my needs, especially with food—thanks, Ed—and to do so without guilt.

Outside of these tools, there was also the relearning and reteaching of how to eat. Probably one of the more tangible tools we were given while at RWC. But forget calling it a tool—this was a gift.

Remember when I said, "Down the hatch in seven minutes," and that we were being monitored beginning with our first meal at RWC?

A couple of days into my stay, someone joined us at mealtime, an expert in mindful eating strategies. She had a way of emphasizing the importance of taking time, not just in theory but in precise numbers. "Lauren, your first lunch here took seven minutes. Do you know how long it should take? Ideally, about thirty."

I laughed, thinking she couldn't be serious—thirty minutes? Most days, I barely had ten! But she wasn't laughing. The teacher continued, explaining the principles we needed to follow, and there were lots of them. Take at least thirty minutes for a meal; avoid drinking while eating; eat seated, without distractions. We were to savor each bite with no mixing of foods, pausing between each mouthful to set down our forks and chew deliberately, twenty times or more. Even before that first bite, we should pause to give thanks. Tell it out loud: ask our food to nourish us in the way most necessary. We should be enjoying our food because of what was in it, no longer lusting over it because of how it made us feel, as those were short-term gains, and we wanted long-term life-giving nourishment. We were eating to live!

Talk about a full-circle moment. Eating to live!

I'm happy to report my average mealtime when I left RWC was around thirty-five to forty minutes.

As you know, I'd been so afraid rehab would hold me back from real-world challenges, but I was wrong. That was all in my head. Once our leaders thought we were strong enough to do some of those activities, we did! We went out to Jason's Deli—funny how Jason's is such a staple in stories of mine—and our leaders watched as we ordered, offering us support every step of the way. I don't think I've ever sat in Jason's Deli for so long! But it was such a wonderfully redemptive experience for me. It felt like a second chance to connect with food on my own terms.

Mindful eating, I learned, is a conscious effort at every meal. Sometimes, it seems and feels entirely unrealistic, but as long as you have the tools, they do work! And practice doesn't make perfect, but it certainly leads to progress. And this was the case for me.

As the intensive was drawing to an end, RWC encouraged our attendance at either Alcoholics Anonymous (AA) meetings or Overeaters Anonymous (OA) meetings. They hosted some of their own on campus, or you could take a bus to a meeting nearby in town.

That wasn't my first exposure to those meetings, as I'd learned of the fellowship years prior when Diane began going for her own struggles with addiction. I went with her when she received her one-year sobriety chip—a token symbolizing her commitment to recovery.

During that meeting, a man who had been sober for eleven years stood up. Eleven! He wept tears of joy as he spoke about his journey. "I wish I could give all of you this gift," he cried. "I've never felt more free. Freedom is learning to live *with* but not giving *into* addiction."

At that moment, even years before I'd found RWC, I knew I wanted what he had. I didn't know quite how to get to where he was, but I felt I had to. The freedom I saw in him was what I longed for—the same freedom from my own addiction.

Learning to live *with* but not giving *into,* I'd consciously thought to myself. That man's words stuck with me all those years. And now, here I was, tasting just the beginning of what he must have felt.

Patsy encouraged us to become addicted to the fellowship—pun intended—and to find a sponsor. "When you leave here, we require you to attend a meeting the very next day. Begin looking for that sponsor! You won't make it without one."

We all wrote down what meeting we'd attend, its location, and the time.

Preparing to leave RWC was surreal. On one hand, I was desperate to get out, to run down that road and never look back. But sheltered in the cocoon that Patsy and the team had created, I also felt a deep reluctance to leave. I'd come to cherish the safety, the self-work, the things I'd let go of there. Rehab wasn't as terrifying as I'd imagined. Intense, yes. Overwhelming, yes. But in a strange way, even now, I find myself daydreaming about it—thinking of the healing I had there, the layers I shed. Not that I want any of that old baggage back, but there's always more work we can do, right?

As the van door shut and we pulled away from RWC, a cloud of red dust swirled in the air, catching the light through the trees. I looked back at that place where I'd found shade in the Texas heat—shelter from Ed and a path to abstinence, to freedom. I owed my life to Patsy and the entire team who made that possible.

As we merged onto the main road toward the airport, I wiped the last of my tears. I felt something I hadn't in years: hope. I just knew I was better. I was healing.

And for a while, I was.

For lessons learned and insights from this chapter,
visit "ENLIGHTENMENT on DIVORCING ED"

CHAPTER 11

RELAPSE AFTER REHAB

**In this chapter, we'll talk about losing sobriety
and the downward spiral it took me on.**

One of Patsy's teachings stayed with me after I left RWC. Call it a metaphor for transformation or *The Pothole Story*; it was her way of showing just how challenging it is to stay sober or break old patterns for good. The story goes something like this:

A person is walking down a sidewalk and falls into a pothole. They're trapped for months before finally climbing out, but they eventually do. The next time, they walk down the same road and fall into the pothole again. But, having been there before, it's a bit easier to climb out. This time, it takes only a few weeks. Weeks become days, and soon, as they walk the same road, they start to notice the pothole ahead of time, stepping around it to avoid falling in. Eventually, they choose a different road entirely.

I hope this story resonates with you as deeply as it did with me.

The reality of recovery from Ed—and any other addiction—is that it's rarely a straight line. Just having the tools isn't enough to guarantee you won't struggle again.

To avoid relapse, remember what Patsy tasked us with during our departure? Beyond abstinence, there were two things. Get yourself into the fellowship—AA, OA, or any of the twelve-step programs would do—and get yourself a sponsor.

"Do it quick!" she warned as if our lives depended on it. Those were our marching orders. Strict, of course, but Patsy knew what lay in store.

When I got home, I was shocked to discover so many meetings, both for AA and OA, in my area. Eager to start, I chose the first OA meeting I could get to at a nearby hospital. But it was a total letdown, full of folks I didn't connect with, and it was stiff, almost militant. As opposed to my Texas experience, no one was opening up much, and the sharing was vacuous. *Are they all like this?* I wondered.

A day later, I switched gears and decided to attend the next OA meeting at a local church. I know, I know. Lots of meetings. But RWC taught us *a meeting a day to keep Ed away*—or ninety meetings in ninety days, which is common practice after getting out of rehab. Upon walking in, I immediately felt a different, more positive vibe than the last. I couldn't exactly pinpoint where the positive vibe hailed from, but perhaps the less sterile environment was a start.

Not five minutes into this meeting, I found her! I could have picked her out in a crowd. Her name was Lynne, and she was positively radiant. I connected with her—you know, in the way that a shared environment and smile can. She was bubbly and joyful when she spoke, and with anyone's bad, she offered good, whether it be new ideas on how to combat what someone was experiencing or simply love and support. She was light in a room full of dark. She, I thought, had found it. I wasn't sure what *it* was, even at the time. Was she stimulant sober like me? Maybe even just sugar sober? Whatever it was, I knew that was what I wanted. She made claims of *food freedom*, and I couldn't wait to find out what her experience had been.

After introductions were through and more than a few shares, the meeting leader interjected. They'd forgotten to ask about willing sponsors; were there members of the fellowship who were willing to sponsor? Much to my excitement, Lynne lifted her hand! But it was my first meeting there, and I was too shy to say anything. I already knew it, though. I was putting all my laws of attraction tactics to work. Lynne would be my sponsor.

I did it after the very next meeting. I went up to her and asked if she'd be open to sponsoring me. Without hesitation, she said yes! I was so excited. We exchanged numbers and immediately started texting.

We got to know each other better by meeting in town outside of OA meetings. Early on, I gave Lynne the full download of my history and told her what I was looking for. I told her I'd been rather strict with my recovery from Ed, thanks to RWC, and was hoping for her sponsorship to be an understanding one—one that knew I needed to maintain rigidity to make it through sobriety. To stay alive. Abstinence, I touted. That's how I did it and how I believed everyone else should, too.

Lynne went on to encourage me, saying that while being part of OA, my journey might look different from that of others, just as her own wouldn't look identical to mine. She then shared with me her version of food freedom. "I've found a healthy, balanced relationship with food. I can enjoy it without eliminating it. The obsession is no longer there," she said, her relief evident.

You mean some people in OA still have sugar? Sugar was the devil incarnate, after all. I was immediately put off, trying not to eye-roll my way through talks with my newfound sponsor, who I adored but who was confusing the h-e-double-hockey-sticks out of me. This sounded like a whole lotta intuitive-eating hogwash. Regardless of Lynne's amazing qualities, I wondered how she'd be able to sponsor me if she was more free than I was. If I was abstinent, and she wasn't, how would she understand my needs and my temptations if she gave in when I didn't?

In the fellowship's defense, it wasn't all like that; there were some members who were abstinent, sure, but those people—at least at my location—weren't actively up for sponsoring.

Here I was, barely a month out of rehab, already questioning OA as a long-term solution. Texas had encouraged me to dive into the fellowship, but it all felt so similar to the familiar advice I'd heard in therapy for fifteen years, which had never truly stuck. If we were all struggling with Ed, why wasn't everyone on the same page as RWC? Why wasn't everyone following a strict abstinence plan—total stimulant sobriety, or, at the very least, cutting out sugar?

At that moment, though, I needed a program more than I could be without one, so I persisted. I went on, maintaining my relationship with both the fellowship and Lynne while I questioned everything. It was all a little—okay, a lot—frustrating. Why were people sharing stories about their food freedom when they clearly hadn't let some things go? Why were people getting sobriety chips when they'd just shared about eating sugar without feeling guilty?

You see, my sponsor, among others, had already made it to the gray. Lynne had navigated a space I didn't yet understand, one that felt elusive and nearly impossible to achieve. She'd discovered a place between the rigidity of abstinence and the desire to indulge—somewhere between emptiness and fullness. It wasn't all black and white for Lynne; it was more about honoring herself day by day and staying mindful without the obsession. She was finding peace in the present. She seemed unshakable, even in a world where triggers—or Ed—lurk around every corner.

I was still struggling with absolutes, believing recovery required black-and-white rules to stay on track. In my mind, you were either abstinent or in relapse. You were following the program, or you weren't. So when others in the group shared about their *food freedom* while admitting they'd had a cookie, I was stunned. Didn't they understand? To me, it seemed like they were rationalizing behaviors that kept Ed alive. If someone in AA had just had a beer, they wouldn't get their sobriety chip—so why was food treated differently?

However, Lynne and others like her showed a different perspective. She understood that, with food, it wasn't just about abstaining from certain foods forever. It was about learning to navigate the urges and cravings without allowing them to control her. She was living proof that you could engage with life's grays, the middle ground between hard lines of abstinence and outright indulgence, and—guess what—still thrive. Lynne had embraced *one day at a time* in a way that allowed her to make choices based on the moment, trusting herself to know her limits without needing an all-or-nothing rule.

As much as I doubted the gray approach, and let's be real, it would still be years before I got there myself, I also craved the freedom I saw in Lynne—one that came from living *with* the reality of addiction, not constantly battling *against* it. For me, though, embracing the gray felt risky, like opening a door I might not be able to close. So, for now, I clung to the structure of RWC rules, finding comfort in their certainty while still showing up to meetings and listening to Lynne's guidance. Perhaps one day, I'd also be ready to trust myself in that same way.

But let's talk about the RWC way for a moment because following it was no easy task. Sugar, the biggest no-no in the RWC playbook, is literally everywhere. If you've ever read a nutrition label, you already know this: sugar is in everything, woven into the fabric of nearly every processed food on the shelf.

Baby food and formula? It's there.

Bread? In America, absolutely.

Bacon? Not naturally, but in the grocery store, almost always.

Vegetables in a can? For sure.

Your protein bar? Might as well be candy.

Salad dressing? Bet your ass.

You name it, it's got it. And honestly, I get it; sugar is hard to avoid. It adds flavor, extends shelf life, and enhances texture.

While exact numbers are tricky to pin down, studies estimate that sugar is present in more than half of all processed foods, making it nearly inescapable.

And it doesn't stop there. White flour and caffeine are also everywhere in our food system. While the exact percentage of foods containing white flour isn't clear, it's safe to say it's a key ingredient in a significant portion of processed foods, from baked goods to pasta. As for caffeine, it may be harder to estimate, but it's widely found in coffee, tea, sodas, and energy drinks—approximately 20% of beverages.

The result is a processed food industry that leans heavily on these stimulants, creating products that are tough to quit and easy to overconsume. For me, it only reinforced why the RWC abstinence model was essential.

Despite the lukewarm OA experience, I was able to remain victoriously stimulant-sober for five whole months after leaving RWC. My time in Texas had armed me with tools and strategies to be prepared for Ed any time he started acting up and getting rowdy.

I couldn't believe it. Abstinence *was* possible, and when abstinent for that long, you feel great. I'm sure you're thinking this isn't rocket science: I'd effectively kicked processed foods to the curb for five months; of course I was feeling great. But let me tell you, for someone who had lived with Ed for almost fifteen years, this was no small feat. If there was a black-and-white to overcoming Ed, I'd found success and was rocking it.

Can you be high from being sober? If so, that's exactly how I felt. It changed everything. Energy level: amazing. Sex drive: fantastic. Optimism: through the roof. Relationships: solid. Debts: paid. And the weight I'd gained between college and RWC? Naturally falling off, not too fast, not too slow.

It was exhilarating. Remember that, sometimes, saying no is easier than saying yes. That's how long-term sobriety was feeling for me. Every time I said no, I felt empowered. I felt stronger than the time before.

And those food lessons on mindful eating we were taught? They stuck with me, too. Sit down, thank God, smell your food, chew it thoroughly, set down your fork between bites, and wait to drink until after eating. I was beginning to master it. Matthew even joined me in these habits, and it felt like health—among many other things—was finally finding me after so long. I was on top of the world.

Until life threw me a curveball that Texas hadn't quite prepared me for. I guess nothing can, though.

Matthew and I had been trying to conceive for a few years at this point and were convinced my history with Ed had likely affected my ability to get pregnant. To my surprise and shock, exactly five months into my sobriety after leaving RWC, I knew something was different. I missed a period. Ed causes amenorrhea, or the absence of periods, and for two years into our relationship, my periods remained a thing of the past. I had surgery to correct this, though, and ever since then, I'd been regular, so a missed period was new territory. *Hmmmm.*

The night I got back from a trip to Finland, I wondered if I was pregnant. I found an old test under the sink, and Matthew and I waited impatiently. I saw something. Could it be? A faint blue line. Two of them. *Ahhhh!*

We stared at each other in shock for what seemed like ten whole minutes. We were going to be parents!

I couldn't contain my excitement. On the heels of my sobriety high, I felt pride in knowing I'd finally hacked Ed. It was as if life was rewarding me for choosing health, sobriety, and a new beginning. Now I wouldn't only have my own life to live fully but a new life to nurture, free from the shadows of my past.

Then the so-called morning sickness hit me. Except, this was an all-day, relentless assault, freaking misery that went on for weeks. Around the eight-week mark, I was doubled over with the kind of nausea that felt like I'd swallowed ten simultaneous stomach viruses. It was a crushing wave that left me reeling. Just when I'd gotten a moment of relief, it would come back stronger, like a sucker punch.

Remember Dustin, my amazingly cool boss who didn't so much as bat an eye when I told him I needed to check myself into rehab? Thankfully, he was still around, willing to cover for me when my morning sickness was only made tolerable by long, medication-induced naps that took up chunks of my entire day.

I couldn't bear the thought of opening a refrigerator, much less eating food. And don't even think about going into a grocery store. The smell alone could bring me to my knees. I would gladly have sniffed roadkill before stepping into a supermarket.

Still, I had commitments, and as I dabbled in photography on the side, one of them was photographing Lynne's family in the mountains. I couldn't possibly cancel. This was going to be a massive shoot for her entire family, both immediate and extended, and it was very different from rescheduling a session for one family. This would be like canceling on four. So I loaded up my mom to come with me. She'd assist with lighting and holding my extra lenses. And holding my hair back if needed. Morning sickness didn't just put a damper on my life; it was trying to break me.

On the way up to the north Georgia mountains, I was as pale as a ghost, barely holding it together. Every little thing—the hum of the road, the whisper of the air from the vents—felt amplified as if I were sitting inches from a roaring locomotive. Even the gentle music on the radio seemed deafening, so I begged for silence, needing every bit of calm I could get to keep the nausea at bay.

Silence, though, wasn't exactly Brenda's strong suit, and she's the type who has the Lord on speed dial and believes prayer is the answer to everything—even my morning sickness. So there she was, fervently whispering prayers, convinced they'd help, while I tried to tune her out, wondering if maybe, just maybe, she was making it worse.

As we pulled into the town near our final destination, my mom looked at me, "Honey, it hurts me to see you this way. Especially when I know just what the fix is. You need some fizz, baby girl."

Some fizz?

"I don't know what it is, but those bubbles do something just right. Your nausea will be gone. I wish you would—" she pleaded. "Just pull into that Zaxby's on up the hill, there."

I hadn't had anything fried and definitely no soda in a long time. This would undo every bit of progress I'd worked so hard to achieve after leaving RWC. I couldn't. But I was desperate, and if Zaxby's was the cure, then fine. I'd risk it all in the name of "Please, take this morning sickness from me!"

Before I could even think, smell, or give thanks for the food in front of me, it was gone. Just like old times, I scarfed that food down in record time, and I drank the cherry-flavored Diet Dr. Pepper while I ate my fries, not after. I didn't think about the number of chews, and there certainly wasn't a fork to put down between mouthfuls; my order conveniently didn't need one. Did I check in? To see if my mom had some extra sauce for me, maybe.

And just like that, my sobriety was shattered. The surge of caffeine and sugar ran through my veins, hitting me like a high-speed rush, almost like being an addict wired up to a drip of their drug of choice. This dopamine hit was unlike any other as my brain lit up like a Christmas tree. Pleasure, motivation, and reward all turned on at once. Memories, fond ones, flooded in, reminding me of what Ed had given: the release, the escape. Oh, I'd missed this!

I hadn't just given in; I'd relapsed. Something I'd sworn would never happen after leaving RWC.

I suppose he'd never left in the first place, but I'd just given Ed permission to take center stage and was gripped by him once again. Forget it, I thought. It made me feel good for the first time since I'd gotten pregnant, so I'd keep on. And keep on, I did. During that pregnancy, I'd go on to gain back every healthy ounce I'd lost since rehab and then some, all due to the same old cyclical bingeing habits I'd had before RWC.

As easily as I'd stepped into RWC—okay, that's a joke because it took me years to check myself in—I slipped into relapse, and it would be a long one, postpartum and beyond. The proverbial pothole had me. I'd keep climbing out of it and falling into it for four long years and some months.

I was only bingeing this time around, though. Of course, bingeing can still be as physically and mentally taxing as purging, with devastating side effects in the short and long term. But I'd left purging at RWC, never to return. I'm not sure exactly why that is, but I was thankful that part of Ed was gone forever.

I fell back into binge cycles tied to days of the week, a throwback to my old weight-loss program habits. I'd choose a fresh start day—usually Monday, especially if the weekend had gotten out of hand—so I could reset at the beginning of the week. If I managed to have two good days, like Monday and Tuesday, and binged on Wednesday, I'd continue the cycle until the next Monday's fresh start, bingeing from Wednesday through Sunday. As the days wore on, each episode would spiral, becoming more extreme as I neared the end of the cycle.

Brain fog, pounding headaches from the sugar, and stomach issues became constants. Emotionally, I was all over the place, feeling the highs and lows as I struggled to get back on track, only to fall off again. This continued beyond the birth of our son.

I cried, aching for RWC. I knew that if I could return, I'd find my way to sobriety once again. Do you want to know why RWC worked—at least in my experience? It's not a one-size-fits-all answer, of course; there are many types of treatment facilities, each effective in their own way. But at RWC, I was surrounded by community. A community that gives you all the tools you need to be successful, and when you leave, you have the power that the program has given you. We aren't meant to bootstrap addiction recovery alone. I'm sure if there was a rehab facility where you could pay rent and raise a family, it would be a thriving business. It's hard coming back and navigating post-rehab life. *Real* life is scary as hell.

The thought of leaving my baby was even scarier, though. Utterly devastating. Sure, being on this earth and not dead from Ed was more important than the risk of missing my baby for another intensive treatment, but I just couldn't do it. I couldn't leave him. I couldn't leave Matthew. I thought that surely I could bootstrap my way back to abstinence again.

But that wasn't realistic for me, just as it hadn't been after I read *Better than Before*.

Something had to give. Something, perhaps, a bit more permanent.

For lessons learned and insights from this chapter,
visit "ENLIGHTENMENT on DIVORCING ED"

CHAPTER 12

BECOMING A BARI BABE

This chapter explores my experience with bariatric surgery and examines its role as a tool, rather than a cure, in managing struggles with food and weight.

An Important Disclaimer

Before you dive in, let me be very clear: **bariatric surgery is not a tool for overcoming an eating disorder, and it's not something I would ever recommend as a solution to those struggling.**

I mean, okay, I'm not a babe. I've never been a babe, I don't think. Babe has always been reserved, in my mind, for an elite class. Blonde hair, tan skin, striking. I do call my girlfriends babe from time to time. I got that from California Hillary, God rest her soul, and it made its mark on me. In that context, babe just makes you feel good, ya know? It's like telling your friends they should feel as good about themselves as you do about them.

So I've definitely never called myself a babe. That is, until now, so hang in here with me. And as if I hadn't exposed enough of myself, we're about to go even deeper. To set the scene, let's rewind to 2020, three years after my time at RWC. I probably don't need to remind you what happened that year, especially in March. But let's revisit it anyway because that year would become a defining chapter in my journey.

I was still traveling for work almost weekly. Chicago office, Denver office, trips to see business partners, trips with my team. That particular week, my calendar of meetings started in New York, and I remember it as if it were yesterday. My business development rep and I had buttoned up some successful meetings that day and were out late being typical tourists. I was standing in Times Square taking a selfie to send back to Matthew, time-stamped 10:52 pm, dated March 9, 2020.

Early the next morning, March 10, we boarded a train to Boston for another series of meetings, only to arrive and find the city eerily deserted. Though COVID-19 had been in the news, I still downplayed its significance, thinking it wasn't that big of a deal. I knew it was spreading in California and New York, but I hadn't yet grasped the scale of devastation on the horizon. As we exited the train, the quiet streets and wary glances of the few people around should have been a sign that something more serious was unfolding.

My phone vibrated. A message from Dustin: *"Wrap up your meetings and get on the next flight home."*

Still processing, I replied, *"What about our meeting tomorrow morning?"*

"Up to you, but get yourself home. Stay safe."

The priority was clear.

After meetings that day and our final corporate dinner at Legal Sea Foods—the last for years—I checked into my hotel, the Marriott. As I dropped my bags, a text from James, the biz dev rep who had accompanied me, popped up. *"Turn on the news. Any channel."*

And there it was. The very hotel I was staying in had hosted the recent Biogen conference, likely linked to a surge in cases. The same sinking feeling I'd had after Dustin's message hit me again. The gravity of COVID was becoming all too real.

The following morning, the Marriott felt as empty as the city outside. The only guest appeared to be me. A sparse staff, a quick bite, and I wanted to quickly wrap up the coming meeting and head home if an earlier flight was available.

At our partner's headquarters, they wouldn't let us inside without hesitation, much less with handshakes. The World Health Organization (WHO) had just declared COVID-19 a global pandemic, they informed us. We proceeded with the meeting, but they promised to cut it short, as they were likely going to send their employees home, and we already had our marching orders to get back. James and I headed for the airport after our brief meeting and quick goodbyes, and luckily, both of us were able to catch the next flight.

After arriving home safely, I found Matthew's mindset shifted into full-blown crisis mode. Every bit of him sounded almost apocalyptic, "We're hunkering down and staying in!"

And his concerns weren't unfounded; the world had turned upside down overnight, and the uncertainty was palpable. The next morning, as shocking as it was to see the Marriott on the news the first time, this time, it was even clearer what anguish COVID had introduced. Headlines screamed, "Marriott Long Wharf to close."

Y'all, I'd just checked out the day before. What in the world was happening? Panic bubbled up inside me. Had I unknowingly put my family at risk by staying there? I tried reassuring myself that the event in question—the Biogen conference—had taken place weeks earlier, so surely everything had been sanitized since then. But my thoughts spiraled. What about the meeting in Boston? What about the people I shared a plane with on the way home?

Matthew's unease mirrored my own but was channeled differently. He wasn't just concerned; he was preparing for the worst. Stockpiling supplies, tracking every news update, and making it clear that our home was now our fortress.

We pulled our little one from daycare and dove headfirst into our new COVID lifestyle. Work travel came to a screeching halt, and our once-busy routine shifted to days spent almost entirely at home. At first, the shift felt drastic. Suddenly, though, we were settling into the slower pace of life. Matthew, despite his initial doomsday-level preparedness, seemed to find comfort in this new sense of control—our little world locked down, safe, and contained.

Just over a month after checking out of the Marriott and watching our lives change almost overnight, we got a surprising bit of news: we were expecting our second child. It happened easily—almost too easily, given the whirlwind of everything else happening—and it brought a mix of excitement and urgency.

Then came the realization: our cozy home, though perfect in so many ways, might not be enough for a growing family. And a month after finding out I was pregnant, with shelter-in-place restrictions easing, we decided to put our home up for sale. The idea felt borderline chaotic; were we seriously going to uproot during a pandemic? But the pull for something more was undeniable.

The mission was clear: we wanted land, a great school district, and a builder who could bring our vision to life. North of town promised all of that and more. And before we knew it, we were on the hunt.

And let me tell you, things moved fast. Exceedingly fast. Within forty-eight hours, our home was under contract, and just as quickly, we stumbled upon what would soon be our next one. It all started with a Zillow alert: a home recently built by a local custom builder. That particular property was already spoken for, but when I reached out, I learned the builder had even more land available nearby. And not just any land—the perfect spot for a ranch home.

A ranch! Have you noticed how rare ranch-style homes are these days? It had been my dream for as long as I can remember, and the opportunity felt too good to pass up. Without hesitation, we signed on the dotted line.

With a quick closing date on our current home, we had to move fast. We packed up everything we owned and crammed it into two storage units. COVID was still a major concern, so we decided to simplify things by limiting contact to immediate family—and to our builder and realtor, of course. Some exceptions just can't be helped, right? For the time being, we couch-surfed while we figured out a more permanent living arrangement.

It was about ten weeks into my pregnancy, only a month after we'd put a contract on our home build, and we were heading north for a meeting with our builder when my phone rang. It was the nurse from my OB's office, and the news hit like a ton of bricks. "Your hormone levels aren't strong enough," she said, explaining that my progesterone was too low to sustain my pregnancy. A wave of grief washed over me. I couldn't hold back the tears. As we pulled up to the land where our future home would be, the weight of it all was unbearable. We sat there, feeling a deep and overwhelming sadness, as Matthew did his best to comfort me while sharing my pain. The moment we got out of the car, our builder, who had been through a similar loss with his wife years before, wrapped us both in a hug, understanding what we were going through.

Over a week later, however, as I sat in the OB's office awaiting results and a path forward from loss, I received news that turned everything upside down—my baby was alive. Somehow, despite the initial scare, my body had begun to do what it needed to and produce. It was nothing short of a miracle. What had felt like a devastating loss transformed into something hopeful, a continuation of life.

But the emotional ride wasn't over. Throughout the rest of my pregnancy, I battled anxiety and compulsive eating, desperately trying to soothe the ever-present fear of losing him again. The bingeing that had plagued me before this chapter resurfaced in full force. Though purging didn't return, Ed was still very much with me. I'd transitioned from bulimia to binge eating disorder and felt myself continuously slipping further and further away from the person I'd worked so hard to rebuild.

Determined to find a way back to abstinence—not just for myself, but for the health of my baby—I turned to social media, typing in specific hashtags for eating disorder recovery and food addiction solutions. I was hoping to find a community that could guide me. While scrolling, I stumbled upon something unexpected: posts about bariatric surgery. It wasn't the recovery support I was initially looking for, but there was something compelling about the similarities between the two communities. Both were filled with stories of people navigating complicated relationships with food and their bodies, along with the emotional hurdles of trying to heal.

As bizarre as it may seem, in the chaotic world of social media, there are spaces where people are sharing their struggles and finding real support—even in the most unexpected of places.

And that's where I first encountered the term *Bari Babe*—a trendy label for individuals who had undergone bariatric surgery and were embracing a new life. While it wasn't an option for me at the time, being pregnant and all, the idea planted itself in my mind. I still had my doubts about the actual success of that type of procedure, but I quietly began following accounts, tucking the information away for later, reviewing others' journeys and the ups and downs they shared post-surgery.

Meanwhile, life continued to throw challenges our way. The morning sickness wasn't as bad as my first pregnancy, but I still felt awful most days. If I wasn't eating, I felt worse. So I ate—and I ate a lot. With our home sold and everything in storage, our daily routine became monotonous: wake up, work from home, eat out, bath, bed. It wasn't sustainable, but with all our belongings in storage and no kitchen to call our own, eating out felt inevitable.

Then August came. On the thirteenth, less than seventy-two hours after being tested for COVID at a drive-thru clinic, we received the results: positive, every one of us. While I had a relatively mild case, Matthew and our firstborn struggled. Matthew's symptoms resembled the flu, and our son suffered his highest fever yet, complete with hallucinations. It's funny now, but back then, it was terrifying; he thought Matthew and I were bees trying to sting him.

Three months later, Matthew was hospitalized, and the grim reality of Long COVID hit. What began as a battle we thought we could fight with IV fluids and some basic meds turned into a nightmarish struggle. His body was failing as his kidneys and liver responded negatively, a direct result of the aggressive treatment with remdesivir. The days blurred together, and his recovery was anything but easy. Slowly, he did improve and was discharged, but not without a trail of physical and emotional scars.

Just when we thought things might finally settle, the pandemonium increased—a whirlwind, to say the least—as we moved into our new home just seven days before our second baby was born.

Even after he'd turned six months old, I found myself still struggling with Ed. By then, our builder had become more like family to us. I don't remember exactly how the conversation began, but one evening, over dinner, he shared his weight-loss journey with us. A few months prior, he'd shown me a *before* photo, and I'd noticed his careful, deliberate eating habits, small portions, always eating slowly and quickly satisfied. This time, though, he opened up about the major catalyst for his transformation.

"I had surgery," he said.

The words hit me like a lightning bolt. I knew exactly what he meant before he even finished explaining. Thanks to my deep dive into social media almost a year prior, I was no stranger to the basics of bariatric surgery. I'd even spoken to friends and colleagues who'd gone through it. But hearing our builder speak so candidly, without any shame or hesitation, took me by surprise. It made everything feel suddenly so real, so personal.

He suggested I visit him later to collect all the information he had. In that tattered navy blue folder was everything—notes, documents, and details from his journey. I poured over its contents that night, diving deeper into my research, weighing the pros and cons, and balancing the risks against the rewards.

And let's be honest, bariatric surgery often gets a bad rap. There's always someone waiting to call it the easy way out to point to the few who have regained the weight, bolstering the stigma that surrounds it. It's a poorly informed narrative I knew all too well. I'd heard my mom and others repeat it: "You know so-and-so had gastric bypass, and now they've gained all their weight back."

These misguided judgments like to hang around, don't they? I can't stand it, but people love to talk about someone's failure and rarely their triumph. It's like endless bad reviews, always undermining the decision to invest in a transformative tool like bariatric surgery.

But in listening to our builder share his experience, something shifted. I found myself questioning everything I'd believed, reconsidering what I'd dismissed, and opening myself to a new reality, one I hadn't thought possible. Sure, I'd stored all that social media influence for a rainy day, a glimmer of hope tucked into the back of my mind, but I never fully considered it. His story challenged my preconceived notions and brought everything I'd researched into sharp focus, inviting me into a world of possibilities. It was something I'd never seriously explored before, maybe becoming a Bari Babe after all.

Then, as I dug deep, the facts became undeniable. This wasn't just a last resort. Bariatric surgery was a proven, effective tool for significant and sustained weight loss. Studies show that over 90% of patients lose at least 50% of their excess weight within the first year. Even more compelling, long-term success rates hover around 60–70%, with many maintaining substantial weight loss for a decade or more. That. Speaks. Volumes.

But here's the thing about bariatric surgery that's often not exactly overlooked but maybe not emphasized enough. It's not a mental fix. It's an anatomical change, a powerful tool, but not a magic wand. A surgeon doesn't operate on your mind or habits—they alter your body, your digestive system. This means that while the surgery can physically limit how much you eat and how your body processes food, the mental and emotional relationship with food still needs addressing. Without that partnership of commitment to mental and emotional growth—whether that be through therapy, support groups, or lifestyle changes—those old patterns can creep back in. The journey doesn't end in the operating room. Got it.

From improved quality of life to the resolution of health conditions, I discovered the physical benefits of bariatric surgery were irrefutable. The more I learned, the clearer it became. This wasn't about taking the easy way out; it was about equipping myself with a tool—a partnership between science and personal responsibility. This could be the path forward I'd been searching for.

It felt like a door was opening, but I hesitated. I wanted to bring it up with Kristen, my therapist, but fear held me back. What would she think? Would she judge me? Would she also dismiss it as the easy way out? Kristen had been with me since just after my initial relapse. What's wild is that I'd also found her through hashtags on social media! She'd been there every step of the way, supporting me as I struggled to regain control over my eating disorder and return to abstinence.

To my surprise, Kristen's response was nothing like I'd imagined. She didn't dismiss the idea or react with judgment. Instead, she helped me process everything. She educated me on how bariatric surgery could help or hurt depending on the individual. She emphasized the need for serious commitment, both physically and mentally.

"You're likely ready for this tool," she said with conviction.

Her support was a revelation. She even connected me with two of her clients who had undergone the surgery: one had a bad experience, the other a great one. One had been post-op for over eight years, and the other had recently undergone the procedure.

Talk about helpful.

Armed with all of it, conversations with our builder, talks with Kristen, and the feedback from the referrals, I decided to reach out to our builder's surgeon. It was August, and I was eight months postpartum. I wasn't sure if they'd even schedule an evaluation, given the timing, but to my surprise, they welcomed me without hesitation. I counted down the days, eager to learn about my options.

When I was deep in binge mode, there were times I'd already be eating before I realized it. Shame would follow swiftly, but now I saw a beacon of hope. Bariatric surgery could give me that pause—a tool to connect my body and mind when they weren't in sync. A physical change, an anatomical shift that could help me break the cycle.

As you know, I'd left purging behind, but bingeing still held me captive. I believed this could be the final piece of the puzzle, the tool I could carry with me everywhere. Ed would be quiet because, physically, I wouldn't be able to feed him anymore, not with the restriction surgery would provide.

My surgeon and his staff took excellent care of me, just as our builder had assured me they would. They were genuinely interested in learning about my story and my struggles.

I had questions, so many questions. How long does recovery take, and what will it feel like? What kind of support will I need after surgery, both physically and emotionally? How will my relationship with food change after surgery? How do I stay motivated to maintain my weight loss long-term? What happens if I don't lose the expected amount of weight after surgery? Will I need to take supplements? What will my follow-up care look like, and how often will I need check-ins? I wanted to know everything.

After discussing the pros and cons of vertical sleeve gastrectomy (VSG) versus gastric bypass, I felt confident in my decision. VSG, where up to 80% of the stomach is removed, forming a tube-like shape that limits the amount of food and liquid the stomach can hold, seemed like the better fit for me. Aside from my obesity, I was otherwise healthy, and gastric bypass—where the stomach is divided into a small pouch that's then connected to the small intestine—seemed more risky, particularly with the potential for malabsorption issues. I wasn't diabetic, and I didn't suffer from acid reflux—except during pregnancy; thanks, kids! Given all this, VSG was the clear choice for me.

One last question from my surgeon: "Do you plan on having any more babies?"

"Pffff. Of course not," I scoffed. I most certainly wouldn't be permanently changing my anatomy if I wanted to have more babies.

"Great. We want to give you the best chance of success, and having a baby after this surgery isn't advisable. Or at least not in the next couple of years."

I moved forward, covering all the necessary pre-surgery requirements in record time. I was an eager beaver, waiting on binge-free me.

Enthusiastically, I scheduled the surgery for just before Thanksgiving, believing this would be my best holiday yet, free from the fear and shame that food often brought during the holidays.

Since I'd be post-op at the time, I'd go through the holidays on a liquid diet, which would be the biggest blessing in my life. We have three or four Thanksgiving get-togethers on our route, but I wouldn't have to think about food this year. It was going to be the best Thanksgiving ever, a full-circle moment to the time I met Belle at Thanksgiving.

But as I was wheeled into the operating room in early November after a quick picture with my doc for the gram, an anesthesiologist paused. "You're wheezing," he said. "Have you been sick?"

I knew I'd definitely had a baby sinus infection, but I desperately wanted today to be the day. "Yes and no. Nothing crazy," I quickly responded. I couldn't wait a day longer for my destiny.

"I hate to do it," he said, "but I'm sending you home. I can't take this risk. You could get pneumonia, and you'd be way worse off and still in the hospital this time next week."

He'd just killed every bit of holiday hope I had.

In the end, though it delayed my plans, it gave me more time to focus on my health. Thanksgiving still came despite the setback, but I was on the mandatory pre-surgery diet, so it wasn't all that bad, and I persisted right through.

Finally, I ended up going in on December 3, 2021. My surgeon would perform the vertical gastric sleeve on my tum drum. Directly after surgery, I'd go from being able to tolerate around thirty-two ounces in my stomach—maybe more when I was bingeing—down to two or three ounces.

I woke up feeling like I'd been hit by a truck. I kinda had, I suppose. I mean, my stomach had been cut on, and the excess disposed of. I wonder where that stuff goes, anyway?

Going in, I thought I was totally mentally prepared for the surgery. But let me just say this. No matter how many conversations you have with your therapist or bariatric specialist, nothing can prepare you for the adjustment to life post-surgery. It rocked my world.

The psychological response to my physiological change was unreal. Straight out of surgery, even something as simple as drinking water felt terrifying. *Will this be more than my new stomach can handle? Will I be able to keep anything down?* Small sips, I kept reminding myself as I adjusted to the new limits of my body and the fear that came with them.

Once I was home, the physical pain hit me hard. Between the punch in the gut—literally—and the relentless gas pains, all I could do was walk. Walk and walk and walk. It became the only thing that helped ease the discomfort. I was recovering in our pool house—more like a barndominium—away from our boys, who were still too young to understand the fragility of my healing body. Each day, I made my protein shakes, mixing them into those small to-go ketchup containers—just one to two ounces, and perfect for my post-surgery recovery diet. I stacked them up in the fridge like little trophies, my surgical badges of honor. I'd just given myself a win, after all. A shiny new tool in my arsenal to battle Ed.

I slowly moved from clear liquids to soft foods and eventually to solids. The strangest thing was the fullness sensation. You don't fill up the way you used to—your stomach isn't a giant reservoir anymore, and that leaves a heavy, odd feeling in your throat. It's like you can't get the rest of your food down. It gets stuck. At least, that was my experience. But then, I'd also had hernia surgery to go along with my new stomach, so maybe that was a factor.

After the surgery, my check-ins with my surgeon were brief. They started off quarterly, then would be bi-annually, and eventually just once a year. The meetings always included a nutritionist but never the mental support I truly needed. Kristen had been instrumental in helping me tackle my emotional triggers and disordered eating patterns before the surgery, but I let that relationship lapse, convinced I'd finally divorced Ed, thanks to my new tool. What I knew but chose to ignore was that successfully losing weight after surgery didn't mean my mind didn't still require care. Without Kristen, I neglected the guidance I needed to navigate the emotional hurdles that followed—a mistake I'd later learn was deeply detrimental.

And remember the last question my surgeon asked me before I left the pre-surgery evaluation? Did I plan on having more children? Well, two months before my one-year surgiversary, as the bari babes call it, I found out I was pregnant with our third. How did *that* happen? Well, I know exactly how. Matthew— Okay, I'll stop there; you know the details.

I was ashamed. Not of the baby; I was thrilled about our new addition. But I felt embarrassed by my confidence that I'd follow every instruction given to me. I'd been so sure about sticking to the plan, so sure that I'd have control. I mean, of course, I'd dreamed of a bigger Thanksgiving table and wondered if my family was complete. But to go back to my surgeon and tell him I was pregnant? I'd rather just not have shown up.

Of course, that's Ed talking again. My surgeon and his staff were nothing but supportive, even if I wasn't the textbook patient we'd envisioned. And thank goodness for that because I needed help. I needed guidance on how to nourish both myself and the baby. I needed reassurance that the drastic change I'd made to my body wouldn't get in the way of navigating my new reality.

After the surgery, my ability to consume calories was limited, which made pregnancy a strange journey. In the beginning, I felt hungry, but I couldn't eat enough. Later, during my second and third trimesters, I had no hunger at all. I had to force myself to eat, doing my best to fuel the baby in the healthiest way possible. This was the kind of pregnancy I'd always envisioned—where I took the best care of myself and the baby, where I ate clean and well. It was the only way I *could* eat.

With my boys, I hadn't had that opportunity. But with my third babe, a girl? Redemption. I missed that chance because of Ed, and I'll admit, it pains me to say that out loud. But surgery gave me this second chance with my third, a fully health-focused pregnancy.

Once my baby girl was born and I started breastfeeding, my appetite returned in full force. It came on fast, and I had questions. Could I eat enough? Could I make room for the calories I needed to sustain my milk supply and my new body? Surprisingly, there was no restriction. I could eat. And I did, devouring food like a woman who'd been starved.

I was still shedding weight quickly, faster than I ever had before. But things didn't stay that way. When my milk supply dried up, my appetite didn't. And before I knew it, the weight started piling on again—and fast.

At one year postpartum and two-and-a-half years after surgery, I'd gained back around twenty percent of what I'd lost. To add to this number sandwich, and since I don't believe in talking in pounds, I've successfully lost around seventy percent of the weight I had to lose. So I guess you could say I'm still a positive statistic, but I'd never recommend VSG as a solution for Ed because bariatric surgery isn't brain surgery.

Here's the heavy truth; I still struggle with Ed. He finds a way to stay:

You can

Take prescription drugs, but Ed doesn't leave,

You can

Have plastic surgery to alter what you see in the mirror, but Ed still sees you,

You can

Spend years in therapy, but Ed waits in the shadows,

You can

Check into rehab, but Ed will pack a bag and tag along,

You can

Remove part of your stomach, but it doesn't remove Ed,

You can

Have all the tools, but Ed isn't going anywhere.

The tools we're given, every tool we fight for, they aren't the solution. They're only part of it. The rest is up to us. It's up to us to evolve, to survive, to keep going even when Ed is relentless and his shadow looms large.

This isn't a one-size-fits-all or single-solution journey. I wish it were. But the battle doesn't end there. It's about showing up for yourself, over and over again, even when Ed feels louder than hope. Surviving isn't about being perfect or finding *the* cure—it's about refusing to quit.

For lessons learned and insights from this chapter,
visit "ENLIGHTENMENT on DIVORCING ED"

CHAPTER 13

MAGIC IN THE MIDDLE

Here, we'll explore the constant evolution of recovery and what happens when you start living life in the gray.

This final chapter reflects my continued journey through recovery, my current relationship with Ed, and living life in the gray today. It's deeply personal and written from my perspective. While I do hope it resonates with you, it's important to remember that every recovery journey is unique.

If you find yourself currently struggling with an eating disorder or facing immediate physical or emotional danger, this section could be triggering or frustrating. My story isn't a one-size-fits-all guide to healing, nor is it a substitute for professional care.

Please prioritize your well-being and, if you need to, seek support from a trusted therapist, physician, or network.

The "Resources Guide for Mental Health and Eating Disorders" below provides support organizations to help you start your journey.

My intention here isn't to present the *right* way to recover but to share my imperfect progress with the hope that it will bring you comfort, reassurance, and understanding. Please read with care, and remember: *your* story, *your* journey, and *your* well-being matter most.

Here We Are

I've got to tell you, writing the final chapter of a memoir is a lot of pressure. Like, *a lot*. Ever since I began writing, with the immense weight of ending on a high note, I've been mulling over how to end *Big-Boned*. Somehow, some way, I'm supposed to craft an ending out of something that feels like it's just beginning.

So, spoiler alert: this chapter may strike you as an overstuffed suitcase. I'm throwing in everything I don't want you to leave without. It's bursting at the seams with no way to zip it up. But it's full of the things you mustn't leave behind, including the hope you *must* carry with you. So here goes.

For years, I held off on writing *Big-Boned*. Twenty or more. I convinced myself I couldn't tell this story—not yet. Not until I was "better." Not until I'd figured out how to rid myself of Ed for good or serve him divorce papers he couldn't ignore. Not until I'd achieved some imaginary, picture-perfect recovery.

But here's what I've learned: the story people need isn't the one with a tidy ending. It's the story told from the middle—the messy, complicated, uncertain middle. One that serves up a lot of trials and a little triumph.

For so long, I believed I had to be *perfect* to share my story. I felt strongly that perfection, whatever it even meant, was the cost of being worthy of a reader's time or trust. I was wrong. The truth is, the middle does matter. The in-between is where real transformation takes hold.

Have you heard the saying, "It's about the journey, not the destination?" Well, I wholeheartedly agree. Recovery is the same and doesn't come with a clean slate or a cure. It's a living, breathing process.

There's no real beginning or ending to a story like this, and that's okay. What matters is the space in between. The now. And people don't need perfect stories; they need honest ones.

Living in the Gray

A teacher once told me, "The only people who believe in black and white are those who haven't used their gray matter."

That quote has stuck with me in more ways than one. If I apply the saying to recovery alone, it couldn't ring truer with my own journey. So let's use our gray matter for a minute and be honest with ourselves and others.

What if we accept that recovery—or heck, even life—isn't so black or white, all or nothing? What if we accept that it isn't all that intuitive, either, when you're still learning to trust yourself? Living in the gray means accepting that recovery isn't linear and that it might not fit into neatly packaged solutions for treatment or follow a universal roadmap to healing.

There's no *right* way to recover, only the way that works for you today!

For me, the gray means some days are abstinent days. Other days, I practice moderation, maybe because I feel emotionally balanced because I want to enjoy something without overthinking it, or because I know my limits and can enjoy moderation in the moment without it becoming overwhelming. Neither is better or worse; simply, they're what I can do *just for today.*

When I started writing this book over a year ago, I was deep in a season of moderation. It felt right then. It was the path that kept me steady. On some days, practicing moderation feels okay when I feel connected to my goals, in tune with my body, or when indulging feels like an act of self-care rather than self-sabotage. And moderation can still have hard stops, like grabbing it in a drive-thru instead of bringing it into my house.

But for today, going back to abstinence feels like the better fit. It gives me the space to stay grounded as life swirls around me.

Last night, though? Abstinence went out the window. I said yes to the goodies at Bunco, and I'm not sure why. Was it the stress of finishing this book, prepping my kids for school, or planning an international trip? Maybe. Or maybe it was one of those moments when Ed whispered a little too loudly. Either way, I'm learning to make peace with it, knowing that *not* knowing the why is okay, too. It's about listening to yourself, honoring where you are, and trusting that every day brings new opportunities to move forward.

That's what living in the gray looks like. It's not about having it all figured out. It's about getting out of the pothole and taking a new path next time.

The gray is knowing what you need for today. Not tomorrow. Not two weeks from now. Today! I love that. Isn't there something so calming when we take the pressure off? We don't have to think lifetime; we just have to think about now. Once we have now in front of us, we address it with how.

The How: Integrating the Gray

Living in the gray means recognizing that Ed's voice will try to sneak in. It's what he does. The trick is learning how to drown him out before he gets too loud. It's not about *listening to your body* because, let's face it, Ed likes to hijack that conversation. Instead, it's about making decisions early, when you're clear-headed, and setting yourself up for success before weakness has a chance to creep in.

I'll get into the weeds with this later on in the Enlightenment section, but the cliff notes are things like deciding your non-negotiables in advance, creating white noise for Ed, building a toolkit for weak moments, focusing on adding things to your life instead of taking them away, and respecting yourself.

The how isn't perfect either. It's messy, unpredictable, and sometimes exhausting. But when you set yourself up with a plan and tools to quiet Ed's voice, you create space for progress.

So what about you? *For today,* are you a moderator or an abstainer? That's the more appropriate question, at least for those of us struggling with Ed. The pressure of the black-and-white statement—are you a moderator or an abstainer?—leaves too much unknown. Too many variables.

It changes with the seasons of your life. There's no formula, no single solution. What worked yesterday might not work today. What feels impossible now might feel manageable a year from now.

I'm saying recovery will always be fluid, like life.

It's not abstinence *or* moderation. It's not black *or* white.

It's all just—shades of gray.

Now, I know Ed might never completely disappear. Recovery isn't about erasing him; it's about integrating your life with him. Learning to coexist. It's about quieting his voice and amplifying your own. Ed is no longer the very air you breathe but a separate, distant presence because the healthiest version of you gradually begins to take center stage.

The key isn't perfection; it's persistence. Living in the gray means finding balance beyond extremes. It's about showing up for yourself, day after day, no matter how messy or imperfect the process might be.

The Magic in the Middle

The magic in the middle is the outcome of living in the gray.

If I'm coming off a touch repetitive, it's because I am, and there's a reason for that. Some lessons aren't one-and-done—remember the pothole story. They need to be said again and again until they truly sink in, especially with Ed hanging around. Repetition becomes a reminder, a reinforcement, a way to hold steady. It's about coming back to what matters, over and over, until it becomes part of you.

Truth is, the middle isn't just a checkpoint; it's the heart of the journey. The middle is where you learn who you are. It's where you discover that strength doesn't come from perfection; it comes from perseverance. It's where you realize that the gray—the in-between—isn't just a place you pass through; it's where the magic lives.

I spent so many years thinking I had to reach the end of my story before I could share it. But now I see that the middle is what people need most. They don't need the polished version of you wrapped up with a bow. They need the raw, vulnerable, honest you, the one who's still figuring it out.

The magic in the middle is that it gives others permission to be in the middle, too. It says, "You don't have to be perfect to be enough. You don't have to be at the end of your journey to share your story. You just have to keep going."

The middle is enough.

You are enough.

Your Story Matters

Part of my *keep going* is being here and writing this book—not from the other side of recovery but from the thick of it. Writing it scared. Writing it imperfect. Writing it because my messy, unfinished, somewhere-in-between story might help you with yours.

And now, I'm asking you to trust your story, too. You don't have to wait until you have it all figured out to start living fully. You don't need to wait for Ed to disappear completely to make progress. True progress comes from embracing the journey—messiness, uncertainties, and all—rather than chasing the illusion of some unattainable perfection.

I don't need this final chapter—or even this whole book—to be what matters. I need *you* to know that *you* matter. Honor where you are today, knowing today doesn't define forever. The gray is where you grow, where you learn, where you find your way forward.

The End is Just Your Beginning

None of this happened **to** *you; it happened* **for** *you.*

For a long time, I thought big-boned was a label—a judgment about who I was and what I lacked. But now, I see it differently. To me, big-boned is about being strong, about carrying the weight of my journey while still moving forward. It's about embracing the parts of me that once felt too much or too little and realizing they were always exactly enough.

And finding the magic in the middle doesn't mean life will be any easier than before. It means life will be wonderfully human. That's where freedom lives—not in perfection, but in progress.

I hope *Big-Boned* has shown you that recovery isn't about erasing Ed entirely. It's about living alongside him, putting yourself in the driver's seat, and finding your balance day by day.

The journey ahead won't be perfect, but it'll be yours. And that's more than enough to begin.

No matter what challenge comes your way, you have the strength within you to overcome—even if it's gray—or maybe *especially* if it's gray.

Because big-boned isn't just about carrying weight; it's about carrying hope. Whether you're carrying too much or fighting to carry enough, this journey is about realizing you've always had the strength to write your next chapter—and it's going to be one worth telling.

You're enough. You've always been enough. And your story? It's just beginning.

For lessons learned and insights from this chapter,
visit "ENLIGHTENMENT on DIVORCING ED"

ENLIGHTENMENT

things I learned | take them with you

A NOTE ON ENLIGHTENMENT

As the name suggests, this next section of *Big-Boned* is purely informative—no storytelling. I shared my story first, hopefully in a readable format, so you and I could build a connection. I guess you could say this is the self-help portion of my self-help memoir.

Enlightenment suggests a deep understanding and wisdom that comes with acquiring knowledge, and it speaks to a positive transformation that comes with that knowledge. Therefore, I wish to shed light on many things I learned from my experiences, as documented in the prior chapters of *Big-Boned*. Things I learned that I wished I'd known at the time. Things I hope to share with you now—before you need them, or exactly when you do—rather than after the fact.

Whether you've got a relationship with Ed or not, buckle up; this next section covers a lot of ground. We're not just diving into the differences between types of eating disorders and their treatments, but also religious hurt, spiritual abuse, and how certain relationships can creep into someone's recovery and sometimes seriously overstay their welcome. It's probably more than you bargained for, but life covers a lot of territory, so why not talk about it all? Consider this the cramming of a bit more into that overstuffed suitcase I left you with in Chapter 13.

If you feel you already have a useful amount of knowledge on the subject(s), this section may be redundant information for you. Or if you feel like you aren't in a space where you can receive this information at this time, you can come back to it when you're ready.

I've split up the content to easily tie back to the three sections of *Big-Boned*: Discovering Ed, Dating Ed, and Divorcing Ed.

For the sake of flow and context, you may notice some overlap in topics throughout this section. I've included relevant details in each chapter, so if you only read one part, you won't miss out on essential information. For example, in the chapter "ENLIGHTENMENT on DATING ED," under *All About Eating Disorders,* I'll touch briefly on treatment options. Later, in the chapter "ENLIGHTENMENT on DIVORCING ED," I'll dive deeper into those options as they better fit the concept of divorcing Ed.

So while some topics may appear in multiple places, they're there intentionally, ensuring every section stands alone while contributing to the bigger picture.

From this point on, I'll be referring to ED in all caps rather than as "Ed." While I used the name Ed in the memoir portion to reflect a personal, subjective experience—Ed being a character in my story—this section is far less subjective and more informational, so I'm calling it what it is.

Let's get into it.

CHAPTER 14

ENLIGHTENMENT on DISCOVERING ED

Quick Reference Page Guide

BIG-BONED DEBUNKED

Let's talk about it. After all, this book is named after—and thematically inspired by—the age-old euphemism, to be "big-boned."

The Science of Being Big-Boned

If you've never heard of the term big-boned, consider yourself lucky. For most of us, it's a phrase we've heard or used to describe individuals perceived as larger or heavier, supposedly because of their bone structure.

But let's clear this up: **being big-boned as a determinant of body size or weight is a myth.**

Yes, bone structure and density vary between individuals, and some people do have denser bones than others. But bones are not the reason behind someone's body size, shape, or weight.

Scientifically speaking:

- There's no ICD-10 code or medical diagnosis for being big-boned.
- Bones don't have the capacity to dictate someone's overall body composition.
- Factors like muscle mass, body fat percentage, and genetics play a much larger role in determining size and shape.

So the idea of being big-boned as an excuse—or explanation—for weight or size simply doesn't hold water. If we're going to talk about weight and health, let's keep it grounded in real science and leave bones out of it.

To Those Familiar with the Term

If you've been on either the giving or receiving end of this phrase, it's time to have a real conversation.

For Those on the Giving End

Let's cut to the chase: stop saying it.

Using big-boned as a descriptor oversimplifies the complex factors that contribute to body diversity. When you tell someone they're big-boned, you plant the idea that their body is unchangeable—that they're stuck as they are because of anatomy. This can be incredibly harmful, especially for young and impressionable individuals.

Here's why it's time to retire this phrase:

- It perpetuates myths about weight and health.
- It's an outdated, oversimplified explanation that refutes the existence of body diversity.
- It keeps fueling harmful stereotypes, reinforcing the idea that larger bodies are inherently flawed or abnormal.

As a description of anyone, big-boned is a tired euphemism. Stop relying on old sayings and ill-informed narratives and embrace body diversity instead. Let's celebrate that bodies come in all shapes and sizes and reject the urge to define or judge people based on their appearance.

Society is moving toward greater acceptance, but we still have a long way to go. Be part of the change by promoting body positivity—or at least neutrality—and focusing on overall health and kindness over judgment.

From all of us mid- to extended-size humans, thank you for helping us feel seen, respected, and understood.

For Those on the Receiving End

If you've ever been labeled big-boned, I'm sorry.

Comments like these can stick, sometimes for years, even though they have more to do with the person saying them than with you. People often project their insecurities onto others, and phrases like big-boned are their way of avoiding their own discomfort.

Here's what I want you to know:

- It's not about you. The phrase and those words don't define you or your worth.
- You're allowed to let them go. Forgive and move on. Don't let someone's ignorance live rent-free in your mind.
- If you're in a position to educate, do so with empathy. Respond with kindness and use the moment to shift the narrative.

And if you feel bold enough, maybe even suggest they work on their own insecurities or find a good therapist to help them do so. You're doing your work to heal. Maybe it's their turn.

A Call to Change

Let's charge up the conversation, shall we? Let's begin to understand body diversity and size instead of leaning on tired euphemisms like big-boned.

Here's an easy place to start:

- Stop perpetuating harmful stereotypes.
- Celebrate the diversity of human bodies.
- Promote health, kindness, and acceptance.
- Debunk the myths and embrace science.

This work begins with us. It starts when we reject judgment, embrace acceptance, and prioritize the things that matter, like kindness, respect, and well-being. The journey isn't always easy, but it's worth it.

Because every body—yours included—is worth celebrating.

IDENTIFYING AN EATING DISORDER
Supporting Yourself

If you think you might have an eating disorder, it's essential to take proactive steps toward understanding your experience and seeking help—*as soon as possible.* While the journey may vary based on your age and circumstances, below is a concise step-by-step list of things you can do to start navigating the process.

What to Do if You Think You Have an Eating Disorder

1. Educate Yourself

- Learn about eating disorders. Research their signs, symptoms, and treatment options.

2. Reach Out for Support

- Talk to someone. Share your concerns with a friend, family member, or someone else you trust. Opening up can be the first step toward seeking help.
- Consider age-specific approaches:
  - *Teens and young adults*: Involve a trusted parent, teacher, or school counselor.
  - *Adults*: Reach out to a close friend, partner, or family member for support.

3. Seek Professional Help

- Schedule an appointment with a healthcare provider specializing in eating disorders, such as a therapist, counselor, or physician.

- Be honest about your food behavior and eating habits, including your thoughts and feelings. This will ensure accurate assessments and effective recommendations.

  (As a side note, this is extremely important. Oftentimes, we feel embarrassed to share. It's totally natural to want to downplay or leave out details, but doing so could delay an accurate diagnosis or lead to treatment plans that don't fully address what you need.)

4. Track Your Patterns and Behaviors

- Start journaling all of it: your thoughts, emotions, and eating behaviors. This can help you identify triggers, patterns, or moments when you feel weak and struggle the most.
- Share these insights with your healthcare provider to help inform your treatment plan.

5. Explore Treatment Options

- Work with your provider to create a treatment plan tailored to your needs, finances, and goals. Treatment options may include:
  - Therapy
  - Nutritional counseling
  - Medical monitoring for physical health
  - Support groups or online communities
  - Medication management

6. Find Your Village

- Surround yourself with supportive friends, family members, or peers who respect and encourage your journey.
- Consider joining a support group or online community to connect with others who share similar experiences and can offer understanding.

7. Limit Negative Influences

- Identify and reduce exposure to things that might perpetuate unhealthy thoughts or behaviors, such as triggering social media accounts, toxic relationships, or environments that focus heavily on weight or appearance.

- Replace these with positive influences that promote body neutrality, health, and self-compassion.

8. Prioritize Self-Care

- Engage in activities that nurture your physical, emotional, and mental well-being, such as:
  - Relaxation techniques like deep breathing, meditation, or mindfulness.
  - Hobbies that bring you joy and a sense of accomplishment.
  - Physical activities that make you feel good, not punished, like walking, yoga, or dancing.

9. Practice Patience and Self-Compassion

- Remind yourself that recovery is not linear and often comes with setbacks.
- Treat yourself with kindness during difficult moments, recognizing that progress is more important than perfection.

10. Stay Committed

- Understand that recovery is an evolution of self. It's not about an endpoint but about building a healthier relationship with yourself and food over time.
- Celebrate small victories, and remind yourself that every step forward, no matter how small, is important.

Seeking help for an eating disorder is an act of bravery. It's the most important step! Remember, you're not alone. There are people, resources, and professionals ready to support you every step of the way.

Take the first step today—you deserve it.

IDENTIFYING AN EATING DISORDER
Supporting a Child

If you suspect a child may have an eating disorder, your approach can make a significant difference in their recovery.

It's important to address the situation with sensitivity and understanding. Some of this will be similar to what's above, but that's because a lot of this material applies universally, regardless of whether you're supporting a child or yourself. That said, children require a unique level of care, given their potential inability to fully articulate what they're going through or to seek help on their own.

Your role is crucial in recognizing the signs, fostering a supportive environment, and guiding them in the right direction. Below is a tailored guide to help you get started in this situation.

1. Educate Yourself

- Learn about eating disorders, including their signs, symptoms, and treatment options.
- Understanding the complexities of eating disorders will help you provide informed support and recognize when professional help may be necessary.

2. Approach with Care

- Express your concerns calmly in a non-judgmental way.
- Allow them to talk openly about their feelings, experiences, and struggles without fear of criticism or blame, creating a safe space.

3. Reassure Them of Your Support

- Let the child know they're valued and supported regardless of their struggles and that your support is unconditional.
- Reinforce that they're not alone and that you're there to help them navigate this journey.

4. Encourage Professional Help

- Help connect the child to a therapist, counselor, or healthcare provider specializing in eating disorders.
- Offer assistance in finding resources, scheduling appointments, or accompanying them if appropriate.

5. Foster Open Communication with Professionals

- Work with therapists or healthcare providers to create healthy communication boundaries.
  - For example, ensure parents or guardians are informed of any life-threatening concerns while also respecting the child's need for privacy in their therapeutic process.

6. Be a Positive Role Model

- Exhibit healthy behaviors around food, self-care, and body image.
- Avoid making negative comments about your weight or appearance or that of others.

7. Monitor Behavioral and Emotional Changes

- Pay attention to shifts in the child's behavior, mood, or eating habits.
- Warning signs might include restrictive eating, preoccupation with weight, emotional withdrawal, or drastic changes in physical appearance. Seek professional help immediately if concerning patterns emerge.

8. Create a Safe Environment

- Remove or limit exposure to triggering influences, such as social media accounts promoting harmful diet culture or toxic environments focused on appearance.
- Promote body neutrality and a culture of acceptance within their immediate surroundings.

9. Practice Patience and Consistency

- Understand that recovery is not a linear process. It takes time, and setbacks are normal.
- Be consistent in offering empathy, encouragement, and a non-judgmental presence.

10. Seek Support for Yourself

- Acknowledge that supporting a child with an eating disorder can be emotionally challenging.
- Access resources, support groups, or counseling for yourself to process your emotions and remain a stable source of support.

Supporting a child with an eating disorder requires compassion, patience, and persistence. Just by being present, informed, and understanding, your actions can profoundly impact their recovery journey because you provide the stability and encouragement they need to heal.

Even small steps can make a big difference, so keep showing up, offering support, and fostering hope.

IDENTIFYING AN EATING DISORDER
Supporting Others

If you know someone—friend, coworker, peer, neighbor, relative—who may have an eating disorder, your support can be instrumental in their recovery. Offering understanding and care, even in small ways, can make a significant difference. While the above two lessons—supporting yourself or a child—do have a few repeat steps in the guide below, there are also some outliers unique to supporting others. Relationships like these often require a delicate balance of compassion, respect for boundaries, and proactive encouragement. Your role may not be as central as a parent's or as personal as your own journey, but it's still vital.

Below is a tailored guide to help you navigate these relationships and offer meaningful support in ways that honor both their journey and your connection to them.

1. Express Concern

- Let them know you've noticed changes—either in their behavior, mood, appearance, or any combination of these—and that you're sorry they're going through a tough time.
- Avoid accusations or criticism; keep the focus on them and their well-being.

2. Listen, Don't Judge

- Be a safe, empathetic space for them to share their feelings and experiences.
- Resist the urge to fix. Sometimes, your presence and willingness to listen are enough.

3. Educate Yourself

- Learn about eating disorders, including their signs, symptoms, and treatment options.
- Make sure to rely on credible sources, as there's plenty of misinformation online. A well-informed approach will help you offer more meaningful support.

4. Encourage Professional Help

- Let them know it's okay to seek help from trained professionals like therapists, counselors, or healthcare providers.
- Offer assistance, such as helping them locate resources, scheduling appointments, or providing emotional support throughout their journey.

5. Regular Check-ins

- Stay connected, letting them know you care about their overall health and well-being.
- Simple messages of encouragement, like "I'm thinking of you" or "I'm here if you need anything," can mean the world.

6. Avoid Triggering Topics

- Be mindful of your words and actions. Avoid comments about their appearance, weight, or food choices.
- Refrain from discussing dieting, calorie counting, or other potentially harmful topics.

7. Encourage Positive Activities

- Suggest activities that promote self-care and well-being, such as spending time with loved ones, pursuing hobbies, or practicing relaxation techniques.
- Refer them to resources like breathing and grounding exercises.

8. Be Patient

- Recovery is not linear, and setbacks are part of the process. Avoid showing frustration if they struggle or resist help.
- Continue offering your support consistently, even if they aren't ready to make changes.

9. Avoid Making It About Yourself

- It's natural to feel upset, worried, or even frustrated when someone you care about is struggling. Keep the focus on them.
- Avoid saying things like, "You're worrying me," or "I just want you to be better," as this can make them feel guilt or pressure.

10. Take Care of Yourself

- Supporting someone with an eating disorder can take an emotional toll on you. Make sure you're leaning on your own support network, practicing self-care, or seeking guidance from a therapist or counselor if needed.
- You can't pour from an empty cup. Your well-being is just as important.

Supporting someone with an eating disorder requires patience, empathy, and persistence. While you may not be able to change their situation, your steady presence and encouragement can provide the foundation they need to start their recovery journey.

By showing up with compassion and understanding, you're making a bigger difference than you realize.

THE WEIGHT OF WORDS: WHY NUMBERS CAN BE HARMFUL

Okay, hear me out. I'm *definitely* guilty of being an open book about most things—probably too much sometimes. Oversharing? It's practically a personality trait. But when it comes to numbers—calories, weight, body measurements—that's where I draw the line. And honestly? You should, too.

Why? Because the details, even the little ones that seem harmless, can have serious consequences for someone struggling with or at risk of developing an eating disorder. It's not just a little slip; it can truly hurt. Here's why it's so important to stop the share!

Why Sharing Numbers Can Be Harmful

1. Triggering Harmful Comparisons

- People may compare themselves to your numbers, leading to feelings of inadequacy, shame, or competition.
- This can intensify disordered eating behaviors and harm mental health.

2. Fueling Obsession

- Numbers often become a fixation for those with eating disorders, encouraging an unhealthy focus on weight, food, or body image.
- This reinforces cycles of obsession that make recovery more difficult.

3. Encouraging or Normalizing Harmful Behaviors

- While likely unintentional, sharing details about extreme calorie restriction or weight loss might validate or glamorize dangerous habits.
- This sends the message that unhealthy behaviors are acceptable or desirable.

4. Provoking Misinterpretation

- Using what could be distorted numbers as benchmarks for self-worth can create harmful misperceptions. In reality, no one needs numbers to define or rank their value in the first place.
- The broader context of health and well-being is often lost in the fixation on specifics.

5. Causing Safety Concerns

- Sharing specific details may give vulnerable individuals ideas for dangerous weight-loss practices.
- These behaviors can escalate into severe physical or mental health risks.

What to Share Instead

1. Promote Body Acceptance

- Focus on encouraging self-care, self-compassion, and holistic health rather than numbers.
- Highlight the value of mental and emotional well-being over appearance.

2. Share Recovery Stories Thoughtfully

- Discuss personal growth and progress without relying on triggering details.
- Inspire hope by emphasizing resilience and the benefits of seeking help.

3. Encourage Professional Help

- Redirect people to trusted resources, therapists, or healthcare providers for expert guidance.
- Highlight the importance of personalized care over comparisons.

4. Create Safe Spaces

- Avoid discussions about weight, dieting, or body size in conversations or social settings.
- Encourage open and non-judgmental dialogues focused on support and understanding.

5. Be Mindful of Your Impact

- Consider how your words might affect someone who's struggling.
- When in doubt, choose compassion over specifics—uplift rather than unintentionally harm.

Instead of sharing numbers, focus on fostering support, encouragement, and understanding. Promote professional help and highlight the importance of self-care and body acceptance. Eating disorders are complex mental health conditions, and recovery requires compassion, support, and qualified care.

If you or someone you know is struggling, seek help from healthcare providers who specialize in eating disorder treatment.

Your words matter—use them to uplift, not harm.

THE COST OF COMPARISON

Why do I feel envy? Jealousy? Or sometimes both?

First, let's get one thing straight. Feeling envy or jealousy doesn't make you a bad person; it makes you human. These emotions are baked into us at a primal level, hardwired from our earliest ancestors in the hunter-gatherer stage of human evolution.

Back then, comparison wasn't just natural; it was essential. It helped us gauge our survival skills—who was the best at gathering food, hunting prey, or protecting the tribe? These comparisons determined who thrived and who struggled. They were necessary for survival.

Fast forward to now, and while the stakes have shifted, the instinct remains. We're no longer competing for survival in small tribes, but the urge to measure ourselves against others still lingers. For many, social media amplifies this instinct, putting curated lives and highlight reels in constant view.

But even without social media—back when my world was smaller and my circles more intimate—the comparison trap still found me.

My Own Experience: Ashley and the Weight of Comparison

When I think back to my early days with Ashley, I can admit, now with some perspective, that I felt both envy and jealousy. They showed up in different ways for different reasons, but they were undeniably there.

I envied her success: the visible weight loss, the discipline, and the way her hard work was paying off in ways I couldn't seem to replicate. But there was jealousy, too. I wasn't just longing for her results; I was frustrated by the attention and validation she received. Why wasn't anyone noticing me the way they noticed her?

Even without the ever-present scroll of social media, the comparison instinct was alive and well in my mind. It left me questioning my worth and trapped in a cycle of feeling I wasn't enough.

And yet, here's what I've learned. The key isn't to eliminate these feelings entirely; it's to understand them, give them context, and learn how to manage them in a way that allows you to grow.

What's the Difference Between Envy and Jealousy?

While envy and jealousy often overlap, they're distinct emotions with different roots.

Envy is about wanting something you *don't have*, while jealousy is about feeling threatened over something you *do have*.

Envy

- Envy happens when you *want something someone else has*.
- It's often rooted in a sense of lack—like feeling you're missing out on success, possessions, or qualities that another person has.
- Example from my story: I envied Ashley's ability to lose weight and the visible changes in her body. I wanted those results for myself but felt like they were out of reach.

Jealousy

- Jealousy arises when you *fear losing something you already do possess* to someone else.
- It's often tied to interpersonal dynamics and involves insecurity about being overlooked or replaced.
- Example from my story: I was jealous of the attention Ashley received from others—time with my friends, my connections,

and the space I held. It wasn't just about her weight loss; it was about how her transformation seemed to outshine me, making me feel I was losing my place.

Why These Feelings Show Up

Both envy and jealousy are linked to comparison and insecurity, but they manifest in different ways. Envy reflects a longing for something you feel you're missing, while jealousy stems from the fear of losing something you already possess and value—like relationships, status, or recognition.

Social Media's Role in the Comparison Trap

These emotions were tough enough to navigate in my experiences with Ashley, but today? Social media pours fuel on the fire. Constant exposure to curated, filtered, and idealized images of others makes it nearly impossible to avoid the comparison trap.

That's why it's so important to recognize these emotions for what they are: natural responses to a world that's constantly asking us to compare.

Managing Envy and Jealousy

Understanding these emotions is the first step in managing them. Here's how to move forward:

1. Acknowledge and Accept Your Feelings

- Recognize jealousy and envy as normal emotions.
- Avoid judging yourself for feeling this way—these feelings are human and universal.
- Label the emotion and take a moment to sit with it instead of trying to push it away.

2. Identify Your Triggers

- Pay attention to the situations, people, or platforms that spark feelings of envy or jealousy.
- Write down patterns you notice—this can help you anticipate and prepare for triggering moments.
- Recognize whether these triggers are internal—your own insecurities—or external—social media, comparisons, and so on.

3. Reframe Your Thoughts

- Challenge assumptions that fuel your jealousy or envy. Are you comparing yourself to an idealized or incomplete version of someone else's reality?
- Replace envy-driven thoughts like "They're better than me" with more empowering ones, such as "Their success doesn't diminish mine."
- Remind yourself that everyone faces challenges, even if they're not visible.

4. Limit Comparison Traps

- Minimize exposure to environments that encourage unhelpful comparisons, like social media platforms promoting unrealistic standards.
- Curate your social feeds, prioritizing content that inspires you rather than triggering envy or insecurity.
- Take breaks from social media or step away when you feel overwhelmed.

5. Cultivate Gratitude

- Shift your focus to what's going well in your life. Every day, write down three things you're grateful for. If that doesn't seem manageable, one will do!
- Reflect on your strengths, achievements, and positive qualities.

- Gratitude doesn't erase envy, but it helps shift your mindset from scarcity to abundance.

6. Celebrate Others Without Losing Yourself

- Practice congratulating others genuinely, *even* if you feel envious. Their wins don't make you a failure.
- Think of success as an infinite resource—someone else's achievements don't take away your potential.
- Focus on collaboration over competition when possible.

7. Build Self-Esteem and Confidence

- Engage in activities you love and excel at—this helps you feel capable and valued.
- Set small, achievable goals that align with your values and work toward them consistently.
- Recognize and celebrate even the smallest wins.

8. Focus on Your Own Journey

- Redirect energy from comparing yourself with others to working on your personal growth.
- Reflect on what success means to you, not on someone else's definition.
- Engage in hobbies or passions that bring you joy and fulfillment.

9. Practice Empathy

- Try to view others' successes with empathy rather than resentment. Remind yourself that they have struggles you may not see.
- Remember that envy often tells you what you value, so use it as a guide to focus on areas for personal growth.

10. Seek Support When Needed

- Talk to trusted friends, family, or a therapist about your feelings. External perspectives can provide clarity and validation.

- Consider joining a support group or community that fosters positivity and shared experiences.
- If jealousy impacts relationships, work on open and honest communication to build trust and resolve insecurities.

When I reflect on my feelings toward Ashley back then, I can see how envy and jealousy worked together to trap me in comparisons. But I also see how understanding those emotions and reframing them, even now, has helped me grow.

Feeling envy or jealousy doesn't make you weak; it makes you human. The trick is recognizing them for what they are and refusing to let them define your worth. By focusing on your own journey, you can step out of the comparison trap and embrace the path that's uniquely yours.

CHAPTER 15

ENLIGHTENMENT on DATING ED

Quick Reference Page Guide

ALL ABOUT EATING DISORDERS

What Are Eating Disorders?

Eating disorders are psychiatric conditions marked by severe disturbances in eating behaviors and related thoughts and emotions. These conditions often involve an unhealthy obsession with food, weight, and body image, and they can have devastating physical and psychological consequences.

Eating disorders affect individuals of all genders, ages, and backgrounds. They're not a choice or a lifestyle but rather complex mental health conditions that require professional intervention.

Types of Eating Disorders

Following the Diagnostic and Statistical Manual of Mental Disorders (DSM-5) and the International Classification of Diseases (ICD-11), we recognize the following major types of eating disorders:

1. Anorexia Nervosa

Key Characteristics:

- Restriction of energy intake leading to significantly low body weight
- Intense fear of gaining weight or being fat, even when underweight
- Distorted perception of body weight or shape, with undue influence on self-esteem

Behaviors:

- Restrictive eating or food avoidance
- Obsessive calorie counting
- Excessive exercise

Physical and Emotional Consequences:

- Malnutrition and severe weight loss
- Fatigue, dizziness, and cold intolerance
- Preoccupation with food and eating rituals
- Depression, anxiety, and social withdrawal

2. Bulimia Nervosa

Key Characteristics:

- Recurrent episodes of binge eating with a sense of loss of control
- Compensatory behaviors to prevent weight gain, such as vomiting, laxative use, fasting, or over-exercising
- Body image heavily influencing self-esteem

Behaviors:

- Secretive binge-eating episodes
- Feelings of shame, guilt, or distress after binge episodes

Physical and Emotional Consequences:

- Electrolyte imbalances leading to cardiac complications
- Gastrointestinal problems such as esophageal tears
- Chronic dehydration and dental issues

3. Binge Eating Disorder (BED)

Key Characteristics:

- Recurrent episodes of consuming large quantities of food in a short time

- Feeling a lack of control during eating episodes
- No compensatory behaviors such as purging or fasting

Behaviors:

- Eating when not physically hungry
- Eating alone due to embarrassment
- Experiencing guilt or disgust after binge episodes

Physical and Emotional Consequences:

- Weight gain and related health risks, such as diabetes or heart disease
- Emotional distress, shame, or social isolation

4. Other Specified Feeding or Eating Disorders (OSFED)

Key Characteristics:

- Eating disorder symptoms that don't meet the full criteria of other disorders

Examples of OSFED:

- Atypical Anorexia Nervosa: All the features of anorexia nervosa, but the individual isn't significantly underweight
- Purging Disorder: Recurrent purging behaviors without binge eating
- Night Eating Syndrome: Consuming a significant portion of daily food intake during nighttime hours

Consequences:

- Similar physical and emotional impacts as other eating disorders, varying according to specific presentation

5. Avoidant/Restrictive Food Intake Disorder (ARFID)

Key Characteristics:

- Avoidance of food based on sensory characteristics, fear of choking, or lack of interest in eating
- Significant weight loss, nutritional deficiencies, or reliance on nutritional supplements

Behaviors:
- Extreme food selectivity
- Reluctance or refusal to eat food with certain textures or flavors

Consequences:
- Growth delays in children
- Physical weakness and immune suppression
- Impaired daily functioning

Causes and Effects of Eating Disorders: Understanding Without Getting Stuck

When faced with any of these eating disorders, it's natural to wonder, "Why did this happen to me?" Identifying causes can provide insight and validation, but it's important to avoid becoming fixated on the why. Don't let cause hold you back. Trying to pinpoint the root of an eating disorder can feel like searching for a needle in a haystack—overwhelming and unproductive.

Eating disorders arise from a complex web of factors, including genetics, biology, psychology, environment, and social influences. They can rarely be traced to a single cause, and dwelling on the why can sometimes create more frustration than clarity. Instead of focusing exclusively on identifying the causes, it's far more helpful to explore how these factors have impacted you and to dive into healing work that allows you to move forward.

The Multifaceted Causes of Eating Disorders

While no two experiences are identical, eating disorders often emerge from multiple factors.

1. Biological and Genetic Factors

- **Family History:** Genetic predispositions to eating disorders or co-occurring conditions like anxiety, depression, or OCD.
- **Brain Chemistry:** Neurotransmitter imbalances, particularly with serotonin and dopamine, can influence mood, appetite, and reward systems.
- **Body Image Perception:** Some people may be more biologically prone to perceive their bodies negatively or develop perfectionist tendencies.

2. Psychological Factors

- **Low Self-Esteem:** Struggles with self-worth can make individuals more vulnerable to disordered eating as a coping mechanism.
- **Trauma or Emotional Pain:** Experiences of abuse, bullying, or significant life stressors can trigger an eating disorder as a way to regain control or to numb feelings.
- **Perfectionism and Control:** A drive for perfection can lead to rigid dieting, obsessive exercise, or other unhealthy patterns.

3. Environmental and Social Influences

- **Family Dynamics:** High expectations, over-criticism, or lack of emotional support can increase vulnerability—though supportive families aren't immune.
- **Cultural Pressure:** Unrealistic societal standards for beauty, often perpetuated by social media and advertising, exacerbate body dissatisfaction.
- **Peer Influence:** Bullying, fat-shaming, or peer comparison can deeply affect self-esteem and eating behaviors.

4. Life Transitions or Stressors

- **Major Changes:** Starting college, moving cities, or experiencing a breakup can act as triggers for disordered eating.
- **Grief or Loss:** Significant loss, whether of a loved one, job, or identity, can lead individuals to turn to food-related behaviors for comfort or control.

5. Dieting Culture

- **Diet Obsession:** Exposure to diet fads and clean eating culture can normalize restrictive eating and unhealthy weight-loss practices.
- **Fear of Food:** Moralizing food—for example, labeling foods as *good* or *bad*—fosters a destructive relationship with eating.

The Effects—or Consequences—of Eating Disorders: Why Action Matters More Than Analysis

While exploring the causes can provide perspective, focusing on the effects of eating disorders will highlight why healing is urgent. Eating disorders are among the most lethal of all psychiatric conditions. They can lead to severe physical, emotional, and social consequences. Understanding the impact helps shift the focus from analyzing the past to addressing the present and planning for the future.

Short-Term Effects of Eating Disorders

Behavioral Effects

- **Extreme Dieting**: Severe food restriction can lead to irritability, fatigue, and obsessive thoughts about food.
- **Binge Eating**: Overeating large amounts of food in a short time is often followed by feelings of guilt or shame.

- **Purging**: Self-induced vomiting or misuse of laxatives/diuretics can cause immediate physical harm.
- **Compulsive Exercise**: Excessive physical activity that can lead to exhaustion and injury.

Physical Effects

- **Malnutrition**: Weakness, fatigue, and impaired immune function from a lack of essential nutrients
- **Electrolyte Imbalance**: Irregular heartbeat, muscle cramps, and even cardiac arrest
- **Gastrointestinal Issues**: Bloating, constipation, and abdominal pain from disrupted digestion
- **Dehydration**: Issues with kidney function and overall health caused by purging or insufficient fluid intake
- **Weight Fluctuations**: Rapid weight loss or gain that destabilizes physical health
- **Dental Problems**: Enamel erosion and cavities from frequent vomiting in bulimia
- **Hair and Skin Problems**: Dryness, hair thinning, and brittle nails due to nutrient deficiencies

Mental and Emotional Effects

- **Anxiety and Depression**: Mood swings and increased risk of depressive episodes
- **Obsessive Thoughts**: Preoccupation with food, body weight, and appearance
- **Social Withdrawal**: Avoiding social gatherings, especially those involving food
- **Impaired Cognitive Function**: Difficulty concentrating, remembering, or making decisions due to malnutrition
- **Low Self-Esteem**: Persistent feelings of inadequacy or poor self-worth

Long-Term Effects of Eating Disorders

The long-term consequences of eating disorders can be devastating, with physical and psychological effects that may last a lifetime.

Physical Health Effects

- **Cardiovascular Problems**: Heart palpitations, arrhythmias, low blood pressure, and heart failure due to malnutrition and electrolyte imbalances
- **Gastrointestinal Damage**: Chronic bloating, constipation, and, in severe cases, intestinal rupture
- **Osteoporosis**: Loss of bone density, increasing the risk of fractures
- **Nutritional Deficiencies**: Long-term shortages of vital nutrients, leading to conditions like anemia and impaired immune function
- **Menstrual Irregularities**: Loss of menstruation—amenorrhea—with potential long-term impacts on fertility

Psychological and Emotional Effects

- **Chronic Depression and Anxiety**: Persistent mood disorders that may require lifelong management
- **Obsessive-Compulsive Behaviors**: Continued preoccupation with food, weight, or body image
- **Low Self-Esteem**: Feelings of inadequacy and poor self-worth
- **Social Isolation**: Difficulty maintaining relationships due to long-term emotional strain

Behavioral and Cognitive Effects

- **Impaired Cognitive Function**: Reduced concentration, memory, and decision-making capabilities due to long-term malnutrition

- **Chronic Dieting Patterns**: Persistent disordered eating habits that can hinder recovery and quality of life

Medical Complications

- **Increased Risk of Chronic Diseases**: Metabolic changes cause higher susceptibility to conditions like diabetes, cardiovascular disease, and cancer.
- **Premature Death**: Eating disorders, especially anorexia, have one of the highest mortality rates of any psychiatric illness, often due to cardiac complications or suicide.

The Shift From "Why?" to "What Now?"

While identifying contributing factors can provide a foundation for understanding, it's what you do next that truly matters. Healing begins when you stop dwelling on the origin or the why and start focusing on actionable steps. By moving into action, you can reclaim control and empower yourself to change your story.

We'll dive deeper into treatment options, but before we do that, let's address some quick but crucial steps you can take right now to begin your recovery journey.

Actionable Steps for Moving Forward

1. Focus on the Present:

- Acknowledge how your eating disorder is affecting your life today—physically, emotionally, and socially. Use this awareness to set specific recovery goals. Identifying where you are now will help you determine the next steps forward.

2. Embrace Early Intervention:

- The sooner you seek help, the better. Early intervention can prevent long-term physical and emotional complications and increase the likelihood of a successful recovery.

3. Shift to Action Mode:

- Healing doesn't happen in a vacuum. Start small by making one proactive choice each day, whether it's reaching out to a friend, eating a balanced meal, or journaling. Small steps create momentum.

4. Build a Support Network:

- Recovery is not a solo mission. Surround yourself with people who encourage and uplift you, whether it's friends, family, or a support group. Connection is essential for long-term healing.

5. Prioritize Healing Over Perfection:

- Recovery isn't about achieving flawlessness; it's about finding a sustainable, healthier balance. Embrace the idea that progress is the ultimate goal.

6. Challenge Negative Thoughts:

- Notice when you fall into patterns of self-blame, comparison, or unworthiness. Counter these with affirmations of self-compassion and focus on the progress you're making.

7. Set Tangible Goals:

- Break down your recovery into manageable steps. Celebrate small victories along the way to stay motivated and remind yourself of the progress you're making.

8. Stay Open to Professional Help:

- Treatment is a crucial part of recovery. Therapists, nutritionists, and medical professionals can provide personalized guidance to help you address both the physical and emotional aspects of your eating disorder.

9. Practice Patience with Yourself:

- Recovery is a journey, not a race. There will be setbacks, and that's okay. Be gentle with yourself as you navigate the process and focus on long-term growth.

10. Prepare for Treatment:

- Whether you're starting therapy, joining a support group, or considering other interventions, take a moment to prepare mentally for the journey. This can include writing down questions, identifying your goals for treatment, or simply acknowledging your readiness to take this step.

When you're ready to take the next step, know that you don't have to do it alone. Support is available, and taking action now is a courageous and vital choice for your health and well-being.

How Are Eating Disorders Treated?

Treatment requires a multidisciplinary approach tailored to the individual. Treatment isn't one-size-fits-all, but a combination of strategies can help address the unique needs of the person seeking recovery. Have a look at the full section on treatment in Chapter 16: *Understanding Treatment: Exploring Options for a Healthier You.*

Key components of treatment include:

Psychotherapy

- **Cognitive-behavioral therapy (CBT)**: Helps identify and change disordered thoughts and behaviors surrounding food, body image, and self-esteem

- **Dialectical behavior therapy (DBT)**: Focuses on emotional regulation, stress management, and building mindfulness skills to navigate challenging emotions

Nutritional Counseling

- A registered dietitian can provide personalized guidance to restore balanced eating habits and address nutritional deficiencies.

Medical Monitoring

- Regular check-ups with a healthcare provider are crucial to track weight, heart health, and other vital signs impacted by the disorder.

Medication

- Antidepressants, anti-anxiety medications, or other psychiatric medications may be prescribed as part of a comprehensive treatment plan.

Support Groups

- Fellowship programs like **Overeaters Anonymous (OA)** or **Alcoholics Anonymous (AA)** offer free, accessible peer support. These groups often meet both virtually or in person and can be a lifeline for those seeking community and accountability.

The road to recovery may feel overwhelming, but each step forward, no matter how small, is a testament to your resilience. In the section on treatment, we'll explore ways to access treatment, including affordable and accessible options for those who may not have the means to pursue traditional paths. Help is always within reach, no matter what.

A Final Note on Recovery

Early intervention is crucial when addressing eating disorders. The sooner help is sought, the better the chances of preventing long-term physical and emotional complications. Eating disorders are complex conditions that don't always have a definitive *cure*. However, healing is possible, and progress can happen at any stage of the journey.

Recovery doesn't mean erasing every struggle or returning to a past version of yourself. Instead, it's about reclaiming your health, rethinking your relationship with food, and learning how to integrate it into your life in a way that supports your overall well-being. It's not about perfection or an endpoint—it's about creating a new, healthier balance that works for you.

While the path may not be linear, every small step forward—no matter how imperfect—is progress. With the right support, tools, and patience, you can rebuild your connection with your body and food in a way that fosters resilience and self-compassion.

Recovery isn't a one-size-fits-all journey, but it's always worth taking.

ESSENTIAL FACTS ABOUT EATING DISORDERS

What are some statistics surrounding eating disorders?

Understanding the scope of eating disorders is crucial for raising awareness, reducing stigma, and encouraging timely intervention. Below are key statistics that highlight the impact of eating disorders on individuals and society.

General Statistics

1. An estimated 1 in 7 people are affected by eating disorders.
2. 9% of the US population—28.8 million people—will experience an eating disorder in their lifetime.
3. By the time women are in their 40s or 50s, 15% will have had an eating disorder, but only 27% of these seek treatment.
4. Eating disorders are increasingly prevalent among males, breaking past misconceptions of being a *female-only* condition.
5. Fewer than 6% of people with eating disorders are medically diagnosed as underweight, challenging the stereotype of who struggles with these conditions.
6. People in larger bodies face the highest risk of developing eating disorders. Among them, the higher the BMI, the greater the risk.

Mortality and Suicide Rates

1. Anorexia nervosa has the highest mortality rate of any mental illness.

2. 10,200 deaths occur annually in the US due to eating disorders—one death every 52 minutes.
3. Individuals with severe eating disorder symptoms are 11 times more likely to attempt suicide.
4. Even those with sub-threshold symptoms are 2 times as likely to attempt suicide as those without symptoms.
5. Patients with anorexia face an 18 times higher risk of suicide than the general population.

Financial and Societal Costs

The financial burden of eating disorders in the US totals $64.7 billion annually. This includes healthcare costs, lost productivity, and indirect impacts on families and communities.

Why These Facts Matter

These statistics aren't just numbers—they reflect the urgent need for greater understanding, compassion, and action. By highlighting these truths, we can empower those currently struggling, support those in recovery, and advocate for systemic change to help future generations.

DISORDERED EATING:
The Gray Area Between Health and Illness

What Is Disordered Eating?

Disordered eating is a term often used to describe a range of irregular eating behaviors that don't align with the norms of balanced, healthy eating. This can include behaviors like restrictive dieting, skipping meals, binge eating, or an intense preoccupation with food, calories, and weight. While these habits might not meet the full criteria for a diagnosable eating disorder, they can still have significant impacts on both physical and mental health.

Casual Use of the Term

People often use the term *disordered eating* casually when they don't feel ready—or able—to acknowledge that they might have an eating disorder. It's seen as a softer label, less clinical, or even less intimidating. For many, admitting to disordered eating feels easier, like dipping a toe into acknowledging that their relationship with food isn't healthy without jumping straight into the deep end of diagnoses like anorexia or bulimia.

Disordered eating also appeals to those who feel they don't fit the mold of an eating disorder stereotype, such as being underweight or engaging in extreme behaviors. It's important to validate that disordered eating can look different for everyone and that its impacts are no less real.

How Is Disordered Eating Different From an Eating Disorder?

Here's how disordered eating and eating disorders compare:

- **Disordered Eating:**
  - Encompasses a broad range of unhealthy eating behaviors
  - Is often situational, tied to stress, cultural trends, or short-term goals
  - Can include irregular meal patterns, emotional eating, or obsessing over clean eating
  - Lacks the severity, consistency, and diagnosable criteria of an eating disorder.

- **Eating Disorders:**
  - Are classified as psychiatric conditions in the DSM-5
  - Include specific diagnoses like anorexia nervosa, bulimia nervosa, and binge eating disorder
  - Are defined by chronic and severe patterns of disordered thoughts and behaviors around food, weight, and body image
  - Often involve long-term health risks and require professional intervention

In short, disordered eating behaviors might start casually or temporarily but, without intervention, can escalate into eating disorders.

Why Address Disordered Eating?

Disordered eating isn't harmless just because it doesn't have a label. Here's why it's critical to address:

1. Precursor to Eating Disorders:

- Disordered eating can progress into full-blown eating disorders over time. Identifying and addressing it early can prevent further physical and emotional harm.

2. Mental Health Impacts:

- Constant preoccupation with food and weight can lead to anxiety, guilt, shame, and reduced self-esteem.

3. Physical Risks:

- Irregular eating patterns can result in nutritional deficiencies, fatigue, digestive issues, and other health complications.

4. Cultural Normalization of Harmful Behaviors:

- Many disordered eating patterns, like restrictive dieting or obsessing over clean eating, are normalized in our culture. This can make it harder to recognize when these behaviors cross into unhealthy territory.

5. Better Relationships with Food and Body:

- Early addressing of disordered eating can help build a healthier relationship with food and a more compassionate view of your body before destructive habits take root.

Taking Steps Forward

If you think your behaviors might fall under disordered eating:

- Reflect honestly on your relationship with food and your body.
- Recognize patterns that cause physical, mental, or emotional distress.
- Seek support from a trusted friend, counselor, or healthcare provider.
- Understand that disordered eating is common but doesn't have to be your norm. It's okay to ask for help.

Disordered eating sits in a gray area, but that doesn't make it any less important to address. It's a signal that your relationship with food and body image needs attention, and addressing it now can prevent a deeper struggle down the road.

THE BINGE SPECTRUM:
From Occasional Episodes to Binge Eating Disorder (BED)

Binge eating exists on a spectrum. For some, it's an occasional behavior tied to emotional or situational triggers. For others, it becomes a diagnosable condition with severe consequences. Understanding this range is critical to recognizing when binge eating becomes more than a fleeting behavior.

What Is Binge Eating?

Binge eating is the consumption of large amounts of food in a short time, often accompanied by a sense of loss of control. Binge episodes can be occasional or habitual and don't always involve emotional distress or guilt.

- Common Triggers for Binge Eating:
  - Emotional triggers like stress, sadness, or boredom
  - Situational triggers such as celebrations or loneliness
  - Physical hunger from restrictive dieting or skipping meals

What Sets Binge Eating Disorder Apart?

- Diagnostic Criteria for BED:
  - Recurrent episodes of binge eating at least once a week for three months

- ◦ Associated emotional distress, including guilt, shame, or embarrassment
- ◦ No compensatory behaviors like purging, which distinguishes BED from bulimia nervosa
- Behavioral Indicators of BED:
  - ◦ Eating when not physically hungry
  - ◦ Eating rapidly or to the point of discomfort
  - ◦ Consuming food in secret due to embarrassment

How Binge Eating and Obesity Intersect

- Shared Space, Different Experiences:
  - ◦ Binge Eating and Obesity:
    - □ Some individuals with obesity engage in binge eating, contributing to weight gain. However, not all individuals with obesity binge eat.
  - ◦ BED Across All Weight Ranges:
    - □ BED doesn't discriminate by weight. It affects individuals who are underweight, average weight, overweight, or obese.
- The Vicious Cycle:
  - ◦ Binge eating episodes can lead to weight gain, and societal stigmas around weight can exacerbate emotional distress, perpetuating the cycle of binge eating.

Consequences of Binge Eating and BED

The physical and emotional toll of binge eating and BED can be significant:

1. Physical Health Risks:

- Increased likelihood of obesity-related conditions such as type 2 diabetes, heart disease, and hypertension

- Gastrointestinal issues from consuming excessive amounts of food in one sitting
- Potential for sleep apnea or joint pain associated with weight gain

2. Emotional and Mental Health Challenges:

- Heightened risk of anxiety and depression
- Low self-esteem fueled by guilt and shame surrounding eating habits
- Social isolation or withdrawal due to embarrassment

Why Early Recognition and Action Matter

- Understanding Patterns:
  Occasional binge eating may not immediately seem problematic, but repeated episodes and associated emotional distress can signal BED.

- Seeking Help:
  Recognizing the difference between binge eating and BED allows individuals to seek the appropriate level of care, whether that's support for emotional eating or targeted treatment for BED.

Key Takeaway

Binge eating exists on a spectrum, but no matter where it falls, it's essential to address it, just as we do with other forms of disordered eating. Occasional binge episodes can be an opportunity to reflect on triggers, while BED requires a more structured, clinical approach. Both are valid experiences that benefit from compassionate care and intervention.

Next Step: Explore treatment options, from therapy to support groups, and build a toolkit to address binge behaviors effectively.

OBESITY:
Beyond the Scale

Obesity is a medical condition that carries immense social, psychological, and health implications. It's more than just a number on a scale or a BMI chart—it's a complex issue often influenced by genetics, environment, behavior, and systemic factors. In the context of eating disorders, obesity often occupies a misunderstood and underrepresented space despite its overlap with disordered eating behaviors.

What Is Obesity?

- **Defined by Body Fat:**
  Obesity is characterized by excessive body fat accumulation that negatively impacts health.

- **BMI as a Measure:**
  While Body Mass Index (BMI) is often used to categorize obesity, it has significant flaws. BMI doesn't account for:
  - Muscle mass—athletes, for example, may be misclassified as obese
  - Ethnic and genetic differences in body composition
  - Holistic health markers like metabolic function or physical fitness

- **Key Takeaway:**
  Obesity is not just a weight issue. It is a multifaceted health condition influenced by numerous factors beyond diet or exercise.

How Obesity Relates to Eating Disorders

- **Shared Behaviors:**
  Disordered eating patterns like binge eating can contribute to obesity. However, not all individuals with obesity engage in disordered eating.

- **Weight Bias in Eating Disorder Treatment:**
  - Individuals with obesity may not recognize they have an eating disorder because symptoms like binge eating are often dismissed as *just overeating*.
  - Healthcare providers can overlook or misdiagnose eating disorders in people with obesity, focusing solely on weight loss rather than addressing underlying behaviors or mental health.

- **Stigma and Its Role:**
  - Societal weight stigma can worsen mental health, leading to emotional eating and reinforcing the cycle of weight gain.
  - Stigmatization may discourage individuals from seeking help for either obesity or disordered eating.

What Causes Obesity?

Obesity results from a web of interconnected factors, making it far more complex than simple calories in calories out.

1. Genetic Influences:

- A family history of weight-related issues can predispose individuals to obesity.
- Certain genetic mutations can affect appetite regulation and metabolism.

2. Behavioral Factors:

- Overeating, often influenced by emotional or situational triggers
- Sedentary lifestyles exacerbated by technology and modern work environments

3. Environmental Factors:

- **Food Deserts, or Grocery Gaps:** Limited access to affordable, nutritious food
- **Socioeconomic Status:** Financial inaccessibility of healthy food options and fitness resources
- **Cultural Norms:** Food consumed as a celebration, coping mechanism, or status symbol

4. Medical Conditions:

- Chronic illnesses like hypothyroidism and polycystic ovary syndrome (PCOS)
- Certain medications, including antidepressants and corticosteroids

Health Risks Associated With Obesity

Obesity is not just about aesthetics or societal judgment; it significantly impacts physical and mental health.

Physical Risks:

1. **Metabolic Issues:**
   - Type 2 diabetes and insulin resistance
2. **Cardiovascular Conditions:**
   - Heart disease, hypertension, and stroke
3. **Cancer:**
   - Higher risk of cancers such as breast, colon, and endometrial cancer

4. **Respiratory Problems:**
   ◦ Sleep apnea and asthma

5. **Orthopedic Issues:**
   ◦ Osteoarthritis from joint stress caused by excess weight

Mental Health Risks:

- **Depression and Anxiety:**
  ◦ Weight stigma and societal judgment can exacerbate emotional distress.

- **Eating Disorders:**
  ◦ These include emotional eating, binge eating, and restrictive dieting cycles.

Sobering Statistic:

Obesity contributes to approximately *2.8 million deaths worldwide* each year.

Obesity: A Systemic Problem

We live in a world that sets us up to fail:

1. **Marketing of Unhealthy Foods:**
   Processed, calorie-dense foods are often cheaper and more accessible than healthier alternatives.

2. **Sedentary Lifestyles:**
   Jobs, entertainment, and transportation increasingly require little physical activity.

3. **Diet Culture:**
   The societal pressure to achieve thinness often promotes unhealthy dieting, which can lead to weight cycling and worsen metabolic health.

How Is Obesity Treated?

There's no one-size-fits-all solution to obesity. Treatment must consider the individual's physical, emotional, and environmental circumstances.

1. Lifestyle Modifications:

- **Dietary Changes:**
  - Focus on balanced, nutrient-dense meals rather than restrictive dieting.
- **Physical Activity:**
  - Participate in regular exercise tailored to individual ability and interests.

2. Behavioral Therapy:

- Cognitive-behavioral therapy (CBT) can address emotional eating and self-sabotaging behaviors.

3. Medical Interventions:

- **Medication:** FDA-approved weight-loss medications may be considered for some individuals.
- **Bariatric Surgery:** Reserved for severe cases, it can help manage weight and associated health conditions.

4. Community Support:

- Free resources like Overeaters Anonymous (OA) or other virtual and in-person fellowship groups can provide a sense of belonging and shared understanding.

In the context of eating disorders, obesity intersects with disordered eating, societal stigma, and biases within the healthcare system, highlighting the need for compassion and a focus on both physical and mental health.

Moving forward

The focus for those navigating obesity, eating disorders, or both should be on fostering self-acceptance, prioritizing overall well-being, and building a sustainable, positive relationship with food and movement.

UNDERSTANDING THE ADDICTED BRAIN:
Why It Matters

When discussing eating disorders and disordered eating patterns, understanding how the brain functions in the context of food addiction is essential. Recognizing the neurological underpinnings of these behaviors can help remove stigma, provide clarity, and guide effective treatment strategies. The addicted brain doesn't simply operate on willpower. It involves complex neurobiological and psychological mechanisms that make overcoming these challenges more nuanced than many realize.

How Does an Addicted Brain Work, Specifically with Food?

1. **The Reward System Activation**
   The brain's reward system, particularly its response to highly palatable foods—those high in sugar, fat, and salt—plays a central role. Consuming these foods triggers the release of neurotransmitters like **dopamine**, which are linked to pleasure and reward. Over time, repeated exposure reinforces cravings and can lead to compulsive eating behaviors. This is why certain foods feel almost impossible to resist—they hijack the brain's reward pathways.

2. **Neurotransmitter Imbalances**
   In an addicted brain, the balance of key neurotransmitters, such as dopamine and serotonin, may be disrupted. **Dopamine dysregulation**, for instance, can amplify the brain's desire for

reward, creating a cycle of seeking out pleasurable foods even when the consequences are harmful.

3. **Hypothalamic Dysfunction**

   The hypothalamus, the part of the brain that regulates hunger, satiety, and energy balance, can be affected. Dysregulated signaling in this region may result in difficulty recognizing fullness or controlling food intake. This biological malfunction often contributes to overeating and disordered patterns.

4. **Sensory Processing**

   Heightened sensitivity to food cues—like the sight or smell of palatable foods—and an enhanced pleasure response can drive individuals to consume these foods despite negative outcomes. This sensory-driven urge highlights how the brain's hedonics—the pleasure you derive from food—can overpower logical decision-making.

5. **Neuroplasticity and Habit Formation**

   Chronic exposure to highly rewarding foods or overeating can reshape the brain's neural circuits. This **neuroplasticity** strengthens habits and cravings, reinforcing addictive behaviors while diminishing the brain's capacity for self-regulation and decision-making.

6. **Emotional Regulation and Stress Response**

   Emotional eating often stems from using food to cope with stress, anxiety, or other negative emotions. This reinforces the behavior, as the brain begins associating food with temporary relief. Over time, this pattern can hardwire a reliance on food as a coping mechanism.

Why Understanding This Matters

Understanding the addicted brain shifts the conversation from blame to science. These behaviors aren't a lack of willpower but rather the result of deeply ingrained neurobiological and psychological processes. This perspective is critical for:

- **Reducing Stigma:** Recognizing the biological basis helps foster compassion for individuals struggling with these challenges.
- **Targeting Treatment:** Treatment approaches can be tailored to address the specific mechanisms at play, from emotional regulation to neural rewiring.
- **Promoting Early Intervention:** Recognizing the signs of food addiction or disordered eating can lead to earlier, more effective support.

Treating Food Addiction and Disordered Eating

Effective treatment requires a multifaceted approach that addresses both the brain and the behaviors. Some key strategies include:

- **Behavioral Therapies:** Cognitive-behavioral therapy (CBT) or dialectical behavior therapy (DBT) can help individuals reframe thought patterns and develop healthier coping mechanisms.
- **Nutritional Counseling:** A registered dietitian can guide individuals toward balanced eating habits and help reduce reliance on trigger foods.
- **Emotional Support:** Addressing underlying emotional factors, such as trauma or stress, through therapy is vital for long-term recovery.
- **Medical and Psychiatric Support:** In some cases, medications may help regulate neurotransmitter imbalances or address co-occurring conditions like anxiety or depression.
- **Support Networks:** Joining communities, such as Overeaters Anonymous (OA) or other peer support groups, provides connection, accountability, and encouragement.

Moving Forward

Understanding the addicted brain underscores the complexity of food-related challenges and the importance of targeted, compassionate care. With the right tools, support, and awareness, individuals can reclaim their relationship with food and build healthier, more sustainable patterns—free from guilt and empowered by knowledge.

GOOD FOOD, BAD FOOD:
Shifting the Narrative

How should we think about food, and how can we model positive food behavior for ourselves and those around us? Whether you're working on your own relationship with food or teaching children about it, adopting a neutral, balanced approach is key. Let's break it down.

The Problem with *Good* and *Bad* Food

Why Food Labels Don't Work

Food is often labeled as good or bad, but this oversimplification ignores context. I recently heard a beautiful perspective about a donut that illustrates this point:

- **To one person,** a donut represents disaster, a step toward severe obesity and poor health.
- **To another,** it symbolizes a victory in recovery, a huge milestone after years of battling ED.
- **To someone else,** it's just a tasty snack they enjoy occasionally, without guilt.
- **For one struggling financially,** it may be the only meal they can afford that day.
- **For another person,** it's a small but much-needed source of joy during a difficult time.

The donut didn't change. The donut's *meaning* to the consumer did. Food itself is neutral; the value we assign to it is shaped by individual context.

Once you understand this, you can laugh at the idea of bad or good foods and move on.

How to Adopt a Neutral Approach to Food

Thinking neutrally about food means recognizing that no food, albeit donut or vegetable, has moral value. Here's how you can shift your mindset:

1. Be Present When Eating

- Focus on the sensory experience: taste, texture, and smell.
- Avoid judging yourself for your food choices in the moment.

2. Recognize Food as Fuel

- Food doesn't have power over you—you have power over it.
- Consider how your overall eating patterns, not just a single food choice, impact your health.

3. Practice Self-Compassion

- When negative thoughts about food arise, ask yourself: Would I say this to a friend? If not, don't say it to yourself

4. Ask, "How Does This Serve Me?"

- Evaluate food based on how it supports your health and well-being:
  - Does it provide energy?
  - Does it make you feel good physically or emotionally?
  - How will it make you feel after you eat it?

5. Challenge Food Messaging

- Question societal beliefs or diet fads.
- Remember, there's no one-size-fits-all when it comes to nutrition.

6. Seek Support if Needed

- If you're struggling to maintain a neutral perspective on food, consider reaching out to a dietitian or therapist for guidance.

Modeling Positive Food Behavior for Children

For those raising children, the stakes feel higher. You want to foster healthy attitudes toward food without passing on your own struggles. Here are actionable strategies:

1. Use Food as a Teaching Tool

Teach kids about food's benefits in a positive, engaging way:

- "This apple is full of fiber—fiber helps keep your body strong and healthy!"
- "Spinach has nutrients that make your brain super sharp."
- "Did you know that sugar gives us quick energy? But it's best paired with foods like nuts or cheese that help keep us full for longer."
- "What foods can give us long-lasting energy today?"
- "Some foods have added dyes to make them colorful. While they don't give our bodies the same kind of benefits as natural colors from fruits and vegetables, it's fun to learn about what's in our food and make choices that help us feel our best."

2. Involve Them in the Process

- Take them grocery shopping and let them pick out fruits and vegetables.
- Include them in meal prep to build excitement and ownership around healthy eating.

3. Avoid Using Food as a Tool

- Don't use food as a reward, bribe, or punishment.
- Call food by its name: ice cream is ice cream, *not a treat.*

4. Watch Your Own Behaviors

- Avoid weighing yourself in front of children or talking about food in negative ways.
- If kids see a scale, talk about weight in terms of strength: "Look how strong you are!"

5. Don't Stress About Food Phases

- Kids go through phases where they'll only eat certain foods. It's okay—it's part of parenting survival mode.

For Everyone—With or Without Kids

Whether or not you're a parent, modeling healthy eating behaviors benefits everyone. Here's what to focus on:

- Be flexible. Eating patterns don't have to be perfect to be healthy.
- Celebrate variety. Expose yourself to diverse foods and cuisines.
- Focus on balance. A donut isn't *bad*, just like a salad isn't a moral victory. They're both *just food*.

The Bottom Line

Food isn't the enemy. It's not *good*, *bad*, or anything else. It's just food. By approaching food neutrally and modeling positive behaviors, we can foster healthier, more balanced relationships with what we eat. Whether for ourselves or the next generation, this shift can break cycles of guilt, shame, and negativity and lead to a more empowered way of thinking about nutrition.

BODY TALK: PARTS 1 AND 2

Exploring the complex relationship between how we perceive our bodies, how we change them, and the psychological impacts of it all.

Part 1: All About Dysmorphia

Understanding Body Dysmorphic Disorder and Its Impact

What Is Body Dysmorphic Disorder (BDD)?

BDD is a mental health condition defined by an obsessive preoccupation with perceived physical flaws, often exaggerated or nonexistent, causing emotional distress and disrupting daily life.

Key Features of BDD:

- **Preoccupation with Appearance:**
  - Focused obsession with specific body parts or aspects—for example, skin, nose, hair, body size
  - Flaws minor or unnoticeable to others that dominate the individual's thoughts
- **Repetitive or Compulsive Behaviors:**
  - Mirror checking or avoiding mirrors entirely
  - Excessive grooming, reassurance-seeking, or comparison to others

- **Avoidance Behaviors:**
  - ◦ Skipping social events or activities due to fear of judgment
  - ◦ Withdrawal from work, school, or personal relationships
- **Emotional Distress:**
  - ◦ Intense feelings of shame, embarrassment, and low self-worth
  - ◦ Often coexists with anxiety, depression, or OCD
- **Impaired Insight:**
  - ◦ A belief that perceived flaws are severe and obvious to others despite evidence to the contrary

Why Understanding BDD Matters:

- **Not Vanity:** It's a serious mental health disorder with far-reaching effects on quality of life.
- **Impacts Relationships and Functioning:** Social isolation and emotional distress are experienced, and daily routines are impaired.
- **Increases Risk of Co-Occurring Disorders:** These include depression, anxiety, and OCD.

How Is BDD Treated?

- **Psychotherapy:**
  - ◦ *Cognitive-Behavioral Therapy (CBT):* Reframing distorted thoughts and reducing compulsive behaviors
  - ◦ *Exposure and Response Prevention (ERP):* Encouraging facing fears without engaging in rituals
- **Medication:**
  - ◦ *Selective Serotonin Reuptake Inhibitors (SSRIs):* Helping manage obsessive thoughts and compulsions

- **Lifestyle and Support:**
  - Building a network of support and prioritizing self-care over appearance
- **Avoid Harmful Behaviors:**
  - Discouraging unnecessary cosmetic surgeries or excessive social media use that can reinforce insecurities

Part 2: Changing and Rearranging

Exploring Appearance Changes and Their Impacts

How Rapid Changes Affect Body Image:

Physical changes—whether through weight loss, gain, or cosmetic interventions—can influence body image in profound ways.

Key Impacts of Rapid Changes:

1. **Unrealistic Expectations:**
   - Alterations may create false ideals of how one *should* look, perpetuating dissatisfaction with natural features.
2. **Increased Risk of Body Dysmorphia:**
   - Physical changes may heighten insecurities, especially in those predisposed to obsessive focus on appearance.
3. **Fragile Self-Worth:**
   - Reliance on external changes for validation can undermine intrinsic self-confidence.
4. **Identity Challenges:**
   - Young individuals may struggle to reconcile changes with their developing self-identity.
5. **Health Risks:**
   - Extreme dieting, excessive exercise, or surgeries can pose physical and emotional challenges.

The Role of Plastic Surgery:

While plastic surgery can address aesthetic concerns or health issues, it's essential to approach it cautiously, especially for younger individuals.

Key Considerations for Plastic Surgery:

1. **Physical Maturity:**
   - Wait until the body has fully matured, as this is crucial for predictable results.

2. **Emotional Readiness:**
   - Ensure motivations stem from personal desire or medical need, not societal pressure.

3. **Long-Term Implications:**
   - Consider the permanence of results and how they may change with aging.

4. **Psychological Risks:**
   - Dissatisfaction or regret can exacerbate existing insecurities.

5. **Financial Costs:**
   - Elective procedures are rarely covered by insurance and can be expensive.

Alternatives to Surgery:

1. Non-invasive treatments
2. Therapy or counseling to address body image concerns
3. Lifestyle changes focused on health and well-being over aesthetics

Final Thoughts

Our relationship with our bodies is complex, shaped by how we perceive ourselves internally and the changes we make externally. Body dysmorphic disorder (BDD) highlights how our minds can distort reality, fixating on flaws that often don't exist.

Pursuing rapid changes, like extreme weight shifts or cosmetic interventions, can deepen insecurities when driven by distorted self-perception. These issues are interconnected, and often, trying to fix external appearance without addressing internal thoughts leads to more dissatisfaction.

True growth comes from shifting focus—from striving for perfection to embracing inherent self-worth rooted in our unique strengths and value. By prioritizing mental health, self-acceptance, and emotional well-being, we can break free from the cycle of dissatisfaction and reclaim the energy and joy lost in the pursuit of unattainable ideals.

LOVE AND VALIDATION:
How Eating Disorders Intersect with Relationships

Our relationships, especially those shaped by love and validation, can be profoundly impacted by the vulnerabilities that accompany eating disorders. These vulnerabilities often make individuals more susceptible to unhealthy or dysfunctional partnerships.

This section explores the complex dynamics of love, validation, and relationships through the lens of eating disorders, highlighting the challenges, impacts, and possibilities for growth and healing.

The Vulnerable Heart: Why ED Can Make Love Risky

1. Seeking Validation to Fill a Void:

- **Low Self-Esteem:** Individuals with eating disorders often struggle with self-worth and may seek validation from partners to compensate for perceived inadequacies.
- **Body Image Struggles:** A distorted sense of self can lead to craving external affirmation, believing that love from others can fix internal battles.

2. Emotional Vulnerabilities:

- Eating disorders are often linked with underlying emotional issues like anxiety, depression, or trauma, which can make individuals more prone to forming relationships that exploit these insecurities.

- Emotional pain or unhealed wounds from past relationships or life experiences can make individuals gravitate toward unhealthy dynamics.

3. Codependency in Relationships:

- **Overreliance:** Individuals may develop patterns of excessive reliance on their partner for identity, approval, or validation, blurring boundaries and fostering unhealthy dynamics.
- **Desire to Please:** A tendency to put the partner's needs above their own can lead to enabling others or neglecting personal well-being.

4. Escapism Through Love:

- Romantic relationships can become a coping mechanism to avoid confronting the deeper pain or trauma tied to an eating disorder.
- While this may offer temporary distraction, it often perpetuates the cycle of both unhealthy eating behaviors and dysfunctional relationships.

The Impact of Dysfunctional Love

How Toxic Relationships Hurt Self-Worth

Toxic or abusive relationships significantly damage self-esteem and reinforce the negative thought patterns that accompany eating disorders. Key impacts include:

- **Emotional Abuse:** Constant criticism, gaslighting, or manipulation chips away at self-confidence and amplifies feelings of worthlessness.
- **Loss of Autonomy:** Controlling behaviors in a partner can erode independence, making the individual overly reliant on the abuser for validation.

- **Internalized Negativity:** Victims may begin to believe harmful messages, such as "I'm not good enough" or "I deserve this," further entrenching their insecurities.
- **The Trauma Bond:** Emotional attachments to abusive partners—fueled by cycles of conflict and reconciliation—create a deep, toxic dependency that's difficult to break.

The Bright Side: Romantic Relationships and Recovery

Can Committed Relationships Be a Source of Healing?

A committed relationship can be a double-edged sword for someone with an eating disorder. While it can amplify challenges, it also has the potential to be a powerful source of support and healing when approached healthily.

1. Foundations of Support

- A loving, empathetic partner can create a safe environment for open communication about struggles, triggers, and progress in recovery.
- Partners who prioritize patience and understanding foster a sense of security and reduce shame around the eating disorder.

2. Collaborative Growth

- Couples who work together to manage daily routines—like meal planning, social activities, and trigger management—strengthen their bond and reduce stress on the individual with ED.
- Committed relationships offer opportunities to build a support system, including seeking therapy together or establishing boundaries with external family influences.

3. Couples Counseling and Therapy

- Professional guidance can help address the unique challenges ED introduces into relationships, from intimacy struggles to differing recovery expectations.

- Therapy equips couples with tools to improve communication, manage triggers, and maintain a healthy dynamic.

The Happy Ending? A Balanced Perspective

Rewriting the Narrative of Love and Healing

While committed romantic relationships aren't a *cure* for eating disorders, they can play a pivotal role in the journey toward recovery—provided both partners commit to understanding, compassion, and collaboration.

Ultimately, recovery from an eating disorder requires the individual to build self-worth independent of external validation. Relationships can support this growth, but they can't replace the inner work necessary to heal. A healthy partnership complements this process, encouraging resilience and self-acceptance rather than dependency or dysfunction.

When approached with honesty, empathy, and shared accountability, love can indeed be transformative—not as a fix but as a foundation for mutual growth and healing.

RELIGIOUS ABUSE AND THE CHURCH:
Exploring the Intersection
with Eating Disorders

Before we dive in, here are two important notes:

1. **This may feel like a detour.** Perhaps the section on love and relationships felt the same way. If so, you're likely getting comfortable with these side roads by now. Still, it would be remiss of me not to include this topic and share the insights I've discovered, along with the hope I've found.

2. **I'm speaking from a Christian perspective; however, I firmly believe religious abuse transcends denominations, faiths, and traditions.** If necessary, adjust these reflections to fit your own understanding of God or spirituality.

While many find solace and support in their faith communities, it's crucial to recognize the harm that can arise when religious teachings or authority are misused. Religious abuse can profoundly impact mental health, self-worth, and physical well-being. Here, we'll explore its connection to eating disorders and outline steps for healing and spiritual growth.

What Is Religious Abuse?

Religious abuse refers to the misuse of spiritual beliefs, practices, or authority to manipulate, control, or harm individuals or groups. It can occur in organized religions, cults, or other spiritual communities and manifests in several ways:

Forms of Religious Abuse

- **Coercive Control:** Using fear, guilt, or shame to enforce strict rules and maintain obedience, often extending to relationships, finances, and personal decisions
- **Emotional Exploitation:** Manipulating followers' emotions to gain control or compliance, such as using guilt, fear, or shame to enforce loyalty or extract personal sacrifices
- **Psychological Harm:** Promoting rigid beliefs that instill fear, self-doubt, or guilt, leading to anxiety, shame, or feelings of unworthiness
- **Isolation:** Discouraging contact with the outside world to maintain control, making it difficult to seek help or alternative perspectives
- **Physical Harm:** Inflicting punishment, forced fasting, or labor under the guise of religious discipline
- **Sexual Exploitation:** Coercing followers into sexual favors or assaulting vulnerable individuals, often under the pretext of spiritual authority
- **Sexism and Gender Inequality:** Restricting women's rights, autonomy, or roles under the guise of religious doctrine. While some women may embrace these roles as an expression of faith, others experience these restrictions as oppressive, limiting their opportunities and autonomy.
- **Suppression of Critical Thinking:** Discouraging questioning, limiting information, and demanding unquestioning obedience

Impacts of Religious Abuse

Religious abuse can have long-lasting effects, including:

- **Trauma:** Symptoms of anxiety, depression, or PTSD
- **Loss of Trust:** Difficulty trusting others, authority figures, or even oneself
- **Identity Confusion:** Struggles with self-worth, purpose, and autonomy

- **Spiritual Disconnection:** Internal conflict about faith or religion
- **Family Strain or Separation:** Rigid beliefs and expectations can create distance or break families apart when values clash

The Connection Between Religious Abuse and Eating Disorders

Religious abuse and eating disorders can intersect in complex ways, especially in environments that promote control, shame, or rigid beliefs about morality and the body. While not a direct cause, religious abuse can exacerbate vulnerabilities that lead to disordered eating behaviors.

How Religious Abuse Contributes to Eating Disorders

1. **Strict Dietary Rules:**
   - Religious fasting or dietary restrictions can create unhealthy relationships with food. When unable to adhere to rigid expectations, individuals may develop guilt or shame, making them vulnerable to eating disorders.

2. **Idealized Beauty Standards:**
   - Thinness may be equated with moral virtue or self-discipline, fostering negative body image. Pressure to conform to these ideals can lead to restrictive dieting, over-exercising, or purging.

3. **Shame and Guilt:**
   - Teachings emphasizing sin or punishment can heighten feelings of inadequacy, and eating disorders may develop as coping mechanisms in response to these emotions.

4. **Manipulation and Control:**
   - Leaders or authority figures may dictate personal behaviors, including appearance and e*ating habits, creating a toxic environment that contributes to eating disorders.

5. **Religious Trauma Syndrome (RTS):**
   ◦ Trauma from religious abuse can manifest as anxiety, depression, or eating disorders as individuals struggle to reconcile faith with harmful experiences.

Healing from Religious Abuse: Rebuilding Faith and Self-Worth

Breaking free from religious abuse and fostering a healthier relationship with spirituality is a deeply personal process. Healing involves reclaiming autonomy, rediscovering self-worth, and rebuilding trust in oneself and others.

Steps Toward Healing

1. **Acknowledge the Abuse:**
   ◦ Recognize and validate your experiences without minimizing their impact. Abuse is never justified.

2. **Seek Support:**
   ◦ Reach out to trusted friends, family, or support groups. Professional therapy, particularly with someone experienced in religious trauma, can provide essential guidance.

3. **Question Harmful Beliefs:**
   ◦ Critically examine imposed beliefs that feel coercive or damaging. Explore alternative perspectives that align with your values.

4. **Reconnect with Spirituality:**
   ◦ Redefine your connection to the divine in a way that feels empowering and authentic. This may involve exploring other faith traditions or spiritual practices.

5. **Set Boundaries:**
   ◦ Limit or cut ties with toxic individuals or environments. Prioritize your safety and emotional well-being.

6. **Practice Self-Compassion:**
   ◦ Be gentle with yourself as you navigate the healing process. Accept that recovery takes time and includes a range of emotions.

7. **Build Healthy Relationships:**
   ◦ Surround yourself with supportive, nurturing people who respect your autonomy and worth.

8. **Engage in Self-Care:**
   ◦ Mindfulness, meditation, or other self-care practices can help you find inner peace and resilience.

9. **Educate Yourself:**
   ◦ Learn about religious trauma, manipulation, and strategies for recovery through books, workshops, or online resources.

10. **Celebrate Growth:**
    ◦ Recognize your progress and the courage it takes to rebuild your relationship with faith and yourself.

Moving Forward: Finding Peace in Faith

Healing from religious abuse doesn't mean abandoning faith—it means reclaiming it in a way that nurtures your well-being. Faith, at its best, should uplift, empower, and connect you with something greater than yourself. By separating the divine from the damage inflicted by humans, you can begin to cultivate a spirituality rooted in love, acceptance, and healing.

Let this journey remind you that faith and self-worth aren't mutually exclusive. You deserve both.

CHAPTER 16

ENLIGHTENMENT on DIVORCING ED

Quick Reference Page Guide

UNDERSTANDING TREATMENT:
Exploring Options for a Healthier You

The information shared here is based on personal experience and general research. While I've done my best to provide an overview of treatment options, availability and accessibility vary widely depending on location, provider, and individual circumstances.

If traditional treatment feels out of reach, there are often low-cost or no-cost alternatives to explore, such as community clinics, nonprofit organizations, or peer support groups. These options may not provide the full spectrum of care but can be an excellent starting point for finding support and making progress.

Always consult directly with providers for the most accurate and personalized information.

How are eating disorders treated?

Treating eating disorders requires a **multidisciplinary approach** that addresses the physical, emotional, and psychological aspects of recovery. Options vary greatly, and no single approach works for everyone.

Key Components of Treatment

1. **Psychotherapy: Rewiring Thought Patterns**
   - **Cognitive Behavioral Therapy (CBT):**
     - **Focus:** Identifying and changing disordered thoughts and behaviors around food, body image, and self-esteem

- □ **Approach:** Structured, goal-oriented sessions that challenge distorted thinking patterns and build healthier habits
  - ○ **Dialectical Behavior Therapy (DBT):**
    - □ **Focus:** Emotional regulation, distress tolerance, and mindfulness
    - □ **Approach:** Skills to manage emotional triggers related to disordered eating; group and individual therapy
  - ○ **Family-Based Therapy (FBT):**
    - □ **Focus:** Empowering families to support recovery, particularly effective for adolescents
    - □ **Approach:** Learning together to oversee meals, address triggers, and rebuild trust

2. **Nutritional Counseling: Food as Medicine**
   - ○ **Focus:** Restoring balanced eating habits and addressing fears or misconceptions about food
   - ○ **Approach:** Personalized plans that meet nutritional needs while addressing emotional barriers to food

3. **Medical Monitoring: Safeguarding Physical Health**
   - ○ **Focus:** Managing health risks like electrolyte imbalances, heart issues, and malnutrition
   - ○ **Approach:** Regular monitoring with labs, weight tracking if appropriate, and guidance on managing physical complications

4. **Medication: Supporting Mental Health**
   - ○ **Focus:** Treating co-occurring conditions like depression, anxiety, or OCD
   - ○ **Approach:** Often combined with therapy to stabilize mood and reduce obsessive thoughts

5. **Support Groups: Finding Connection**
   - ○ **Focus:** Peer-based support for shared experiences and accountability
   - ○ **Approach:** Virtual or in-person meetings, often following a 12-step program or an open-discussion model

Treatment Levels and Curriculum

1. **Residential Treatment:**
   - **Focus:** Immersive 24-hour care for individuals with severe eating disorders
   - **Approach:** Combines medical monitoring, psychotherapy (CBT, DBT), group therapy, and life-skills training

2. **Partial Hospitalization Programs:**
   - **Focus:** Day programs offering intensive care without overnight stays
   - **Approach:** Structured days of therapy, meal support, and group sessions designed to build independence

3. **Intensive Outpatient Programs:**
   - **Focus:** A few sessions per week for therapy and support, allowing individuals to integrate recovery into daily life
   - **Approach:** Emphasis on meal planning, emotional regulation, and relapse prevention

4. **Intensive Inpatient Programs:**
   - **Focus:** Short-term, highly focused treatment programs designed to address immediate and pressing needs. They typically last 7–14 days and provide a structured environment with concentrated support. This option is ideal for those who need significant help quickly but can't commit to long-term residential care.
   - **Approach:** Structured days complete with comprehensive assessments, nutritional rehabilitation, skills training, family involvement, and aftercare planning

5. **Outpatient Care:**
   - **Focus:** Regular check-ins with a therapist, dietitian, or medical professional
   - **Approach:** Sustains recovery by addressing ongoing challenges in a less intensive format

Low-Cost and No-Cost Treatment Options

As mentioned above, if traditional eating disorder treatment feels financially out of reach, there are numerous accessible and affordable alternatives. Here's a clear breakdown of some options:

1. **Community and Public Health Resources**
   ◦ **Community Clinics**: Many local clinics offer free or low-cost therapy, medical evaluations, and nutritional counseling.
   ◦ **Public Health Programs**: Government-funded health initiatives in your area may cover certain treatments or provide access to professionals for free or at reduced cost.

2. **Support from Nonprofits**
   ◦ **National Alliance for Eating Disorders**: Provides free helplines, live chat support, and toolkits to guide you toward affordable treatment options
   ◦ **Project HEAL**: Offers grants and scholarships specifically for individuals seeking treatment for eating disorders

3. **University and Educational Programs**
   ◦ **University Counseling Programs**: Graduate students in counseling or psychology programs often provide low-cost therapy under professional supervision.
   ◦ **Research Studies**: Some universities and institutions offer free treatment for participants in clinical studies related to eating disorders.

4. **Fellowship and Peer Support Groups**
   ◦ **Overeaters Anonymous (OA)**: Free, peer-led support based on the 12-step model, available both in person and online
   ◦ **Alcoholics Anonymous (AA)**: For individuals with co-occurring substance use, offering community and accountability

5. **Affordable Professional Services**
   - **Sliding Scale Providers**: Many therapists, dietitians, and other professionals adjust their rates based on income. Websites like Open Path Collective connect individuals with affordable mental health services.
   - **Teletherapy**: Such platforms often have lower fees than in-person services and sometimes offer payment plans.
6. **Virtual and Online Support Options**
   - **Virtual Support Groups**: Online communities, forums, and group sessions are often free or low-cost and provide connections and shared experiences.
   - **Nonprofit-Funded Apps and Platforms**: Some organizations offer free mobile apps or virtual tools to assist with tracking progress, mindfulness, or accessing support networks.

Making Recovery Accessible

Remember, recovery doesn't have to come with a high price tag. By exploring these low-cost and no-cost options, you can find the help and support you need to heal. Each step forward—no matter how small—brings you closer to a healthier, more balanced life.

Philosophies of Treatment: A Personalized Path

Treatment philosophies often guide how recovery is approached, and they vary based on the provider and the patient's needs. Here are the primary frameworks:

1. **Abstinence-Based Models**
   - **Focus:** Avoidance of *trigger foods* to reduce loss of control
   - **Strengths:** Providing structure for individuals overwhelmed by food-related choices

- ◦ **Limitations:** Can perpetuate fear of certain foods, hindering long-term recovery

2. **Intuitive Eating**
   - ◦ **Focus:** Encourages reconnecting with hunger and fullness cues
   - ◦ **Strengths:** Builds trust in the body and a more relaxed approach to food
   - ◦ **Limitations:** May be too unstructured for those early in recovery

3. **Mindfulness-Based Approaches**
   - ◦ **Focus:** Emphasizes awareness of food-related emotions and behaviors
   - ◦ **Strengths:** Reduces automatic or compulsive eating behaviors
   - ◦ **Limitations:** Requires a high level of emotional regulation to implement

4. **Trauma-Informed Care**
   - ◦ **Focus:** Acknowledges past trauma as a root cause of disordered eating
   - ◦ **Strengths:** Addresses the emotional pain underlying behaviors
   - ◦ **Limitations:** Can take longer to see behavioral improvements

5. **Adaptable Treatment:**
   - ◦ Recognizes that treatment isn't static
   - ◦ Encourages evolving approaches as patients progress, for example, starting with structured abstinence and moving to intuitive eating when ready

A Final Note

There's no single *perfect* path to recovery. What works for one person may not work for another, and that's okay. The key is finding an approach that meets your needs today, knowing it may evolve over time. Remember, recovery isn't just about weight or food—it's about reclaiming your time, joy, and sense of self. Wherever you are in your journey, help is available, and progress is always possible.

MEDICATION:
A Tool, Not a Cure

Medication can play a supporting role in eating disorder treatment by helping to manage co-occurring symptoms like anxiety, depression, or obsessive thoughts. These symptoms can often intensify disordered eating behaviors, and alleviating them may provide the mental clarity and stability needed to engage more effectively in therapy and other treatment approaches. However, medication alone isn't a cure; it's one piece of a larger puzzle.

Why I Don't Focus on Medications Here

While medication can be an important part of treatment for some, I've chosen not to focus on specific medications in this book. Why? Because simply naming or listing medications can be triggering. For individuals struggling with an eating disorder, hearing the name of a medication might lead to obsessive thoughts, compulsive research, or even misuse. These unintended consequences can derail the recovery journey rather than support it.

My goal is to foster a safe and empowering space for healing—one where information provides guidance, not harm. If you're curious about medication as part of your treatment, I encourage you to have an open and honest conversation with your healthcare provider. They can offer tailored recommendations based on your needs and ensure that any decisions about medication are made with careful consideration.

The Dangers of Medication Misuse for Eating Disorders

While medication can provide relief when used appropriately, it's essential to recognize the risks involved, particularly for individuals with eating disorders:

- **Potential for Misuse or Abuse:** Some medications, especially appetite suppressants, stimulant medications, or diuretics, can be misused by individuals with eating disorders in attempts to control weight or appetite. This can lead to dependency or serious health complications.
- **Triggering New Behaviors:** Medications prescribed for unrelated conditions may inadvertently trigger disordered eating behaviors, such as using certain drugs to suppress appetite or as a substitute for purging.
- **Physical Risks:** Misusing medications can lead to severe health consequences, including heart problems, electrolyte imbalances, liver or kidney damage, and increased risk of addiction.
- **Psychological Dependence:** Relying solely on medication to manage symptoms without addressing the underlying causes of the eating disorder can create a false sense of security and prevent deeper emotional healing.

Personalized Care Is Key

The decision to incorporate medication into a treatment plan is deeply personal and should always be made with guidance from a qualified healthcare provider. Everyone's journey is different, and what works for one person may not work—or may not be necessary—for another. Medication is just one of many tools available, and its effectiveness varies from individual to individual.

A Balanced Approach

Medication, when used, is most effective as part of a comprehensive treatment plan. This plan often includes therapy, nutritional counseling, and peer support, all working together to address the root causes of disordered eating. The focus should remain on building long-term skills, resilience, and self-compassion, with medication serving as a supportive tool rather than the central solution.

Empower Yourself Through Questions

If medication is recommended to you, don't be afraid to ask questions:

- What is the goal of this medication?
- How will it support my recovery?
- What are the potential benefits and side effects?
- Are there alternative approaches to addressing my symptoms?

Understanding the role of medication in your recovery can help you feel more confident and in control of your treatment plan.

No One Path Is the Only Path

Not everyone will use medication as part of their recovery, and that's okay. For some, it's a helpful tool; for others, it's not necessary. What matters most is finding a treatment approach that aligns with your needs, values, and goals. Remember, healing isn't one-size-fits-all. There are many paths to getting better, and each step forward, no matter how small, is a victory.

If you have questions or concerns about medication, don't hesitate to reach out to a trusted professional. Your journey is yours, and the best path is the one that feels right for you.

REHAB UNCOVERED:
How It Works and What to Expect

Rehabilitation, or rehab, is an intensive, structured approach to treating eating disorders, substance abuse, or other addictions. It provides individuals with the tools, support, and environment needed to begin their recovery journey. Here's a breakdown of what rehab entails and how to navigate the journey, including the challenges of relapse and post-rehab life.

How Does Inpatient Rehab Work?

Inpatient rehabilitation offers a safe, controlled setting for individuals to focus on recovery without external stressors or triggers. Here's what you can expect:

- **Structured Environment**: Scheduled meals, therapy sessions, group activities, and supervised downtime help establish healthy routines.
- **24-Hour Support**: Multidisciplinary teams—therapists, psychiatrists, nurses, dietitians—ensure round-the-clock care, addressing emotional, medical, and nutritional needs.
- **Medical Stabilization**: Many people with eating disorders require medical monitoring for complications like malnutrition, dehydration, or electrolyte imbalances.
- **Intensive Therapy**: Evidence-based approaches such as Cognitive Behavioral Therapy (CBT), Dialectical Behavior

Therapy (DBT), and Family-Based Therapy (FBT) target underlying issues and provide tools to change harmful behaviors.

- **Nutritional Rehabilitation**: Dietitians create individualized meal plans, guide eating habits, and help rebuild a healthy relationship with food.
- **Peer Connection**: Group therapy and peer support foster a sense of community, reducing feelings of isolation and shame.
- **Family Involvement**: Many programs involve loved ones to strengthen support systems and address family dynamics.
- **Transition Planning**: Before discharge, staff work with patients to create aftercare plans, including outpatient therapy, nutritional counseling, and support groups.

Checking In: Telling Loved Ones or Employers

Telling loved ones or employers about entering rehab can feel overwhelming. Here are tips for approaching the conversation:

1. **Choose the Right Moment**: Find a private, calm time when the other person can give you their full attention.
2. **Be Honest**: Share your struggles and the reasons you're seeking treatment. Transparency builds understanding.
3. **Reassure Them of Your Commitment**: Emphasize that rehab is a proactive step to improve your life and health.
4. **Ask for Support**: Specify the type of help you need from them, whether it's emotional encouragement, practical assistance, or time off work.
5. **Address Concerns**: Be prepared for questions or mixed reactions and respond with patience.
6. **Follow Up**: After the initial conversation, keep loved ones or employers updated about your plans and intended next steps.

I'm Out; Now What? Life After Rehab

Leaving rehab is a significant milestone, but it's just the beginning of recovery. Here's how to navigate life post-rehab:

- **Ongoing Therapy**: Continue with outpatient counseling to address new challenges and reinforce coping skills.
- **Support Systems**: Build a network of friends, family, or recovery peers who understand and respect your journey.
- **Nutritional Support**: Work with a dietitian to maintain healthy eating habits and manage potential triggers.
- **Self-Care Routines**: Prioritize activities like mindfulness, exercise, hobbies, and relaxation to support mental health.
- **Plan for Triggers**: Anticipate challenging situations and develop strategies to handle them proactively.
- **Gradual Exposure**: Ease back into social or food-related environments that once felt overwhelming.
- **Track Progress**: Regularly assess your goals and celebrate milestones, no matter how small.
- **Fellowship Programs**: Engage with Overeaters Anonymous (OA), Eating Disorders Anonymous (EDA), or similar programs for accountability and peer connection.

Relapse: Preparing for Challenges

Relapse doesn't mean failure—it's a common part of recovery. Recognizing potential triggers and preparing for them can help you navigate setbacks with resilience.

Causes of Relapse

1. **Stress**: High levels of stress, whether from work, relationships, or other pressures, can overwhelm coping mechanisms and lead to old patterns.

2. **Triggers**: Environmental cues, such as specific places, people, or routines, can evoke cravings and disordered behaviors.

3. **Overconfidence**: Believing you're cured or beyond the need for vigilance may result in risky behaviors or neglecting your recovery practices.

4. **Complacency**: Skipping therapy sessions, avoiding support systems, or letting healthy habits slide can create vulnerabilities over time.

5. **Life Events**: Major transitions like job loss, divorce, moving, pregnancy, or the death of a loved one can disrupt stability and lead to emotional turmoil, increasing relapse risk.

6. **Underlying Issues**: Unresolved trauma, co-occurring mental health disorders, or unaddressed emotional pain may resurface and challenge recovery.

7. **Positive Events**: Surprisingly, even celebrations like weddings, vacations, or promotions can trigger relapse, as individuals might let their guard down or feel tempted to celebrate in harmful ways.

Preventing Relapse

- **Stick to Aftercare**: Attend therapy, support groups, and medical check-ups.
- **Know Your Triggers**: Identify and avoid situations or people that jeopardize recovery.
- **Build Coping Skills**: Practice mindfulness, relaxation techniques, and healthy outlets for stress.
- **Set Boundaries**: Protect yourself from environments or relationships that undermine your recovery.
- **Stay Connected**: Regularly engage with your support network and recovery peers.

Handling Relapse

If relapse occurs, treat it as a learning opportunity:

- Reflect on what led to the setback.
- Revisit your treatment plan and seek professional guidance.
- Reaffirm your commitment to recovery.

Relapse and the Role of Intensive Programs

While earlier we discussed intensive inpatient programs as a starting point for recovery, these programs can also be an invaluable tool for addressing relapse. Think of them as a reset—a chance to stabilize, refocus, and recommit to your recovery journey.

If you've experienced a setback, a short-term intensive program can provide:

- Rapid medical and psychological assessments to address urgent needs and ensure safety
- Focused therapy sessions to explore underlying causes of relapse and develop new coping strategies
- Motivation and assistance, rebuilding confidence in your ability to move forward

You Can Do It: Setting Yourself Up for Success

Maximizing the benefits of rehab and sustaining progress requires intentional effort:

- **Engage Fully in Aftercare**: Follow through with all recommended treatments and appointments.
- **Foster a Positive Support Network**: Surround yourself with people who uplift and motivate you.
- **Commit to Healthy Habits**: Practice self-care, establish routines, and stay vigilant about your mental and physical health.

- **Embrace Growth**: View challenges as opportunities to strengthen your resilience.
- **Practice Gratitude**: Focus on your progress and celebrate victories, however small.

Remember, recovery is a lifelong journey. Each new day presents an opportunity to grow, heal, and create a life that reflects your resilience and self-worth.

FELLOWSHIP PROGRAMS:
A General Overview

Fellowship programs such as Alcoholics Anonymous (AA), Overeaters Anonymous (OA), and Eating Disorders Anonymous (EDA) share a common foundation of mutual support, structured recovery principles, and the power of community. These programs aren't specific to one type of addiction or disorder; instead, they offer adaptable frameworks for healing and personal growth. Here's a closer look at what they offer and how they work.

Why I Mention Fellowship Programs

In my own journey, fellowship programs provided an essential sense of connection and accountability. While these programs aren't for everyone, their core principles—acceptance, accountability, and service—can offer transformative insights into recovery. Whether you struggle with food, alcohol, or another challenge, exploring a fellowship program could be a valuable step toward healing.

If you're considering a fellowship program, start by visiting a meeting. You don't have to commit; just listen, observe, and see if it resonates with you. Recovery is deeply personal, and you deserve a path that works for you.

What Are Fellowship Programs?

Fellowship programs are peer-support groups designed to help individuals struggling with addiction, disordered eating, or related challenges. These groups are:

- **Nonprofessional**: Led by peers, not medical or mental health professionals
- **Inclusive**: Open to anyone with a desire to recover, regardless of age, education, or background
- **Widespread**: Held virtually and in person around the world, often multiple times a day
- **Self-Supporting**: Funded by voluntary contributions, with no fees or dues for membership

The Core Teachings of Fellowship Programs

1. **Acceptance**: Members begin by admitting they're powerless over their addiction and that their lives have become unmanageable. This step opens the door to transformation by acknowledging the need for help.
2. **Accountability**: Through personal inventory and amend-making, individuals take responsibility for their actions, identify harmful patterns, and work toward repairing relationships.
3. **Community Support**: Fellowship programs foster a sense of belonging through shared experiences, offering members mutual encouragement and understanding.
4. **Spiritual Growth**: The programs emphasize connecting with a higher power to inspire hope and guidance. This is interpreted differently by each person.
5. **Service to Others**: Helping others within the fellowship reinforces one's own recovery while contributing to the well-being of the community.

The Twelve Steps: A Framework for Recovery

The Twelve Steps, originating with Alcoholics Anonymous (AA), have become the backbone of many fellowship programs, offering a structured process for personal growth, healing, and recovery. These steps emphasize humility, accountability, and reliance on a higher power, forming a foundation for profound personal transformation.

Below are the Twelve Steps as written—to maintain integrity—in the Big Book of Alcoholics Anonymous.

We:

1. Admitted we were powerless over alcohol—that our lives had become unmanageable.
2. Came to believe that a Power greater than ourselves could restore us to sanity.
3. Made a decision to turn our will and our lives over to the care of God as we understood him.
4. Made a searching and fearless moral inventory of ourselves.
5. Admitted to God, to ourselves, and to another human being the exact nature of our wrongs.
6. Were entirely ready to have God remove all these defects of character.
7. Humbly asked Him to remove our shortcomings.
8. Made a list of all persons we'd harmed, and became willing to make amends to them all.
9. Made direct amends to such people wherever possible, except when to do so would injure them or others.
10. Continued to take personal inventory and, when we were wrong, promptly admitted it.
11. Sought through prayer and meditation to improve our conscious contact with God as we understood him, praying only for knowledge of His will for us and the power to carry that out.
12. Having had a spiritual awakening as the result of these steps, we tried to carry this message to alcoholics and to practice these principles in all our affairs.

The Twelve Steps are reprinted with gratitude from *Alcoholics Anonymous: The Story of How Many Thousands of Men and Women Have Recovered from Alcoholism*, 4th ed. (Alcoholics Anonymous World Services, 2001).

Specific Fellowship Programs

Alcoholics Anonymous (AA)

As the originator of the Twelve Steps, AA focuses on sobriety and overcoming alcohol addiction. Its spiritual principles and peer-support model have inspired numerous other programs, making it a cornerstone of addiction recovery.

Overeaters Anonymous (OA)

OA adapts the Twelve Steps to address compulsive eating and other disordered eating behaviors. Meetings focus on building a healthier relationship with food, body image, and emotions. Members find strength in sharing their journeys and adhering to structured recovery plans.

Eating Disorders Anonymous (EDA)

EDA provides a safe space for individuals recovering from any eating disorder, from binge eating to anorexia. It emphasizes balance, flexibility, and self-acceptance rather than rigid adherence to rules. Meetings often highlight tools for cultivating emotional resilience.

Why Are Fellowship Programs Effective?

1. **Peer Support**: Members share their experiences, creating a sense of connection and reducing feelings of isolation.
2. **Structured Path**: The Twelve Steps offer a clear, actionable roadmap to recovery.
3. **Accessibility**: Meetings are available worldwide, often for free.

4. **Anonymity**: A safe, private environment encourages honest sharing without judgment.

5. **Community Building**: Helping others reinforces recovery while fostering purpose and belonging.

Considerations for Fellowship Programs

- **Flexibility**: Interpretations of *higher power* can vary, making the programs accessible to people of all or no religious beliefs.
- **Self-Paced**: Members progress through the steps at their own speed, with guidance from sponsors or group members.
- **Supplementary Role**: Fellowship programs often work best when combined with therapy, medical care, and other recovery tools.

FELLOWSHIP FOR LOVED ONES:
Understanding Al-Anon and Alateen

Addiction and eating disorders don't just affect the individual; they ripple through families, friendships, and communities. Recognizing the toll these struggles take on loved ones, fellowship programs like Al-Anon and Alateen provide a space for those on the periphery of addiction to find support, understanding, and healing.

What Are Al-Anon and Alateen?

Al-Anon Family Groups are fellowships for individuals whose lives have been impacted by someone else's addiction. Whether it's a partner, parent, child, or friend, Al-Anon offers tools to navigate the complexities of loving someone with an addiction.

Alateen is a branch of Al-Anon specifically for teenagers affected by a loved one's substance use or addiction. It provides a safe space for young people to share their feelings, find support, and learn healthy coping mechanisms.

What Do Al-Anon and Alateen Teach?

1. **Acceptance and Powerlessness**: Members learn that they cannot control or cure their loved one's addiction. Accepting this truth is a crucial step in shifting focus from the addict to their own well-being.
2. **Detachment with Love**: Al-Anon teaches members to emotionally detach from their loved one's behavior without

abandoning them. This approach fosters compassion while maintaining healthy boundaries.

3. **Self-Care and Personal Growth**: Members are encouraged to prioritize their own mental, emotional, and physical health rather than solely focusing on their loved one's struggles.

4. **Support Through Shared Experience**: Meetings offer a judgment-free environment where individuals can share their experiences and gain insights from others facing similar challenges.

5. **Tools for Healthy Relationships**: Members develop communication skills, boundary-setting techniques, and strategies to maintain healthier interactions with their loved ones.

How Al-Anon and Alateen Work

- **Meetings**: Held in person and online, meetings provide a space for sharing stories, discussing literature, and exploring the principles of the Twelve Steps as they apply to the loved ones of addicts.
- **Anonymity**: Privacy and confidentiality are core principles, ensuring a safe environment for open sharing.
- **Accessibility**: Meetings are free to attend, with voluntary donations supporting the organization.

Why Consider Al-Anon or Alateen?

Living with or loving someone with an eating disorder or addiction can feel isolating and overwhelming. Al-Anon and Alateen help individuals to:

- Reclaim their sense of self and purpose.
- Break free from enabling behaviors or codependency.

- Build resilience and emotional strength.
- Find solace in knowing they're not alone.

A Final Note on Support for Loved Ones

Just as recovery is a journey for those directly facing addiction or eating disorders, it's also a process for those who love them. Al-Anon and Alateen provide a roadmap for healing, empowering individuals to find balance and peace regardless of their loved ones' choices.

If you're struggling with the impact of someone else's addiction, consider attending an Al-Anon or Alateen meeting. Much like other fellowship programs, these groups remind us that healing doesn't happen in isolation and that support is always within reach.

YOUR STORY MATTERS:
The Power of Sharing

Why Share?

Sharing your story can be an act of bravery, healing, and connection. Whether your journey involves overcoming an eating disorder, surviving trauma, or finding resilience, your story holds value—for you and for others. Here's why it matters:

- **Validation for Yourself:** Sharing allows you to honor your experiences and emotions, giving you the chance to own your truth without judgment.
- **Emotional Release:** Speaking your truth can unburden pent-up feelings, making space for healing and growth.
- **Building Connections:** Sharing fosters empathy and community. Knowing others relate to your journey can ease feelings of isolation.
- **Clarity and Reflection:** Narrating your story helps you process your experiences and recognize how they've shaped you.
- **Inspiration for Others:** Your story could offer hope and encouragement to someone struggling with their own challenges.

Where to Start

If you feel inspired to share, consider these steps to ensure your story feels authentic and meaningful:

- **Reflect:** Think about the pivotal moments in your journey and what lessons you'd like to convey.
- **Clarify Your Purpose:** Decide if your message is about hope, resilience, recovery, or breaking stigma. This will guide how you frame your story.
- **Choose Your Medium:** Whether you're writing, speaking, creating art, or making a video, choose the format that feels right for you.
- **Know Your Audience:** Tailor your story to resonate with those you want to reach, whether it's individuals who are struggling, their loved ones, or the general public.
- **Set Boundaries:** Share only what feels comfortable. Protect your privacy by leaving out details you're not ready to discuss.
- **Provide Resources:** If applicable, include information about tools, support systems, or programs that helped you; this could be a lifeline for someone else.
- **Prepare for Reactions:** Some will deeply connect with your story; others may not understand. Stay focused on the positive impact you're making.

A Note on Privacy

While sharing is empowering, it's important to respect the boundaries of others as well. In programs like AA, OA, or EDA, anonymity is foundational. If fellowship programs are part of your journey, speak to their principles or teachings generally, but avoid specifics about people, groups, or stories that aren't yours to tell. This ensures that you honor the safe spaces that helped your recovery.

Sharing With Intention

Sharing your journey isn't about the past. It's a way to shape the future, both yours and—potentially—someone else's.

Remember, you don't owe anyone your story. Share when and how it feels right for you.

Final Thoughts

While *Big-Boned* is a book, ED is just a chapter in my life. It's not my whole story, and I'm confident my story isn't finished yet. Yours isn't either.

Your story is worth telling. You never know who it might inspire—or how much it might heal you. One voice can make all the difference, and that voice could be yours.

LIVING IN THE GRAY:
A 10-Step Guide to Integrating ED Into Your Life

Living with an eating disorder is about finding balance, not living in extremes. *Living in the gray* means embracing flexibility while maintaining the tools and structures that support your well-being. This guide offers steps—actionable ones—to help you integrate ED and progress into your daily life, creating resilience and purpose along the way.

1. Identify Your Non-Negotiables

Set boundaries that prioritize your health and recovery. These non-negotiables help create a foundation for balanced living.

Examples of Non-Negotiables:

- Commit to three balanced meals a day.
- Say no to calorie-counting apps, restrictive diets, or triggering environments.
- Schedule regular therapy or support group meetings.

2. Create a Flexible Routine

Balance structure with adaptability to fit your evolving needs.

- Plan meals and activities to encourage consistency but allow room for adjustments.
- Be spontaneous: accept dinner invitations or skip a workout guilt-free.

- Ask yourself: ***What do I need today?*** Is this a day for abstinence—holding firm to boundaries—or is moderation the better path? Honor your needs without judgment.
- Track mental and emotional health, not just physical behaviors.

3. Build a Strong Support System

Surround yourself with people who respect and uplift your recovery.

Who to Include:

- Trusted friends and family members
- A therapist, dietitian, or recovery coach
- Peers from support groups like OA, EDA, or fellowship programs

4. Define Flexibility vs Boundaries

Determine when to be adaptable and when to hold firm in your recovery.

- **Boundaries:** Avoid restrictive dieting or behaviors linked to ED patterns.
- **Flexibility:** Experiment with new foods or participate in social eating situations as you feel ready.

Reevaluate boundaries periodically as your recovery progresses.

5. Create White Noise for ED

Quiet the intrusive ED voice by creating mental and emotional buffers.

How to Create White Noise:

- Distract yourself with an engaging activity like watching a movie or doing a puzzle.
- Practice grounding techniques like deep breathing or naming sensory details.
- Use music or nature sounds to soothe your mind and focus your energy elsewhere.

6. Build a Toolkit for Weak Moments

Prepare for life's challenges or weak moments with recovery tools personalized for you by you.

Toolkit Ideas:

- Comfort items: A journal, affirmations on notecards, or a stress ball
- Distraction tools: Engaging books, games, or playlist
- Support resources: A list of hotlines or contact info for your network of friends and therapists
- Nutritional support: Snacks or meal plans that align with your recovery

7. Practice Healthy Coping Skills

Develop a variety of techniques to handle stress and emotions without relying on old patterns.

- Journaling to process feelings.
- Mindfulness practices to center your thoughts.
- Physical activities like yoga, walking, or stretching to release tension.
- Creative outlets like writing, doodling, painting, or music. This will help channel emotions.

8. Reconnect With Joy

Focus on parts of life that bring happiness and meaning unrelated to food or appearance.

- Explore hobbies you enjoy or want to try.
- Spend time with people who make you feel valued.
- Pursue personal or professional goals that align with your values.

9. Celebrate Progress and Milestones

Acknowledge progress; even little steps forward are an achievement that matters.

Ways to Celebrate:

- Treat yourself to something meaningful, like a book, gadget, tickets to a show, or a new experience.
- Reflect on your journey through journaling, vision boarding, or capturing progress in photos or artwork.
- Invest in self-care, whether it's a massage, fitness class, or another self-maintenance moment.
- Mark the occasion with an activity you love: a hike, game night, day trip, or museum visit.
- Share your achievements with your support network, or celebrate quietly in your own way.

Celebration doesn't have to be extravagant. It's about honoring your efforts and being proud of how far you've come.

10. Commit to Lifelong Growth

Embrace recovery as an ongoing process of learning and evolving into your best self.

- Know that setbacks can also be opportunities to learn and grow.
- Seek out new strategies to strengthen your recovery.
- Value progress over perfection.

Living in the gray means embracing progress, not perfection, as you navigate the complexities of recovery. By integrating these steps into your life, you can build a sustainable foundation for growth, resilience, and joy.

Remember, recovery is a journey—one where every small victory brings you closer to living with balance and purpose. Keep going; you're worth it!

FINAL THOUGHTS:
Embracing the Gray

I know, I know, this feels like the hundredth time I've said it, but it's worth repeating: living in the gray means stepping away from the extremes and learning to find peace in the middle.

It's not about being perfect—spoiler alert: no one is—or magically having all the answers. If only! Instead, it's about creating a life that's no longer empty because you know you're enough. Think of it as finding your own rhythm. It's steady, sustainable—thank goodness—and uniquely yours.

What Does Living in the Gray Look Like?

- It's giving yourself permission to be human: to feel, to stumble, and to thrive in your own unique way.
- It's letting go of the mindset of all or nothing by embracing flexibility, celebrating progress, and using setbacks as opportunities.
- It's about finding fulfillment in the small, everyday moments and understanding that life's beauty often lies in the gray areas where certainty fades, and possibility begins.

Do You Know What You Need—Just for Today?

Recovery and balance aren't built in one grand moment. They're created in the daily decisions and small acts of self-care. Ask yourself:

- **What would feel nourishing today?** Whether it's a walk, a call to a friend, or a quiet moment to breathe, tune in to what you need right now.
- **What small step can I take toward my goals today?** Remember, even the tiniest effort moves you forward.
- **What can I let go of today?** Identify what's not serving you—self-criticism, unrealistic expectations, or lingering guilt—and release it with compassion.

Life in the Gray Is a Life of Freedom

Living in the gray means finding freedom:

- Freedom from the pressure to perform, prove, or perfect
- Freedom to choose joy over judgment and connection over comparison
- Freedom to live a life that aligns with your values, not someone else's standards

Your Journey, Your Way

Remember, balance doesn't mean everything is perfect all the time. It's about creating space for both the highs and the lows, learning to rest instead of quitting, and always coming back to what matters most.

As you move forward, carry this truth with you: you don't need to have it all figured out. All you need is the courage to take the next step—just for today. The rest will follow.

RESOURCES GUIDE FOR MENTAL HEALTH AND EATING DISORDERS

This guide provides a list of free hotlines, websites, and resources for mental health and eating disorders. While many of these services are based in the United States, there's a dedicated section of international resources below. Your well-being matters, and help is always available wherever you are.

Emergency Help (In the United States)

- **Suicide and Crisis Lifeline**
  - Call or text 988
  - Available 24 hours for anyone experiencing a mental health crisis or suicidal thoughts
- **Emergency Services**
  - Call 911 if you or someone else are in immediate danger.

Eating Disorder Support (In the United States)

- **National Eating Disorders Association (NEDA)**
  - Website: www.nationaleatingdisorders.org
  - Resources: Screening tools, education, and website referrals
- **National Alliance for Eating Disorders**
  - Helpline: Call 1-800-931-2237
  - Website: https://www.findedhelp.com/
  - Resources: Treatment center, practitioner directory, and specialized therapist helpline

- **National Association of Anorexia Nervosa and Associated Disorders (ANAD)**
  - Helpline: 1-888-375-7767
  - Website: https://anad.org/
  - Services: Free peer support and referrals for treatment

- **Project HEAL**
  - Website: www.theprojectheal.org
  - Services: Advocacy and access to treatment for individuals struggling with eating disorders

---

General Mental Health Support (In the United States)

- **Crisis Text Line**
  - Text HOME to 741741 for free, 24-hour support via text.
  - International services are available in Canada, the UK, and Ireland. See *International Resources* below.

- **Substance Abuse and Mental Health Services Administration (SAMHSA)**
  - Helpline: 1-800-662-HELP (4357)
  - Website: www.samhsa.gov
  - Services: Confidential referrals and information on mental health and substance abuse treatment

- **Mental Health America (MHA)**
  - Website: www.mhanational.org
  - Resources: Mental health screening tools, educational resources, and support

- **National Alliance on Mental Illness (NAMI)**
  - Helpline: 1-800-950-NAMI (6264)
  - Website: www.nami.org
  - Services: Peer support, education, and advocacy for mental health issues

---

International Resources

- **Befrienders Worldwide**
  - Website: www.befrienders.org
  - Services: Links to suicide prevention hotlines and mental health services in over forty countries
- **International Suicide Hotlines**
  - Website: www.opencounseling.com/suicide-hotlines
  - Services: Comprehensive list of helplines worldwide
- **Crisis Text Line (Global Services)**
  - Canada: Text CONNECT to 686868
  - UK: Text SHOUT to 85258
  - Ireland: Text HELLO to 50808

Additional Notes

If you're located outside the United States, local resources may vary. There are many international mental health organizations that likely offer free or low-cost support specific to your region. Always check for reputable organizations in your country, and don't hesitate to reach out. Help is closer than you think!

You Are Not Alone

Reaching out for help is a sign of strength. Whether you're struggling with an eating disorder, a mental health issue, or any other crisis, these resources are here to support you. Take the first step!

You are so worth it.

Would you do me a favor?

Thank you for reading!

I hope this journey resonated with you as deeply as it did with me while writing it. Your feedback plays a crucial role in helping others discover impactful, life-changing books. If you have a moment, I'd be so grateful if you could share your thoughts in a review on Amazon— whether it's a few words or more, every review makes a difference! Thank you for your support and for being part of this story.

With gratitude,

Lauren

ACKNOWLEDGMENTS

Some names and details have been changed to protect privacy, but you know who you are; thank you for being part of this story.

Allison, should I just write an entirely separate book documenting us? We've been through some life together. Your absolute self-confidence has taught me so much about what it means to be brought up correctly in a loving and open household. You're not just a name; you're a family, and your family is one the world should study and write books about for years to come—the defining example of remarkable self-worth and confidence through unending love. I'll always wanna be a Burkhalter when I grow up. To the best.

Dr. Bagwell, do you know how special you are? What bravery and compassion it took, as a professor, to confront a struggling student about her apparent eating disorder. Boy, did you have me pegged. But you didn't stop at simply noticing; you took action. You offered compassion when others turned a blind eye, and you presented alternatives when I felt like there were none. You saw me when I felt invisible, and your kindness changed the trajectory of my life. I'll never forget the courage it must have taken to reach out to me and the grace you showed in doing so. You were more than a professor; you were a lifeline. Thank you from the bottom of my heart.

Big, you'll find your letter in these pages. I'll never forget that homecoming night when, because of you, I realized the gig was up. Your honesty shattered me, but in the best way possible. You gave me the reality check of a lifetime, one I desperately needed but didn't know how to face on my own. Your tough love was exactly that—tough—but it was also wrapped in support and care that left a lasting impact on my life. You pushed me toward growth and healing in ways I'll always be grateful for, even if it wasn't easy at the time. You inspire me to this day!

Erin, you said two things in particular that have stuck with me. The first one was, "You need to love you like I love you." Those words were something I'd never heard before but desperately needed to. You also said, "If you don't like where you are, move. You're not a tree." Whoa. Revolutionary. Your insight and support have always been a guiding light. Now, as you help me shape my website, among many other things, your vision and talent are making my next chapter even brighter. Thank you for your part in *Big-Boned* and in so many parts of my life. I'm endlessly grateful for you.

Jackie, you've been telling me since day one to write a book. So here I am, and here she is. At long last! Your constant encouragement and steadfast friendship have kept me going. I'll never forget the day I called to tell you I was checking myself into RWC. I was so afraid, but your words gave me the courage to move forward. You've always had this rare gift of making me feel incredibly comfortable in my own skin, even in the moments when I couldn't recognize myself. Your love, wisdom, and unwavering belief in me have been a guiding light through the darkest times. I love your love. It's extraordinary, just like you. Thank you for being the kind of friend—and sister—who inspires, encourages, and always knows exactly what to say.

Jane, your love knows no bounds, and I'm endlessly grateful for it. You'll see your letter in *Big-Boned*, along with a handful of references to yourself and the incredible friendship we share. That handwritten letter remains one of the most extraordinary and life-altering gestures anyone has ever done for me. Hurtful at the time? Absolutely—but only because every word of it was true, and I needed to hear it. Your courage and honesty, rooted in love, pulled me closer to the truth I was afraid to face. You've given me more than friendship—you've given me accountability and grace. You can count on this: your friendship is one I'll never let go of again. Thank you for standing by me, even in the hardest moments.

Joy, how lucky I am to have found you to be my editor! Your time, energy, and the heart you poured into *Big-Boned* made it what it is today. Your incredible eye for detail, paired with your talent for seeing the bigger picture, is truly unmatched. You haven't only transformed my manuscript but also helped me grow as a writer in ways I never expected. Your encouragement and partnership throughout this journey are gifts I'll always cherish and never forget.

Kasey, you were the one. You found me—or did I find you? I can't remember. Regardless, your openness to seeking help for me was an unexpected depth of friendship that I'll never take for granted. I want to thank you for your unwavering support during one of the darkest chapters of my life. You led me down the initial path of recovery before any clinician or rehab could. No matter the miles or years in between, I'll always be here and think of you with immense gratitude and appreciation.

Kristen, I still can't believe I found you on Instagram through a hashtag. It feels like fate. You were such an integral part of my journey, helping me navigate one of the most pivotal moments in my story. Your unwavering support, thoughtful referrals, and judgment-free guidance made all the difference. I'm so grateful for you and the role you played.

Lisa, though I only found you halfway through writing this book, your guidance has already made a profound difference in my story. You've walked with me through the messy, tangled parts of life—family, food, abuse, and everything in between—with compassion, insight, and unwavering support. Your ability to help me face what I thought at times was too overwhelming has brought not only clarity to my writing but healing to my heart. Thank you for always being a safe space.

Lucas, my incredible, one-of-a-kind ex-boyfriend and forever friend. Our journey together certainly took some unexpected turns, but the bond we share has only grown stronger with time. Your unwavering support, honesty, and laughter have meant the world to me, and I am so grateful for the unique connection we have. Thank you for being a constant in my life, for embracing me in all my chaos, and for reminding me that love—no matter the form—does endure. I'm beyond lucky to have you in my corner, always.

Lynne, thank you not just for your guidance through OA but also for the kindred friendship that shaped my journey. Even though we don't see a lot of each other now and didn't always see eye to eye, you remain a reflection of my recovery. You reached the gray before me, and your example reminded me that it's possible to get there.

Patsy and RWC Staff, I found shade in the sweltering Texas heat because of you. I truly believe I wouldn't be here today—or have the privilege of being a parent—if it weren't for the care, compassion, and guidance I found at RWC. You didn't just save my life; you gave me tools to rebuild it. For that, I'll forever be in your debt.

Rehab Roommates, I'll never forget our journey together—the best of times and the worst of times. In those raw and vulnerable moments, your love, grace, and understanding became a lifeline. We leaned on each other, learned from one another, and found strength in our shared struggles. Though we seldom get to catch up, I think of you a lot and pray that you're all in good places with your recovery. The work we did together was hard, but it was meaningful, and I'm forever grateful we shared it together.

Staff and Surgeon of my Bariatric Clinic in Atlanta, I'm profoundly grateful for the life-changing tools you provide to those of us who need care beyond the standard approaches. The work you do creates not just anatomical change but opportunities for complete transformation—physically, emotionally, and beyond. You empower people like me to reclaim our health and lives in ways we never thought possible.

To everyone else, you know who you are. If we've shared any piece of history together, you hold a special place in my heart. There are so many incredible friends I haven't named here—people I've laughed with, cried with, and grown alongside. Please know that I cherish those moments and the bond we share. Thank you for caring about me, for showing up, and for supporting me in this journey of evolution and continued self-discovery. I'm grateful for you.

ABOUT THE AUTHOR

Lauren Hankins, corporate healthcare ladder-climber, lives in Georgia with her husband, Matthew, their three children, a dog named Delphina, a vegetable garden, and hopefully chickens sometime soon—and a cow, if Matthew would oblige. *Big-Boned* is her first book.

SOURCES

The sources I used throughout *Big Boned* are listed here under their respective chapters or under the ENLIGHTENMENT chapters, where they're directly referenced. Every effort has been made to credit original works where they're used; however, these references may also inform broader themes and discussions elsewhere in the text.

NOTES

About Ed

Jenni Schaefer and Thom Rutledge, *Life Without Ed: How One Woman Declared Independence from Her Eating Disorder and How You Can Too* (New York: McGraw Hill, 2003).

About the Stories in This Book

Emily Swaim, medically reviewed by Matthew Boland, PhD, "Emotions Can Affect Your Memory—Here's Why and How to Handle It," *Healthline*, July 10, 2022, https://www.healthline.com/health/mental-health/how-does-emotion-impact-memory#takeaway.

INTRODUCTION | TRIGGER WARNING

Merriam-Webster.com Dictionary, s.v. "addiction," accessed November 1, 2024, https://www.merriam-webster.com/dictionary/addiction.

"Are Eating Disorders a Type of Addiction?" *Addictions.com*, September 5, 2024, https://www.addictions.com/blog/are-eating-disorders-a-type-of-addiction/.

"Addiction," *Cleveland Clinic*, March 16, 2023, https://my.clevelandclinic.org/health/diseases/6407-addiction.

"Obesity and Overweight," *World Health Organization*, March 1, 2024, https://www.who.int/news-room/fact-sheets/detail/obesity-and-overweight#:~:text=Obesity%20is%20a%20chronic%20complex,the%20risk%20of%20certain%20cancers.

"The Disease of an Eating Disorder Is Not a Choice," *Seeds of Hope Eating Disorder Treatment*, June 11, 2021, https://www.seedsofhopesupport.com/the-disease-of-an-eating-disorder-is-not-a-choice/.

"What To Say to Someone with an Eating Disorder," *Cityscape Counseling*, accessed June 1, 2024, https://www.cityscapecounseling.com/post/talking-to-someone-with-eating-disorder/.

DISCOVERING ED

development of an eating disorder | early influences

CHAPTER 1 | THERE IS NO CURE

Grant, J. E., M. N. Potenza, A. Weinstein, and D. A. Gorelick. "Introduction to Behavioral Addictions." *American Journal of Drug and Alcohol Abuse* 36, no. 5 (2010): 233–41. https://doi.org/10.3109/00952990.2010.491884.

April Smith, "Eating Disorders Are the Most Lethal Mental Health Conditions – Reconnecting with Internal Body Sensations Can Help Reduce Self-Harm," *The Conversation*, January 31, 2024, https://theconversation.com/eating-disorders-are-the-most-lethal-mental-health-conditions-reconnecting-with-internal-body-sensations-can-help-reduce-self-harm-218079#:~:text=Did%20you%20know%20that%20anorexia,to%20starvation%2C%20but%20from%20suicide.

Lorenzo Lucchetti, medically reviewed by Nicole Washington, DO, MPH, "Anorexia Fatality: Statistics, Causes, and More," *Medical News Today*, July 24, 2024, https://www.medicalnewstoday.com/articles/how-many-people-die-from-anorexia.

"Report: Economic Costs of Eating Disorders," *Harvard T. H. Chan School of Public Health*, STRIPED, in collaboration with the Academy for Eating Disorders (AED) and Deloitte Access Economics, accessed June 1, 2024, https://www.hsph.harvard.edu/striped/report-economic-costs-of-eating-disorders/.

Steven Zauderer, "43 Eating Disorder Statistics & Prevalence," *Cross River Therapy*, September 19, 2023, https://www.crossrivertherapy.com/eating-disorder-statistics#:~:text=Eating%20disorders%20affect%20at%20least,population%20suffers%20from%20eating%20disorders.

S. Pai Raikar, "Food Pyramid," *Encyclopedia Britannica*, October 19, 2024, https://www.britannica.com/science/food-pyramid.

Azeen Ghorayshi, "Too Big to Chug: How Our Sodas Got So Huge," *Mother Jones*, June 25, 2012, https://www.motherjones.com/media/2012/06/supersize-biggest-sodas-mcdonalds-big-gulp-chart/#:~:text=1993:%20McDonald's%20launches%20another%20summer,of%20its%20new%20Value%20Meals.

Ann F. La Berge, "How the Ideology of Low Fat Conquered America," *Journal of the History of Medicine and Allied Sciences* 63, no. 2 (April 2008): 139–177, https://doi.org/10.1093/jhmas/jrn001.

Obesity

Karen Fittall, "The History of WeightWatchers," *WeightWatchers*, April 23, 2023, https://www.weightwatchers.com/au/blog/weight-loss/ww-through-decades#:~:text=But%20don't%20just%20take,fad%20diets%20that%20never%20worked.

Grace Niewijk, "Research Shows GLP-1 Receptor Agonist Drugs Are Effective but Come with Complex Concerns," *At The Forefront | The University of Chicago Medicine*, May 30, 2024, https://www.uchicagomedicine.org/forefront/research-and-discoveries-articles/research-on-glp-1-drugs.

W. Latif, K. J. Lambrinos, P. Patel, et al., "Compare and Contrast the Glucagon-Like Peptide-1 Receptor Agonists (GLP1RAs)" [Updated February 25, 2024], in *StatPearls [Internet]* (Treasure Island, FL: StatPearls Publishing, 2024), https://www.ncbi.nlm.nih.gov/books/NBK572151/.

J. Holst, "Incretin Hormones and the Satiation Signal," *International Journal of Obesity* 37 (2013): 1161–1168, https://doi.org/10.1038/ijo.2012.208.

Eating Disorders

Jessica Berens, MS, RD, LDN, "Intuitive Eating & Eating Disorders: Principles, Treatment Challenges & 3 Ways to Implement," *The Renfrew Center / First in Eating Disorders*, 2022, https://renfrewcenter.com/intuitive-eating-eating-disorders-principles-treatment-challenges-3-ways-to-implement/.

K. A. Halmi, W. S. Agras, J. Mitchell, et al., "Relapse Predictors of Patients With Bulimia Nervosa Who Achieved Abstinence Through Cognitive Behavioral Therapy," *Archives of General Psychiatry* 59, no. 12 (2002): 1105–1109, https://doi.org/10.1001/archpsyc.59.12.1105.

Rachael Hartley, "Intuitive Eating in Eating Disorder Recovery," *Rachael Hartley Nutrition*, 2018, https://www.rachaelhartleynutrition.com/blog/intuitive-eating-in-eating-disorder-recovery.

"A Family Guide to the Neurobiology of Eating Disorders," *F.E.A.S.T. Family Guide Series, Puzzling Symptoms: Eating Disorders and the Brain* (2012): 1–5, accessed June 10, 2024, https://eatingdisorders.ucsd.edu/dl/docs/feast-neurobiologyofed.pdf.

G. K. W. Frank, M. E. Shott, and M. C. DeGuzman, "The Neurobiology of Eating Disorders," *Child and Adolescent Psychiatric Clinics of North America* 28, no. 4 (October 2019): 629–640, https://doi.org/10.1016/j.chc.2019.05.007.

Jillian Lampert, PhD, MPH, RD, LD, FAED, "The Impact of Eating Disorders on the Brain and Academic Performance," *The Emily Program*, June 26, 2024, https://emilyprogram.com/blog/eating-disorders-and-the-brain/.

James Greenblatt, MD, "Addicted to Food: My Dopamine Made Me Do It," *Psychiatry Redefined*, August 28, 2020, https://www.psychiatryredefined.org/addicted-to-food-my-dopamine-made-me-do-it/.

Sober.com, "Why Does AA Teach Total Abstinence?" *Sober*, 2024, https://sober.com/why-does-aa-teach-total-abstinence/#:~:text=Acceptance%20is%20Key&text=Therefore%2C%20abstinence%20becomes%20the%20only,begin%20their%20journey%20of%20recovery.

CHAPTER 2 | GROWING UP BIG-BONED

Peninsula Health Center, Contributor, "How Perfectionism Leads to Substance Abuse," *Peninsula Health Center*, January 1, 2024, https://

peninsulahealthcenter.com/2024/07/23/how-perfectionism-leads-to-substance-abuse/#:~:text=With%20perfectionism%2C%20people%20have%20unrealistic,often%20lead%20to%20substance%20abuse.

Erika Krull, MSEd, LMHPL, and reviewed by Emily Guarnotta, PsyD, "How Are Perfectionism and Addiction Connected?" *GoodRx.com*, GoodRx, July 21, 2021, https://www.goodrx.com/conditions/substance-use-disorder/perfectionism-and-addiction.

K. Schaumberg, E. Welch, L. Breithaupt, C. Hübel, J. H. Baker, M. A. Munn-Chernoff, Z. Yilmaz, et al., "The Science Behind the Academy for Eating Disorders' Nine Truths About Eating Disorders," *European Eating Disorders Review* 25, no. 6 (November 2017): 432–450, https://doi.org/10.1002/erv.2553.

CHAPTER 3 | LOVE LETTER TO ASHLEY

Cynthia Bulik, PhD, FAED, produced in collaboration with the Academy for Eating Disorders, "'Nine Truths' About Eating Disorders," *Academy for Eating Disorders (AED)*, January 1, 2014, https://www.aedweb.org/resources/publications/nine-truths.

Walter Vandereycken and Ina Van Humbeeck, "Denial and Concealment of Eating Disorders: A Retrospective Survey," *European Eating Disorders Review* (2008), accessed June 10, 2024, https://doi.org/10.1002/erv.857.

CHAPTER 4 | RIP BELLE

Vanessa Rissetto, MS, RD, CDN, and medically reviewed by Jillian Kubala, MS, RD, "Why Fad Diets Don't Work, Plus 7 Tips for Sustainable, Healthy Eating," *Healthline*, February 7, 2022, https://www.healthline.com/health/why-fad-diets-dont-work#why-fad-diets-dont-work.

DATING ED
living to eat | in the trenches of an eating disorder

CHAPTER 5 | GOODBYE BOOBS, HELLO BULIMIA

Las Vegas Liposuction, Contributor, "How We Can Navigate Mental Health Considerations in Cosmetic Surgery," *Las Vegas Liposuction Specialty Clinic*, January 1, 2024, https://www.vegasliposuction.com/how-we-can-navigate-mental-health-considerations-in-cosmetic-surgery/.

CHAPTER 6 | SKINNY PRIVILEGE

Thigh Society, Contributor, "Navigating Thin Privilege: What It Is and Why It Matters," *Thigh Society*, November 30, 2023, https://www.thighsociety.com/blogs/ts-blog/what-is-thin-privilege?srsltid=AfmBOorRsCBJhJla5SpAVyXVyREWusj0kJGRkXXIO_s1wsk2WViasanH.

J. Lamoure, J. Stovel, and P. Chandarana, "Probable Topiramate-Induced Hemiparesis," *Canadian Journal of Hospital Pharmacy* 63, no. 3 (May 2010): 233–235, https://doi.org/10.4212/cjhp.v63i3.919.

L. B. Finer, "Trends in Premarital Sex in the United States, 1954–2003," *Public Health Reports* 122, no. 1 (January–February 2007): 73–78, https://doi.org/10.1177/003335490712200110.

CHAPTER 7 | LOOKING FOR LOVE IN ALL THE WRONG PLACES

J. Momeñe, A. Estévez, M. D. Griffiths, P. Macía, M. Herrero, L. Olave, and I. Iruarrizaga, "Eating Disorders and Intimate Partner Violence: The Influence of Fear of Loneliness and Social Withdrawal," *Nutrients* 14, no. 13 (June 24, 2022): 2611, https://doi.org/10.3390/nu14132611.

Hertfordshire Domestic Abuse Helpline, Contributor, "Domestic Abuse, Eating Disorders and What Links the Two," *Hertfordshire Domestic Abuse Helpline*, June 22, 2021, https://www.

hertsdomesticabusehelpline.org/blogspot-domestic-abuse/2021/6/22/
domestic-abuse-eating-disorders-and-what-links-the-two.

CHAPTER 8 | SETTLING DOWN AND SAYING I DO

". . . yucky love stuff." *My Best Friend's Wedding,* directed by P. J. Hogan (Columbia Pictures, 1997).

First Christian Church, Contributor, "The Dark Side of Theological Fearmongering: Unpacking Hell Houses," *First Christian Church | Theology Matters,* October 23, 2023, https://www.fccsullivan.org/pastors-reflections/2023/10/16/the-dark-side-of-theological-fearmongering-unpacking-hell-houses.

The University of Queensland, Contributor, "Where Are Memories Stored in the Brain?" *The University of Queensland Australia,* https://doi.org/ABN: 63 942 912 684 CRICOS: 00025B TEQSA: PRV12080.

BGEA Staff, "What Does 'Slain in the Spirit' Mean?" *Billy Graham Evangelistic Association,* June 1, 2004, https://billygraham.org/answer/is-the-experience-of-what-some-call-being/.

Caleb Mathis, "How I Got Over My Church Hurt (Without Losing My Faith)," *Crossroads Church,* 2024, https://www.crossroads.net/media/articles/how-i-got-over-my-church-hurt-without-losing-my-faith#:~:text=So%20when%20what%20we%20experience,to%20that%20in%20a%20minute.

CHAPTER 9 | AHA! ABSTINENCE (my holy shit moment)

Gretchen Rubin, *Better Than Before: Mastering the Habits of Our Everyday Lives* (New York: Crown Publishers, 2015).

DIVORCING ED
eating to live | getting to the gray

Chapter 10 | FINDING SHADE IN THE TEXAS HEAT

STANDS4 LLC, "Never Say Never Lyrics," *Lyrics.com*, 2024, accessed December 1, 2024, https://www.lyrics.com/lyric/23800329/Justin+Bieber/Never+Say+Never.

Stephanie Pappas, "Group Therapy Is as Effective as Individual Therapy and More Efficient. Here's How to Do It Successfully," *American Psychological Association* 54, no. 2 (March 1, 2023), https://www.apa.org/monitor/2023/03/continuing-education-group-therapy.

G. A. Williams, D. L. Hudson, B. L. Whisenhunt, and J. H. Crowther, "An Examination of Body Tracing Among Women with High Body Dissatisfaction," *Body Image* 11, no. 4 (September 2014): 346–349, https://doi.org/10.1016/j.bodyim.2014.05.005.

A. S. Hartmann, E. Naumann, S. Vocks, J. Svaldi, and J. Werthmann, "Body Exposure, Its Forms of Delivery and Potentially Associated Working Mechanisms: How to Move the Field Forward," *Clinical Psychology in Europe* 3, no. 3 (September 30, 2021): e3813, https://doi.org/10.32872/cpe.3813.

B. Konkolÿ Thege, C. Petroll, C. Rivas, and S. Scholtens, "The Effectiveness of Family Constellation Therapy in Improving Mental Health: A Systematic Review," *Family Process* 60, no. 2 (June 2021): 409–423, https://doi.org/10.1111/famp.12636.

Albert Wong, PhD, "Unlocking the Hidden Trauma in the Family System: An Introduction to Family Constellation Work," *Somatopia*, March 4, 2023, https://www.somatopia.com/blog/unlocking-the-hidden-trauma-in-the-family-system-an-introduction-to-family-constellation-work.

H. Orkibi and R. Feniger-Schaal, "Integrative Systematic Review of Psychodrama Psychotherapy Research: Trends and Methodological Implications," *PLoS One* 14, no. 2 (February 19, 2019): e0212575, https://doi.org/10.1371/journal.pone.0212575.

Lisa Cleary, LMSW, "Therapy Session," discussion on therapy session types and intensive treatment for eating disorders, October 22, 2024.

J. B. Nelson, "Mindful Eating: The Art of Presence While You Eat," *Diabetes Spectrum* 30, no. 3 (August 2017): 171–174, https://doi.org/10.2337/ds17-0015.

Ellie Swain, medically reviewed by Annamarie Coy, BA, ICPR, MATS, "Sobriety Milestones (AA Chips)," *Alcohol Rehab Help*, September 15, 2023, https://alcoholrehabhelp.org/treatment/alcoholics-anonymous/chips/.

Steven J. Chen, accessed November 1, 2024, https://www.stevenjchen.com/.

CHAPTER 11 | RELAPSE AFTER REHAB

Nelson (author of *There's a Hole in My Sidewalk: The Romance of Self-Discovery*), "Addiction Pothole Story," *Steven J. Chen, PhD | Licensed Psychologist*, June 29, 2021, https://www.stevenjchen.com/addiction-pothole-story/#:~:text=He%20walks%20down%20the%20road,identify%20the%20steps%20for%20change.

Full Circle, Contributor, "Why 90 Meetings in 90 Days?" *Full Circle*, February 4, 2023, https://fullcircleprogram.com/blog?title=why-90-meetings-in-90-days/.

Nicole Avena, Ph.D., and medically reviewed by Michelle Quirk, "Sugar Is in Almost Everything—Hiding in Plain Sight," *Psychology Today*, February 6, 2024, https://www.psychologytoday.com/us/blog/food-junkie/202401/sugar-is-in-almost-everything-hiding-in-plain-sight#:~:text=Many%20foods%20that%20appear%20to,dependence%20that%20much%20more%20challenging.

Katie Thomson, MS, RD, "The Truth About Sugar in Baby Food," *Square Baby*, 2024, https://squarebaby.com/blogs/news/baby-food-all-about-sugar?srsltid=AfmBOoqN0xjTW2x45ljD-SvQnc92ARKabNPgwmJYkDlkb5lfk_RV1mkW.

Lauren Panoff, MPH, RD, and medically reviewed by Jillian Kubala, MS, RD, "Are Protein Bars Good for You?" *Healthline*, March 16, 2020, https://www.healthline.com/nutrition/are-protein-bars-good-for-you.

Nick Desimone, "Why Supermarket Bread in the US Is So Terrible, According to Reddit," *Mashed*, December 10, 2021, https://www.mashed.com/703871/why-supermarket-bread-in-the-us-is-so-terrible-according-to-reddit/.

Pedersons Farms, Contributor, "Does Bacon Have Sugar?" *Pedersons Farms*, January 1, 2024, https://pedersonsfarms.com/blogs/blog/does-bacon-have-sugar?srsltid=AfmBOooKY0H8-eb8hrGDfQh6DDFCgVpm-nethMdcx1SJnTIWFtrviDYA.

CDC.gov, Contributor, "Spotting Hidden Sugars in Everyday Foods," *CDC | Diabetes*, June 17, 2024, https://www.cdc.gov/diabetes/healthy-eating/spotting-hidden-sugars-in-everyday-foods.html.

Meryl Rowin, "The Upshot: It Isn't Easy to Figure Out Which Foods Contain Sugar," *The New York Times*, May 21, 2016, https://www.nytimes.com/2016/05/22/upshot/it-isnt-easy-to-figure-out-which-foods-contain-sugar.html.

Robert H. Lustig, "Ultraprocessed Food: Addictive, Toxic, and Ready for Regulation," *Nutrients* 12, no. 11 (November 5, 2020): 3401, https://doi.org/10.3390/nu12113401.

E. Martínez Steele, L. G. Baraldi, M. L. Louzada, J. C. Moubarac, D. Mozaffarian, and C. A. Monteiro, "Ultra-Processed Foods and Added Sugars in the US Diet: Evidence from a Nationally Representative Cross-Sectional Study," *BMJ Open* 6, no. 3 (March 9, 2016): e009892, https://doi.org/10.1136/bmjopen-2015-009892.

Carrie Durward, Ph.D., RD, and Keshele Stevens, "Added Sugars: What You Need to Know," *Utah State University Extension*, January 1, 2024, https://extension.usu.edu/nutrition/research/added-sugars-what-you-need-to-know?.

K. C. Berridge, C. Y. Ho, J. M. Richard, and A. G. DiFeliceantonio, "The Tempted Brain Eats: Pleasure and Desire Circuits in Obesity and Eating Disorders," *Brain Research* 1350 (September 2, 2010): 43–64, https://doi.org/10.1016/j.brainres.2010.04.003.

C. A. Roberto, C. M. Grilo, R. M. Masheb, and M. A. White, "Binge Eating, Purging, or Both: Eating Disorder Psychopathology Findings from an Internet Community Survey," *International Journal of Eating Disorders* 43, no. 8 (December 2010): 724–731, https://doi.org/10.1002/eat.20770.

W. Vanderplasschen, K. Colpaert, M. Autrique, R. C. Rapp, S. Pearce, E. Broekaert, and S. Vandevelde, "Therapeutic Communities for Addictions: A Review of Their Effectiveness from a Recovery-Oriented Perspective," *The Scientific World Journal* 2013 (January 15, 2013): 427817, https://doi.org/10.1155/2013/427817.

CHAPTER 12 | BECOMING A BARI BABE

D. Cucinotta and M. Vanelli, "WHO Declares COVID-19 a Pandemic," *Acta Biomedica* 91, no. 1 (March 19, 2020): 157–160, https://doi.org/10.23750/abm.v91i1.9397.

Callum Borchers, "Hotel That Hosted Biogen Gathering Tied to Coronavirus Outbreak Will Close Temporarily," *WBUR*, March 12, 2020, https://www.wbur. org/news/2020/03/12/marriott-hotel-closed-biogen-coronavirus.

C. K. H. Wong et al., "From Social Network to Peer Support Network: Opportunities to Explore Mechanisms of Online Peer Support for Mental Health," *JMIR Mental Health* 10 (February 28, 2023): e41855, https://doi.org/10.2196/41855.

X. Lau and E. H. Y. Cowling, "Remdesivir Use and Risks of Acute Kidney Injury and Acute Liver Injury Among Patients Hospitalised With COVID-19: A Self-Controlled Case Series Study," *Alimentary Pharmacology & Therapeutics* 56, no. 1 (July 2022): 121–130, https://doi.org/10.1111/apt.16894.

A. Aleem, G. Mahadevaiah, N. Shariff, and J. P. Kothadia, "Hepatic Manifestations of COVID-19 and Effect of Remdesivir on Liver Function in Patients With COVID-19 Illness," *Proceedings (Baylor University Medical Center)* 34, no. 4 (March 8, 2021): 473–477, https://doi.org/10.1080/08998280.2021.1885289.

Franciscan Health, Contributor, "Bariatric Surgery: Challenging the 'Easy Way Out' Perception," *Franciscan Health*, August 9, 2024, https://www.franciscanhealth. org/community/blog/bariatric-surgery-myths.

Cleveland Clinic, Contributor, "Bariatric Surgery," *Cleveland Clinic*, June 9, 2022, https://my.clevelandclinic.org/health/treatments/bariatric-surgery.

Gabriela Rodriguez Ruiz, MD, PhD, FACS, "What Is the Success Rate of Bariatric Procedure?" *Vida Wellness and Beauty*, 2024, https://www. vidawellnessandbeauty.com/bariatrics/what-is-the-success-rate-of-bariatric-procedure/#:~:text=The%20long%2Dlasting%20success%20rate,initial%20 period%20of%20weight%20loss.

The London Obesity Group, Contributor, "What Is the Success Rate of Bariatric Surgery?" *The London Obesity Group*, December 12, 2018, https://www. thelondonobesitygroup.co.uk/blog/what-is-the-success-rate-of-bariatric-surgery/.

Mayo Clinic Staff, "Sleeve Gastrectomy," *Mayo Clinic*, August 2, 2024, https:// www.mayoclinic.org/tests-procedures/sleeve-gastrectomy/about/pac-20385183#:~:text=Sleeve%20gastrectomy%20is%20a%20surgical,called%20a%20 vertical%20sleeve%20gastrectomy.

Mayo Clinic Staff, "Gastric Bypass (Roux-en-Y)," *Mayo Clinic*, June 25, 2022, https://www.mayoclinic.org/tests-procedures/gastric-bypass-surgery/about/pac-20385189.

Ron Elli, PhD, "Size of Stomach After Gastric Sleeve Surgery," *Mexico Bariatric Center*, September 13, 2018, https://mexicobariatriccenter.com/size-of-stomach-after-gastric-sleeve-surgery/#:~:text=A%20normal%20adult%20stomach%20size,this%20here%20in%20this%20article.

Christopher Wilson and Anis Rehman, "Counseling Patients on Bariatric Surgery for Obesity," *NIH National Library of Medicine*, September 18, 2022, https://www.ncbi.nlm.nih.gov/books/NBK572056/#:~:text=The%20care%20provided%20should%20be,their%20nutritional%20and%20mineral%20state.&text=There%20is%20no%20difference%20in,following%20a%20bypass%2C%20or%20LSG.

Sara Berg, MS, "What Doctors Wish Patients Knew About Bariatric Surgery," *American Medical Association*, September 8, 2023, https://www.ama-assn.org/delivering-care/public-health/what-doctors-wish-patients-knew-about-bariatric-surgery.

CHAPTER 13 | MAGIC IN THE MIDDLE

Narcotics Anonymous: Just for Today: Daily Meditations for Recovering Addicts. Revised ed. Narcotics Anonymous, 2023.

Anna Kowalski, MA, MFT, CEDS, "Teaching Families That Integration (Not Eradication) Leads to Recovery," *MindWise Innovations*, 2024, https://mindwise.org/blog/disordered-eating/teaching-families-that-integration-not-eradication-leads-to-recovery/.

CHAPTER 14 | ENLIGHTENMENT on DISCOVERING ED

BIG-BONED DEBUNKED

Sean Kennedy, "Big-Boned, Big Myth," *Motion Health*, August 18, 2021, https://motionhealth.net/2021/08/18/big-boned-big-myth/.

"Overweight and Obesity E66-," *ICD10 Data*, August 18, 2021, https://www.icd10data.com/ICD10CM/Codes/E00-E89/E65-E68/E66-.

D. L. Duren, R. J. Sherwood, S. A. Czerwinski, M. Lee, A. C. Choh, R. M. Siervogel, and W. Cameron Chumlea, "Body Composition Methods: Comparisons and Interpretation," *Journal of Diabetes Science and Technology* 2, no. 6 (November 2008): 1139–1146, https://doi.org/10.1177/193229680800200623.

Australian Government Department of Health and Aged Care, Contributor, "Factors That Affect Weight," *Australian Government Department of Health and Aged Care*, July 29, 2021, https://www.health.gov.au/topics/overweight-and-obesity/factors-that-affect-weight#:~:text=weight%20for%20everyone-,What%20affects%20weight,more%20likely%20to%20gain%20weight.

IDENTIFYING AN EATING DISORDER | Supporting Yourself

Melissa Spann, PhD, LMHC, CEDS-S, "What Should I Do if I Think I'm Developing an Eating Disorder?" *Monte Nido | Clementine Programs*, February 25, 2021, https://clementineprograms.com/eating-disorder-developing/.

Mayo Clinic Staff, "Eating Disorder Treatment: Know Your Options," *Mayo Clinic*, July 24, 2024, https://www.mayoclinic.org/diseases-conditions/eating-disorders/in-depth/eating-disorder-treatment/art-20046234.

IDENTIFYING AN EATING DISORDER | Supporting a Child

Priory Group, Contributor, "How to Tell if Your Child Has an Eating Disorder," *Priory Group*, January 1, 2024, https://www.priorygroup.com/blog/how-to-tell-if-your-child-has-an-eating-disorder.

NHS, Contributor, "Advice for Parents – Eating Disorders," *NHS*, January 23, 2024, https://www.nhs.uk/mental-health/feelings-symptoms-behaviours/behaviours/eating-disorders/advice-for-parents/.

Mind Family, Contributor, "Eating Disorders in Children: 10 Warning Signs Every Parent Must Know!" *Mind Family*, January 1, 2024, https://mind.family/articles/signs-of-eating-disorders-in-children/.

Jessica, Contributor, "Nourishing Resilience: Supporting Moms with Children Struggling with Eating Disorders," *Waves of Motherhood*, May 18, 2024, https://www.wavesofmotherhood.com/post/nourishing-resilience-supporting-moms-with-children-struggling-with-eating-disorders.

UP Publication, Contributor, "Guide to Childhood Eating Disorder," *UP Publication*, November 24, 2023, https://upbility.net/blogs/news/guide-to-childhood-eating-disorder.

K. Suhag and S. Rauniyar, "Social Media Effects Regarding Eating Disorders and Body Image in Young Adolescents," *Cureus* 16, no. 4 (April 21, 2024): e58674, https://doi.org/10.7759/cureus.58674.

IDENTIFYING AN EATING DISORDER | Supporting Others

Admin, "Understanding Eating Disorders: A Comprehensive Essay," *EssayPro*, September 16, 2023, https://essaypro.pro/understanding-eating-disorders-a-comprehensive-essay-2/.

NHS, Contributor, "How to Help Someone with an Eating Disorder," *NHS*, August 21, 2023, https://www.nhs.uk/mental-health/advice-for-life-situations-and-events/how-to-help-someone-with-eating-disorder/#:~:text=Give%20your%20time%2C%20listen%20to,for%20them%20is%20what's%20important.

Melinda Smith, M.A., Lawrence Robinson, and Jeanne Segal, Ph.D., "Helping Someone with an Eating Disorder," *HelpGuide.Org*, August 21, 2023, https://www.helpguide.org/mental-health/eating-disorders/helping-someone-with-an-eating-disorder.

THE WEIGHT OF WORDS: WHY NUMBERS CAN BE HARMFUL

K. Suhag and S. Rauniyar, "Social Media Effects Regarding Eating Disorders and Body Image in Young Adolescents," *Cureus* 16, no. 4 (April 21, 2024): e58674, https://doi.org/10.7759/cureus.58674.

Frances Coleman-Williams, "Why Are Numbers Unhelpful When Talking About Eating Disorders?" *Mindful Survivor: Bringing Insight and Creativity Together*, October 24, 2018, https://www.mindfulsurvivor.co.uk/2018/10/24/why-are-numbers-unhelpful-when-talking-about-eating-disorders/.

THE COST OF COMPARISON

Vocabulary.com, Contributor, "Commonly Confused Words Envy/Jealousy," *Vocabulary*, January 1, 2024, https://www.vocabulary.com/articles/commonly-confused-words/envy-jealousy/#:~:text=envy%2F%20jealousy&text=Envy%20is%20when%20you%20want,a%20ride%2C%20you%20feel%20jealousy.

Katharine Chan, MSc, BSc, PMP, and reviewed by Ivy Kwong, LMFT, "Envy Vs. Jealousy: Is There a Difference?" *Verywell Mind*, March 27, 2024, https://www.verywellmind.com/envy-vs-jealousy-is-there-a-difference-7109842.

Anthony Tan, "Envy Is Not Enough," *Medium*, July 5, 2018, https://existony.medium.com/envy-is-the-enemy-a218c6ec7f41.

CHAPTER 15 | ENLIGHTENMENT on DATING ED

ALL ABOUT EATING DISORDERS

US Department of Health and Human Services, National Institutes of Health, "Eating Disorders: What You Need to Know," *NIMH*, NIH Publication No. 24-MH-4901, January 1, 2024, https://www.nimh.nih.gov/health/publications/eating-disorders.

P. Balasundaram and P. Santhanam, "Eating Disorders," *StatPearls [Internet]* (Treasure Island, FL: StatPearls Publishing, 2024), accessed June 26, 2023, PMID: 33620794.

B. Feng, J. Harms, E. Chen, P. Gao, P. Xu, and Y. He, "Current Discoveries and Future Implications of Eating Disorders," *International Journal of Environmental Research and Public Health* 20, no. 14 (July 8, 2023): 6325, https://doi.org/10.3390/ijerph20146325.

P. Hay, "Current Approach to Eating Disorders: A Clinical Update," *Internal Medicine Journal* 50, no. 1 (January 2020): 24–29, https://doi.org/10.1111/imj.14691.

Public-Monthly-FebEatingDisorder, *Waterloo Wellington Diabetes*, https://www.waterloowellingtondiabetes.ca/Public-Monthly-EatingDisorder.htm.

F. Jurado-González et al., "Mapping Bridges Between Anxiety, Depression, and Somatic Symptoms in Primary Care Patients: A Network Perspective," *International Journal of Environmental Research and Public Health*, https://doi.org/10.1007/s12144-023-04657-3.

K. Frank, "The Perfect Storm - A Bio-Psycho-Social Risk Model for Developing and Maintaining Eating Disorders," *Frontiers in Behavioral Neuroscience* 10 (March 10, 2016): 44, https://doi.org/10.3389/fnbeh.2016.00044.

Waves of Hope, Contributor, "What Are the Different Types of Eating Disorders?" *Waves of Hope*, July 3, 2024, https://www.wavesofhopeed.com/blog-posts/different-types-of-eating-disorders.

Waves of Hope, Contributor, "Other Specified Feeding or Eating Disorders (OSFED)," *Waves of Hope*, July 3, 2024, https://www.wavesofhopeed.com/blog-posts/other-specified-feeding-or-eating-disorders-osfed.

Kim Anderson, PhD, CEDS, "These Are the Symptoms of ARFID, an Eating Disorder Linked to Fear and Anxiety," *Eating Recovery Center*, April 18, 2023, https://www.eatingrecoverycenter.com/news/arfid-symptoms-fear-anxiety.

Robert E. Emery and Sari Shepphird, "Anorexia Nervosa," *Britannica*, October 26, 2024, https://www.britannica.com/science/anorexia-nervosa.

Joan Owens, "Unveiling Effective Strategies to Treat Eating Disorders in Therapy," *Bright Globes*, January 1, 2022, https://brightglobes.com/unveiling-effective-strategies-to-treat-eating-disorders-in-therapy/.

ESSENTIAL FACTS ABOUT EATING DISORDERS

Erin Pauling, "Not Sick Enough," *Bloom*, July 13, 2023, https://www.bloomcounselingandnutrition.com/post/not-sick-enough.

National Association of Anorexia Nervosa and Associated Disorders (ANAD), "Eating Disorder Statistics," *ANAD*, https://anad.org/eating-disorder-statistic/?com.

National Eating Disorders Association (NEDA), "Eating Disorders in Men and Boys," reviewed by Douglas Bunnell, Ph.D., FAED, CEDS, https://www.nationaleatingdisorders.org/eating-disorders-in-men-and-boys/?.

Dr. Priyom Bose, Ph.D., "Higher BMI Linked to Increased Risk of Binge-Eating Disorder in Adolescents," *News-Medical.net*, reviewed by Benedette Cuffari, M.Sc., May 28, 2024, https://www.news-medical.net/news/20240528/Higher-BMI-linked-to-increased-risk-of-binge-eating-disorder-in-adolescents.aspx?.

National Institute of Mental Health (NIMH), "Eating Disorders," last reviewed January 2024, https://www.nimh.nih.gov/health/topics/eating-disorders?.

Arnold S, Correll CU, Jaite C, "Frequency and Correlates of Lifetime Suicidal Ideation and Suicide Attempts Among Consecutively Hospitalized Youth with Anorexia Nervosa and Bulimia Nervosa: Results from a Retrospective Chart Review," *Borderline Personality Disorders and Emotional Dysregulation* 10, no. 1 (March 31, 2023): 10, https://doi.org/10.1186/s40479-023-00216-1.

Rebecca King Pierce, "Why We Still Fail Those with Eating Disorders," *Ampersand*, September 22, 2016, https://artsci.washu.edu/ampersand/why-we-still-fail-those-eating-disorders.

Reviewed by Douglas Bunnell, Ph.D., FAED, CEDS, "Statistics," *NEDA Feeding Hope National Eating Disorders Association*, January 1, 2024, https://www.nationaleatingdisorders.org/statistics/.

J. Streatfeild, J. Hickson, S. B. Austin, R. Hutcheson, J. S. Kandel, J. G. Lampert, E. M. Myers, T. K. Richmond, M. Samnaliev, K. Velasquez, R. S. Weissman, and L. Pezzullo, "Social and Economic Cost of Eating Disorders in the United States: Evidence to Inform Policy Action," *International Journal of Eating Disorders* 54, no. 5 (May 2021): 851–868, https://doi.org/10.1002/eat.23486.

J. Qian, Y. Wu, F. Liu, Y. Zhu, H. Jin, H. Zhang, Y. Wan, C. Li, D. Yu, "An Update on the Prevalence of Eating Disorders in the General Population: A Systematic Review and Meta-Analysis," *Eating and Weight Disorders* 27, no. 2 (March 2022): 415–428, https://doi.org/10.1007/s40519-021-01162-z.

Presskreischer R, Steinglass JE, Anderson KE, "Eating Disorders in the U.S. Medicare Population," *International Journal of Eating Disorders* 55, no. 3 (March 2022): 362-371, https://doi.org/10.1002/eat.23676.

DISORDERED EATING: The Gray Area
Between Health and Illness

NEDC, Contributor, "Disordered Eating & Dieting," *National Eating Disorders Collaboration*, January 1, 2024, https://nedc.com.au/eating-disorders/eating-disorders-explained/disordered-eating-and-dieting#:~:text=Disordered%20eating%20sits%20on%20a,irregular%20or%20inflexible%20eating%20patterns.

K. N. Harer, "Irritable Bowel Syndrome, Disordered Eating, and Eating Disorders," *Gastroenterology & Hepatology (N Y)* 15, no. 5 (May 2019): 280–282, PMID: 31360143, PMCID: PMC6589841.

Kristen Fuller, MD, medically reviewed by Margaret Seide, MD, and fact-checked by Aaron Johnson, "The Difference Between Disordered Eating and Eating Disorders," *Verywell Mind*, July 29, 2024, https://www.verywellmind.com/difference-between-disordered-eating-and-eating-disorders-5184548.

THE BINGE SPECTRUM: From Occasional Episodes to Binge Eating Disorder (BED)

Shervan Shahhian, "What Is Binge Eating Disorder?" *Liberty Psychological Association*, May 11, 2023, https://shervanshahhian.com/2023/05/11/what-is-binge-eating-disorder/.

Gripalley5, Contributor, "Five Intriguing Truths About How Does Binge Eating Impact the Body?" *Gripalley5*, October 16, 2022, https://squareblogs.net/gripalley5/five-intriguing-truths-about-how-does-binge-eating-impact-the-body.

OBESITY: Beyond the Scale

X. Lin and H. Li, "Obesity: Epidemiology, Pathophysiology, and Therapeutics," *Frontiers in Endocrinology (Lausanne)* 12 (September 6, 2021): 706978, https://doi.org/10.3389/fendo.2021.706978.

C. M. Apovian, "Obesity: Definition, Comorbidities, Causes, and Burden," *American Journal of Managed Care* 22, no. 7 Suppl. (June 2016): s176–s185, PMID: 27356115.

R. Shruthi, "Transform Your Weight Loss Journey: Watch Our Video for Expert Tips on Reducing Obesity," *Medically Speaking*, October 9, 2024, https://squareblogs.net/gripalley5/https://www.medicallyspeaking.in/fitneshttps://www.medicallyspeaking.in/fitness/transform-your-weight-loss-journey-watch-our-video-for-expert-tips-on-reducing-obesity/s/transform-your-weight-loss-journey-watch-our-video-for-expert-tips-on-reducing-obesity/five-intriguing-truths-about-how-does-binge-eating-impact-the-body.

S. Humphreys, "The Unethical Use of BMI in Contemporary General Practice," *British Journal of General Practice* 60, no. 578 (September 2010): 696–697, https://doi.org/10.3399/bjgp10X515548.

UNDERSTANDING THE ADDICTED BRAIN: Why It Matters

Jason Hreha, "What Is Psychological Dependence in Neuroscience?" *The Behavioral Scientist | Jason Hreha*, January 1, 2024, https://www.thebehavioralscientist.com/glossary/psychological-dependence.

Yale Medicine, Contributor, "How an Addicted Brain Works," *Yale Medicine*, May 25, 2022, https://www.yalemedicine.org/news/how-an-addicted-brain-works.

National Institute on Drug Abuse (NIDA), "Drugs and the Brain," *National Institute on Drug Abuse,* July 1, 2011, https://nida.nih.gov/publications/drugs-brains-behavior-science-addiction/drugs-brain, accessed November 30, 2024.

Harrison Wein, Ph.D., Editor, "Biology of Addiction," *News in Health,* October 1, 2015, https://newsinhealth.nih.gov/2015/10/biology-addiction.

Tabitha M. Powledge, "Addiction and the Brain: The Dopamine Pathway is Helping Researchers Find Their Way Through the Addiction Maze," *BioScience* 49, no. 7 (July 1999): 513–519, https://doi.org/10.2307/1313471.

D. A. Wiss and T. D. Brewerton, "Incorporating Food Addiction into Disordered Eating: The Disordered Eating Food Addiction Nutrition Guide (DEFANG)," *Eating and Weight Disorders* 22 (2017): 49–59, https://doi.org/10.1007/s40519-016-0344-y.

D. Ratković, V. Knežević, A. Dickov, E. Fedrigolli, and M. Čomić, "Comparison of Binge-Eating Disorder and Food Addiction," *Journal of International Medical Research* 51, no. 4 (April 2023): 3000605231171016, https://doi.org/10.1177/03000605231171016.

A. N. Gearhardt, M. A. White, and M. N. Potenza, "Binge Eating Disorder and Food Addiction," *Current Drug Abuse Reviews* 4, no. 3 (September 2011): 201–207, https://doi.org/10.2174/1874473711104030201.

GOOD FOOD, BAD FOOD: Shifting the Narrative

Hosts, Contributor, "Eating a Donut for You Can Mean a Very Different Thing for Someone Else," *Facebook | The Bert Show,* July 15, 2024, https://www.facebook.com/TheBertShow/videos/eating-a-donut-for-you-can-mean-a-very-different-thing-for-someone-else-what-doe/1083425289782872/.

Dawn, "Why It's Time to Ditch the 'Good' and 'Bad' Food Labels," *Northern Arizona University,* October 16, 2023, https://in.nau.edu/ucan/why-labeling-food-as-good-or-bad-isnt-healthy/.

S. Shangguan et al., "A Meta-Analysis of Food Labeling Effects on Consumer Diet Behaviors and Industry Practices," *American Journal of Preventive Medicine* 56, no. 2 (February 2019): 300–314, https://doi.org/10.1016/j.amepre.2018.09.024.

The Found Team, "It's Time to Stop Labeling Foods 'Good' and 'Bad'—Here's Why," *Found*, May 18, 2023, https://joinfound.com/blog/there-are-no-good-or-bad-foods?srsltid=AfmBOoqNDwh3hY1v9Q0yopLWTRG6mY_7SN51VPzTuENOxZfVDA0y55aH.

Frankki Sorce, LPC, "The Impact of Labeling Your Child's Food Choices as Good or Bad," *Mindsoother Therapy Center*, October 25, 2023, https://www.mindsoother.com/blog/the-impact-of-labeling-your-childs-food-choices-as-good-or-bad.

BODY TALK: PARTS 1 AND 2

Part 1: All About Dysmorphia

Tracey L. Kelley, "Understanding Body Dysmorphia," *Cottonwood Tucson - Tucson, Arizona Mental Health Treatment and Substance Use Disorder Treatment*, August 20, 2024, https://cottonwooddetucson.com/understanding-body-dysmorphia/.

K. A. Phillips, "Body Dysmorphic Disorder: Recognizing and Treating Imagined Ugliness," *World Psychiatry* 3, no. 1 (February 2004): 12–17, PMID: 16633443, PMCID: PMC1414653.

A. R. Singh and D. Veale, "Understanding and Treating Body Dysmorphic Disorder," *Indian Journal of Psychiatry* 61, no. Suppl 1 (January 2019): S131–S135, https://doi.org/10.4103/psychiatry.IndianJPsychiatry_528_18.

Georgina Krebs et al., "Epidemiology of Body Dysmorphic Disorder and Appearance Preoccupation in Youth: Prevalence, Comorbidity, and Psychosocial Impairment," *Journal of the American Academy of Child & Adolescent Psychiatry*, forthcoming.

Part 2: Changing and Rearranging

S. Higgins and A. Wysong, "Cosmetic Surgery and Body Dysmorphic Disorder - An Update," *International Journal of Women's Dermatology* 4, no. 1 (November 20, 2017): 43–48, https://doi.org/10.1016/j.ijwd.2017.09.007.

S. Hostiuc, O. M. Isailă, M. C. Rusu, and I. Negoi, "Ethical Challenges Regarding Cosmetic Surgery in Patients with Body Dysmorphic Disorder," *Healthcare (Basel)* 10, no. 7 (July 20, 2022): 1345, https://doi.org/10.3390/healthcare10071345.

R. A. Sansone and L. A. Sansone, "Cosmetic Surgery and Psychological Issues," *Psychiatry (Edgmont)* 4, no. 12 (December 2007): 65–68, PMID: 20436768, PMCID: PMC2861519.

Jade Harris, Assistant Opinion Editor, "The Harms of Teenage Plastic Surgery," *The Chronicle*, November 4, 2022, https://hwchronicle.com/105860/opinion/the-harms-of-teenage-plastic-surgery/.

G. Borah, M. Rankin, and P. Wey, "Psychological Complications in 281 Plastic Surgery Practices," *Plastic and Reconstructive Surgery* 104, no. 5 (October 1999): 1241–1246, https://doi.org/10.1097/00006534-199910000-00002.

LOVE AND VALIDATION: How Eating Disorders Intersect with Relationships

L. Lukas, C. Buhl, G. Schulte-Körne, and A. Sfärlea, "Family, Friends, and Feelings: The Role of Relationships to Parents and Peers and Alexithymia in Adolescents with Anorexia Nervosa," *Journal of Eating Disorders* 10, no. 1 (September 29, 2022): 143, https://doi.org/10.1186/s40337-022-00661-3.

A. A. Gilbert, S. M. Shaw, and M. K. Notar, "The Impact of Eating Disorders on Family Relationships," *Eating Disorders* 8, no. 4 (Winter 2000): 331–345, https://doi.org/10.1080/10640260008251240.

J. Momeñe, A. Estévez, M. D. Griffiths, P. Macía, M. Herrero, L. Olave, and I. Iruarrizaga, "Eating Disorders and Intimate Partner Violence: The Influence of Fear of Loneliness and Social Withdrawal," *Nutrients* 14, no. 13 (June 24, 2022): 2611, https://doi.org/10.3390/nu14132611.

J. A. Siegel et al., "'I Felt So Powerful to Have This Love in Me': A Grounded Theory Analysis of the Experiences of People Living with and Recovering from Eating Disorders While in Diverse Romantic Relationships," *Body Image* 49 (June 2024): 101709, https://doi.org/10.1016/j.bodyim.2024.101709.

N. Kiriike, T. Nagata, H. Matsunaga, W. Tobitan, and T. Nishiura, "Single and Married Patients with Eating Disorders," *Psychiatry and Clinical Neurosciences* 52, Suppl. (December 1998): S306–S308, https://doi.org/10.1111/j.1440-1819.1998.tb03253.x.

J. S. Kirby, C. D. Runfola, M. S. Fischer, D. H. Baucom, and C. M. Bulik, "Couple-Based Interventions for Adults with Eating Disorders," *Eating Disorders* 23, no. 4 (2015): 356–365, https://doi.org/10.1080/10640266.2015.1044349.

RELIGIOUS ABUSE AND THE CHURCH: Exploring the Intersection with Eating Disorders

D. Akrawi, R. Bartrop, U. Potter, and S. Touyz, "Religiosity, Spirituality in Relation to Disordered Eating and Body Image Concerns: A Systematic Review," *Journal of Eating Disorders* 3 (August 15, 2015): 29, https://doi.org/10.1186/s40337-015-0064-0.

Cissy Brady-Rogers, "The Church, Sexuality, and Eating Disorders," *CBE International*, January 30, 2007, https://www.cbeinternational.org/resource/church-sexuality-and-eating-disorders/.

Auna Nygaard, "Religious Trauma: 9+ Signs of Spiritual Abuse & How to Heal," *Sanstone Care*, April 12, 2024, https://www.sandstonecare.com/blog/religious-trauma/.

CHAPTER 16 | ENLIGHTENMENT on DIVORCING ED

UNDERSTANDING TREATMENT: Exploring Options for a Healthier You

Beyond Pain Recovery Strategy | Rehab Walk, https://rehabwalk.co.uk/services/beyond-pain-recovery-strategy/.

A. Toulany et al., "Cost Analysis of Inpatient Treatment of Anorexia Nervosa in Adolescents: Hospital and Caregiver Perspectives," *CMAJ Open* 3, no. 2 (April 2, 2015): E192–E197, https://doi.org/10.9778/cmajo.20140086.

J. Streatfeild et al., "Social and Economic Cost of Eating Disorders in the United States: Evidence to Inform Policy Action," *International Journal of Eating Disorders* 54, no. 5 (May 2021): 851–868, https://doi.org/10.1002/eat.23486.

Christie Calucchia, "The Alarming Cost of Eating Disorder Treatment in America," *Glamour*, March 7, 2023, https://www.glamour.com/story/getting-eating-disorder-treatment-in-america.

A. E. Kazdin, E. E. Fitzsimmons-Craft, and D. E. Wilfley, "Addressing Critical Gaps in the Treatment of Eating Disorders," *International Journal of Eating Disorders* 50, no. 3 (March 2017): 170–189, https://doi.org/10.1002/eat.22670.

A. E. Kass, R. P. Kolko, and D. E. Wilfley, "Psychological Treatments for Eating Disorders," *Current Opinion in Psychiatry* 26, no. 6 (November 2013): 549–555, https://doi.org/10.1097/YCO.0b013e328365a30e.

A NOTE: Medication for Eating Disorders

S. J. Crow, "Pharmacologic Treatment of Eating Disorders," *Psychiatric Clinics of North America* 42, no. 2 (June 2019): 253–262, https://doi.org/10.1016/j.psc.2019.01.007.

Project Heal, Contributor, "Cost of Eating Disorder Treatment as a Barrier to Healing," *Project Heal*, January 1, 2024, https://www.theprojectheal.org/cost-of-treatment.

Non-12-Step Rehab Programs, https://www.prescotthouse.com/blog/non-12-step-rehab-programs.

REHAB UNCOVERED: How It Works and What to Expect

S. Frostad and M. Bentz, "Anorexia Nervosa: Outpatient Treatment and Medical Management," *World Journal of Psychiatry* 12, no. 4 (April 19, 2022): 558–579, https://doi.org/10.5498/wjp.v12.i4.558.

J. M. Walsh, M. E. Wheat, and K. Freund, "Detection, Evaluation, and Treatment of Eating Disorders: The Role of the Primary Care Physician," *Journal of General Internal Medicine* 15, no. 8 (August 2000): 577–590, https://doi.org/10.1046/j.1525-1497.2000.02439.x.

H. Nagy et al., "A Clinical Overview of Anorexia Nervosa and Overcoming Treatment Resistance," *Avicenna Journal of Medicine* 13, no. 1 (December 21, 2022): 3–14, https://doi.org/10.1055/s-0042-1758859.

K. A. Halmi, "The Multimodal Treatment of Eating Disorders," *World Psychiatry* 4, no. 2 (June 2005): 69–73, PMID: 16633511, PMCID: PMC1414734.

G. I. Costandache et al., "An Overview of the Treatment of Eating Disorders in Adults and Adolescents: Pharmacology and Psychotherapy," *Postępy Psychiatrii i Neurologii* 32, no. 1 (March 2023): 40–48, https://doi.org/10.5114/ppn.2023.127237.

V. J. Clemente-Suárez et al., "The Impact of Anorexia Nervosa and the Basis for Non-Pharmacological Interventions," *Nutrients* 15, no. 11 (June 1, 2023): 2594, https://doi.org/10.3390/nu15112594.

R. Murphy, S. Straebler, Z. Cooper, and C. G. Fairburn, "Cognitive Behavioral Therapy for Eating Disorders," *Psychiatric Clinics of North America* 33, no. 3 (September 2010): 611–627, https://doi.org/10.1016/j.psc.2010.04.004.

FELLOWSHIP PROGRAMS: A General Overview

Alcoholics Anonymous World Services, Alcoholics Anonymous: The Story of How Many Thousands of Men and Women Have Recovered from Alcoholism, 4th ed. (New York: Alcoholics Anonymous World Services, 2001).

The Twelve Steps of Alcoholics Anonymous are reprinted with gratitude from the same source.

E. A. Riley, "Eating Disorders as Addictive Behavior: Integrating 12-Step Programs into Treatment Planning," *Nursing Clinics of North America* 26, no. 3 (1991): 715–726, https://pubmed.ncbi.nlm.nih.gov/1891404.

K. Blum et al., "The Molecular Neurobiology of Twelve Steps Program & Fellowship: Connecting the Dots for Recovery," *Journal of Reward Deficit Syndromes* 1, no. 1 (2015): 46–64, https://doi.org/10.17756/jrds.2015-008.

C. L. Johnson and R. A. Sansone, "Integrating the Twelve-Step Approach with Traditional Psychotherapy for the Treatment of Eating Disorders," *International Journal of Eating Disorders* 14, no. 2 (September 1993): 121–134, https://doi.org/10.1002/1098-108X(199309)14:2<121::AID-EAT2260140202>3.0.CO;2-N.

AA, Author, "The Twelve Steps," *AA*, January 1, 2024, https://www.aa.org/the-twelve-steps.

FELLOWSHIP FOR LOVED ONES:
Understanding Al-Anon and Alateen

Neil McKinnell, "The 12 Steps of Al-Anon: A Framework for Addiction Recovery," *Evoke Waltham*, August 23, 2024, https://www.evokewaltham.com/rehab-blog/the-12-steps-of-al-anon-a-framework-for-addiction-recovery/.

C. Timko, M. Halvorson, C. Kong, and R. H. Moos, "Social Processes Explaining the Benefits of Al-Anon Participation," *Psychology of Addictive Behaviors* 29, no. 4 (December 2015): 856–863, https://doi.org/10.1037/adb0000067.

C. Timko, R. Cronkite, L. A. Kaskutas, A. Laudet, J. Roth, and R. H. Moos, "Al-Anon Family Groups: Newcomers and Members," *Journal of Studies on Alcohol and Drugs* 74, no. 6 (November 2013): 965–976, https://doi.org/10.15288/jsad.2013.74.965.

C. Timko, A. Laudet, and R. H. Moos, "Al-Anon Newcomers: Benefits of Continuing Attendance for Six Months," *American Journal of Drug and Alcohol Abuse* 42, no. 4 (July 2016): 441–449, https://doi.org/10.3109/00952990.2016.1148702.

YOUR STORY MATTERS: The Power of Sharing

Cara Spagnola, MSW, LISW, LCSW, "How to Share Your Eating Disorder Recovery Story," *Eating Recovery Center*, December 6, 2022, https://www.eatingrecoverycenter.com/resources/how-share-your-eating-disorder-recovery-story.

The Emily Program, "Five Reasons to Share Your Recovery Story," *The Emily Program*, January 23, 2020, https://emilyprogram.com/blog/five-reasons-to-share-your-recovery-story. Cited in E. Sheens, P. Rhodes, and L. Dawson, "Encountering Anorexia: Challenging Stigma with Recovery Stories," *Advances in Eating Disorders* 4, no. 3 (2016): 315–322, https://doi.org/10.1080/21662630.2016.1217495.

LIVING IN THE GRAY: A 10-Step Guide to Integrating ED Into Your Life

Margarita Tartakovsky, MS, "The Voice of an Eating Disorder & 7 Ways to Shut It Up," *Psych Central*, March 5, 2010, https://psychcentral.com/blog/weightless/2010/03/the-voice-of-an-eating-disorder-7-ways-to-shut-it-up#1.

FINAL THOUGHTS: Embracing the Gray

Alexa Rivera, "Setting Achievable & Effective Eating Disorder Recovery Goals," *Acute*, December 22, 2022, last reviewed December 2023, https://www.acute.org/blog/setting-achievable-effective-eating-disorder-recovery-goals.

GENERAL SOURCES

OpenAI, *ChatGPT* (Nov 2022 version) [Large Language Model], accessed 2024, https://chat.openai.com/chat.

Shout, "Welcome to Shout," *Shout*, https://giveusashout.org/.

Project Heal, "Treatment Placement Program," *Project Heal*, https://www.theprojectheal.org/treatment-placement-program.

Substance Abuse and Mental Health Services Administration (SAMHSA), "Contact Us," *SAMHSA*, https://www.samhsa.gov/about-us/contact-us.

Text About It, "Welcome to Text About It," *Text About It*, https://www.textaboutit.ie/.

National Association of Anorexia Nervosa and Associated Disorders (ANAD), "Eating Disorders Helpline," *ANAD*, https://anad.org/get-help/eating-disorders-helpline/.

The Recovery Village, "Eating Disorder Hotlines," edited by Megan Hull, medically reviewed by Denise-Marie Griswold, LCAS, last updated August 17, 2021, https://www.therecoveryvillage.com/mental-health/eating-disorders/eating-disorder-hotlines/.

National Eating Disorders Association, "Get Help," *National Eating Disorders Association*, https://www.nationaleatingdisorders.org/get-help/.

National Alliance on Mental Illness (NAMI), "NAMI Helpline," *National Alliance on Mental Illness*, https://www.nami.org/support-education/nami-helpline/.

988 Suicide & Crisis Lifeline, https://988lifeline.org/.

Discovery Center, "Five Statistics of Anorexia Nervosa and Its Consequences," *Discovery Center*, 2024, https://centerfordiscovery.com/blog/statistics-behind-anorexia.

Eating Disorders Coalition, "Facts About Eating Disorders," *Eating Disorders Coalition*, https://eatingdisorderscoalition.org/inner_template/facts_and_info/facts-about-eating-disorders.html.

Steven Zauderer, "43 Eating Disorder Statistics & Prevalence," *Cross River Therapy*, September 19, 2023, https://www.crossrivertherapy.com/eating-disorder-statistics#:~:text=Key%20Eating%20Disorder%20Statistics,being%20underweight%20by%20healthcare%20professionals.

J. S. Maden, "Samuel Johnson's Alcohol Problem," *Psychological Medicine*, https://www.cambridge.org/core/services/aop-cambridge-core/content/view/44490E8EFDF8602659D6D384251D6E04/S0025727300011996a.pdf/samuel_johnsons_alcohol_problem.pdf.

Terry Hurley, "'Hitting Rock Bottom' in Addiction Recovery," *English Mountain*, April 4, 2023, https://englishmountain.com/blog/is-hitting-rock-bottom-necessary/.

Nancy Carbone, "Do You Have a Toxic Love Addiction to Abusive Relationships?" *Medium*, March 25, 2021, https://medium.com/@nancy_23310/do-you-have-a-toxic-love-addiction-to-abusive-relationships-a53051af57f8.

Libby Cole, "Review | Better Than Before, Gretchen Rubin," *Literary Treats*, August 30, 2015, https://literarytreats.com/2015/08/30/review-better-than-before-gretchen-rubin/.

Karen M. Horton, MD, and Emily Sespaniak, NP, "The Psyche of Cosmetic Surgery – Expected Ups & Downs," *Dr. Karen Horton's Blog*, 2024, https://www.drkarenhorton.com/dr-hortons-blog/psyche-of-cosmetic-surgery.

Jayme, "A Guide for What to Say and What Not to Say to Someone with an Eating Disorder," *Adventure and the Girl*, February 4, 2022, https://adventureandthegirl.com/2022/02/04/what-to-say-to-someone-with-an-eating-disorder/.

Martha Kauppi, "How You Can Help a Client with Negative Body Image," *Institute for Relational Intimacy*, April 3, 2018, https://www.instituteforrelationalintimacy.com/blog/how-you-can-help-a-client-with-negative-body-image.

Amy Marschall, PsyD, "What Is Family Constellation Therapy?" *Verywell Mind*, updated March 17, 2024, medically reviewed by Steven Gans, MD, https://www.verywellmind.com/what-is-family-constellation-therapy-5217964.

Harvard Health Publishing, "Added Sugar: Where Is It Hiding?" *Harvard Health Blog*, November 9, 2019, https://www.health.harvard.edu/staying-healthy/added-sugar-where-is-it-hiding.

Ann Arbor Women's Group, "The Sidewalk, The Hole and The Insanity," *Ann Arbor Women's Group*, https://a2womensgroup.org/the-sidewalk-the-hole-and-the-insanity/.

Mark Warren, MD, MPH, FAED, "What Purging Is & How Does It Affect the Body?" *The Emily Program*, June 26, 2024, https://emilyprogram.com/blog/what-is-purging-how-affect-body/.

Cleveland Clinic, "Bariatric Surgery," *Cleveland Clinic*, last reviewed June 9, 2022, https://my.clevelandclinic.org/health/treatments/bariatric-surgery.

David J. Alperovitz, PsyD, "Effectively Diagnosing and Treating Eating Disorders," *McLean Hospital*, originally aired November 30, 2023, last updated April 24, 2024, https://www.mcleanhospital.org/video/effectively-diagnosing-and-treating-eating-disorders.

Sarah Klein, "Yes, You Can Be 'Big Boned' (But That's Not Why You're Overweight)," *HuffPost*, November 3, 2014, updated December 6, 2017, https://www.huffpost.com/entry/are-you-big-boned-truth_n_6075706.

Joselyn, Heywise Staff, "Could You Have an Eating Disorder? Take the Test," *Heywise*, https://heywise.com/quiz/do-you-have-an-eating-disorder/?utm_source=adwords.

Dr. Brad Smith, "Wondering if You Have an Eating Disorder?" *Rogers Behavioral Health*, 2024, https://rogersbh.org/edquiz#eatingdisorderquiz.

The Emily Program, "Do You Have an Eating Disorder? Take the Eating Disorder Assessment Quiz," *The Emily Program*, 2019–2024, https://emilyprogram.com/treatment-services/take-the-quiz/.

Mayo Clinic Staff, "Eating Disorder Treatment: Know Your Options," *Mayo Clinic*, July 24, 2024, https://www.mayoclinic.org/diseases-conditions/eating-disorders/in-depth/eating-disorder-treatment/art-20046234.

Stephanie Thomas, "Think Your Friend May Have an Eating Disorder? Here's What You Can Do," *Center for Change*, https://centerforchange.com/think-your-friend-may-have-an-eating-disorder-heres-what-you-can-do/.

Butterfly Foundation, "How to Approach Someone," *Butterfly Foundation*, 2024, https://butterfly.org.au/eating-disorders/concerned-about-someone-you-know/how-to-approach-someone/.

Within Health, "What Not to Say to Someone with an Eating Disorder," *Within Health*, July 22, 2022, https://withinhealth.com/learn/articles/what-not-to-say-to-someone-with-an-eating-disorder.

Sara Smith, BSW, "5-4-3-2-1 Coping Technique for Anxiety," *Behavioral Health Partners Blog*, University of Rochester Medical Center, April 10, 2018, https://www.urmc.rochester.edu/behavioral-health-partners/bhp-blog/april-2018/5-4-3-2-1-coping-technique-for-anxiety.aspx.

Psychic Lauryn, "Childhood Home Meditation & Exercise," *YouTube*, 2021, https://www.youtube.com/watch?v=oY4ntHXChhc.

Adrienne Stinson, "What Is Box Breathing?" *Medical News Today*, updated May 13, 2024, medically reviewed by Timothy J. Legg, PhD, PsyD, https://www.medicalnewstoday.com/articles/321805.

Darius Ghadiali, "A Beginner's First Take on Internal Family Systems (IFS)," *Medium*, November 29, 2023, https://medium.com/@dariusghadiali/a-beginners-first-take-on-internal-family-systems-ifs-338ce8b830d3.

Dr. Alaleh Selkirk, "Welcome to the Plastic Surgery Quiz for Patients," *Introspection Beverly Hills*, https://introspectionbeverlyhills.com/plastic-surgery-quiz-patients/.

Shena Jaramillo, Registered Dietitian, "The Body Dysmorphia Test," *Peace and Nutrition*, last updated June 25, 2024, https://peaceandnutrition.com/do-i-have-body-dysmorphia-take-the-quiz.

Abbie Cochrane, "How to Overcome a Negative Body Image," *Southern Utah University Blog*, March 3, 2022, https://www.suu.edu/blog/2022/03/overcome-negative-body-image.html.

Gretchen Rubin, "Back by Popular Demand: Are You an Abstainer or a Moderator?" *Gretchen Rubin*, October 10, 2012, https://gretchenrubin.com/articles/abstainer-vs-moderator/.

World Health Organization, "Obesity," June 9, 2021, https://www.who.int/news-room/facts-in-pictures/detail/6-facts-on-obesity.

Debra L. Franko, Ph.D., Aparna Keshaviah, Sc.M., Kamryn T. Eddy, Ph.D., Meera Krishna, B.A., Martha C. Davis, B.A., Pamela K. Keel, Ph.D., and David B. Herzog, M.D., "A Longitudinal Investigation of Mortality in Anorexia Nervosa and Bulimia Nervosa," *American Journal of Psychiatry* 170, no. 8 (August 1, 2013), https://doi.org/10.1176/appi.ajp.2013.12070868.

The New York Times, "How to Help Kids Develop Healthy Eating Habits," *The New York Times*, https://www.nytimes.com/article/kids-healthy-eating-habits.html.

Raschelle Sabourin, Registered Dietitian, "What Is Food Neutrality?" reviewed by Nüton's Registered Dietitians, March 23, 2022, https://nuton.ca/what-is-food-neutrality/.

Stuart B. Murray, Eva Pila, Scott Griffiths, and Daniel Le Grange, "When Illness Severity and Research Dollars Do Not Align: Are We Overlooking Eating Disorders?" *World Psychiatry* 16, no. 3 (September 21, 2017): 321, https://doi.org/10.1002/wps.20465.

Nick Fuller, "Using BMI to Measure Your Health Is Nonsense. Here's Why," *The Conversation*, May 1, 2022, 4:06 pm EDT, https://theconversation.com/using-bmi-to-measure-your-health-is-nonsense-heres-why-180412.

Christian Nordqvist, "Why BMI Is Inaccurate and Misleading," *Medical News Today*, updated January 20, 2022, https://www.medicalnewstoday.com/articles/265215.

Stephen Humphreys, "The Unethical Use of BMI in Contemporary General Practice," *British Journal of General Practice* 60, no. 578 (September 1, 2010): 696–697, https://doi.org/10.3399/bjgp10X515548.

Dr. Craig Chang, "Wegovy / Ozempic and Mounjaro for Weight Loss…Facts and Fiction," *ABS Specialists*, 2024, https://www.absspecialists.com/2023/07/wegovy-ozempic-and-mounjaro-for-weight-lossfacts-and-fiction/.

Dawn Branley-Bell, Catherine V. Talbot, James Downs, Carolina Figueras, Jessica Green, Beth McGilley, and Claire Murphy-Morgan, "It's Not All About Control: Challenging Mainstream Framing of Eating Disorders," *Journal of Eating Disorders* 11 (2023): 25, https://jeatdisord.biomedcentral.com/articles/10.1186/s40337-023-00752-9.

Bob Deffinbaugh, "Q. Do Those Who Commit Suicide Go to Hell?" *Bible.org*, December 22, 2022, https://bible.org/seriespage/q-do-those-who-commit-suicide-go-hell.

www.ingramcontent.com/pod-product-compliance
Lightning Source LLC
Chambersburg PA
CBHW071707120626
46550CB00001B/142